The Gallant Pioneers

The Gallant Pioneers

UPDATED!
THE GALLANT PIONEERS

Gary Ralston

Dedication

To Lewis and Jennifer.

Contents

I've had my share of pastime, and I've done my share of toil,
And life is short – the longest life a span;
I care not now to tarry for the corn or for the oil,
Or for wine that maketh glad the heart of man.
For good undone, and gifts misspent, and resolutions vain,
'Tis somewhat late to trouble. This I know –
I should live the same life over, if I had to live again;
And the chances are I go where most men go.

The Sick Stockrider
by Adam Lindsay Gordon, 1833–1870.

The above verse by the Australian poet was read by Tom Vallance on the evening of Wednesday 13 April 1898 at his restaurant, The Metropolitan, in Hutchison Street, Glasgow. The occasion was the 21st anniversary of the 1877 Scottish Cup Final between Rangers and Vale of Leven and 30 former players and friends of both clubs accepted the invite from the first great captain of the Light Blues to attend.
He told his guests: 'The same spirit that characterised football in the old days has gone. It has been reduced to a purely mercenary matter.'

* * * * *

'Our very success, gained you will agree by skill, will draw more people than ever to see it. And that will benefit many more clubs than Rangers. Let the others come after us. We welcome the chase. It is healthy for us. We will never hide from it. Never fear, inevitably we shall have our years of failure, and when they arrive, we must reveal tolerance and sanity. No matter the days of anxiety that come our way, we shall emerge stronger because of the trials to be overcome. That has been the philosophy of the Rangers since the days of the gallant pioneers.'

Bill Struth

Four boys had a dream
To start a football team
They had no money, no kit, not even a ball
But they carried on
And the Rangers were born
54 titles
We're still going strong

Acknowledgements

The Gallant Pioneers was published in the summer of 2009 and my gratitude to all those who contributed to the success of the book remains as strong today as it was back then. Few publishers - sadly, most of them Scottish - were willing to take up an option on the book. They argued an early years history, even of a club with as fascinating a past as Rangers, would not capture the imagination of readers. English publishers Breedon Books (later Derby Books) thankfully saw merit in the project. Several re-prints later and with critical success to match the book's popularity among the Rangers support it became clear editors and commissioning agents had failed to judge their market.

The Gallant Pioneers was always intended as a starting point for further research by fans. Its primary aim was to entertain and educate supporters, but if it was to have true worth it also had to inspire. Over the last few years new details have emerged - a phone call here, an email there - which made an updated version of the book not just more and more likely, but more and more necessary.

However, in truth, my role these last couple of years has been the literary equivalent of the defensive midfield sitter, offering a word of friendly advice and encouragement here, pointing a finger of experience over there. This updated version would never have come to pass had it not been for the more energetic efforts of fans such as Gordon Bell and Iain McColl, ably assisted by Neil Stobie. They have made a mockery of the term 'amateur' when it is coupled next to 'football historian'. Their research, borne of a true passion for Rangers, has been exemplary and professional. If only others associated with the club in recent years could look at their lavishly rewarded efforts and say they shared the same commitment to the Light Blues.

Gordon, in particular, has spent as much time at the Mitchell Library as many of the staff and has never failed to be anything other than keen and willing to share the knowledge of all he has found, which has been significant and fascinating. Iain has worn shoe leather into the ground, walking in the footsteps of giants and plotting the locations of their playgrounds, work, homes and final places of rest. This updated version is as much their book as mine. As a result, it is only fair a percentage of all proceeds from it goes to the Founders Trail so Gordon and Iain can continue their tremendous work in spreading the word of the club's early years history as well as support the many charitable projects they have backed so generously in recent years.

Sadly, in the last few years Rangers have lost their heart and soul at boardroom level. However, the history remains - and in the era of the Gallant Pioneers, what wonderful memories they created and fabulous legacies they laid.

Gary Ralston
November 2013

Foreword

Henry Ford declared all history is bunk. The American industrialist manufactured wonderful motor cars but would have made a rotten Rangers supporter. In recent years fans of the Light Blues have been forced to accept some ugly truths about the men stalking the corridors of power at Ibrox, not least the character of the individuals who are an affront to the founding fathers that established the club in 1872. Craig Whyte, Charles Green, Imran Ahmad and their cronies know so little about Rangers they probably thought the Copland Road Underground was a Govan separatist movement. Bill Struth famously urged tolerance and sanity for the years of failure that would inevitably occur at Ibrox, but promised fans the club would emerge stronger for the experience. After all, he insisted, that has been the philosophy of Rangers since the days of the Gallant Pioneers.

The last few seasons have certainly tested the resolve of the fans beyond all that even Struth dared fear. When he pleaded for patience he was undoubtedly speaking about football and not boardroom politics, even if his role in the coup known as the Battle for the Blue Room in 1947 showed him to be a wily operator beyond the four walls of his Ibrox dressing room. Still, if you take the Founders Trail to Craigton Cemetery and lay your ear against the grass, the sound you will hear is the grand old man of Ibrox spinning in his grave at all that has occurred since Sir David Murray lost control of the destiny of the club and sold it to the odious Whyte for £1 in May 2011.

Rangers fans were lied to by Whyte, who denied raising a mortgage against supporters' cash via future season ticket sales to fund his buyout, which included a pledge to repay £18 million of debt to the Lloyds banking group. He then plunged the club into administration in February 2012 on the back of his failure to pay £9 million in tax and VAT on behalf of the club and its employees. They have been deceived by countless directors and taken for fools by fat cat executives, who have trousered lavish salaries and bonus packages on the back of season ticket sales that have been nothing short of staggering, with more than 38,000 fans committing to the club when it was placed into the Third Division for the start of the 2012/13 campaign.

The financial recklessness of many of the club's custodians has been as unedifying a spectacle as the continuing zeal to deny Rangers their history, even if the decision to begin the process of liquidating the old holding company in June 2012 caused widespread confusion initially. Football fans are tribal and while the gloating gene is rogue to the outside eye, it is, was and always will be an essential mocking molecule of the DNA of the Scottish supporter.

The game's administrators should have known better, however. There was a headlong rush in the summer of 2012 by powers within the SPL, for example, to strip Rangers of five titles from 2003 as part of a five way agreement to transfer SFA membership to the new holding company. It angered many inside Ibrox, none moreso than manager Ally McCoist who fought long, loud and publicly for those championships to be retained.

The SPL stood accused of pre-judging the result of the 'Big Tax Case' into the use of employee benefit trusts from 2001. In November 2012 a First Tier Tax Tribunal ruled the scheme did not breach tax law. Therefore, it came as no surprise in February 2013 when the commission appointed by the SPL to investigate alleged undisclosed payments by Rangers decided the payments were not irregular and did not breach SPL or SFA rules. However, the club should have disclosed details of the letters it sent to players relating to the EBT scheme. The independent commission decided not to strip the club of any titles when it found no sporting advantage had been gained.

A football club is more than bricks and mortar and yet, paradoxically, it is emotionally anchored and fixed in the community in which it is based. It can be officially owned and controlled - and very often protected - by the shell of a holding company, but its heart and soul will never be found in a boardroom or a balance sheet. In the case of Rangers, it is passed from father to son like a comfort blanket weaved from the past on the silken talents of Thornton and Waddell, Henderson and Baxter, Cooper and Laudrup and many others whose spirit never frayed.

Still, there are those who continue to insist the thousands who walk along Paisley Road West with their friends every other Saturday to watch Rangers play within Scottish football at Ibrox Stadium, with the club crest on their blue shirts and in a team managed by Ally McCoist, are delusional. They ignore the European Club Association, the only independent body representing clubs to be recognised by UEFA and FIFA, which confirmed in December 2012 after discussions with the SFA that Rangers remain members of the organisation. Admittedly, their status was downgraded from ordinary to associate members following the transfer of ownership as full members require to be playing in their domestic top league and be licensed to play European football which, as a result in a break in the accounts, Rangers were not.

Nevertheless, an ECA spokesman said: "Rangers are permitted to hold associate membership, which holds no voting rights, as they are one of the founder members of the ECA. The organisation considers the club's history to be continuous regardless of the change of company. Taking into account that the 'new entity' also acquired the goodwill of the 'old entity', it was held by the ECA executive board that the goodwill, taking into account legal and practical arguments, also included the history of the 'old company'. Consequently it was concluded that Rangers FC was entitled to associated membership of ECA as considered to be a founding member."[1]

In September 2012 Lord Nimmo Smith also backed the club's right to retain its history following his appointment as chair of the independent committee established by the SPL to investigate the use of those controversial EBTs. However, his announcement came with a sting in the tail - 'newco' Rangers could have the history, but it could also be held liable for any punishments dished out for 'oldco's' actions, should the committee so decide.

Lord Nimmo Smith said: "In common speech a club is treated as a recognisable entity which is capable of being owned and operated, and which continues in existence despite its transfer to another owner and operator. In legal terms, it appears to us to be no different from any other undertaking which is capable of being carried on, bought and sold."[2]

The SFA transferred full membership from 'oldco' Rangers to 'newco' in August 2012 and history was the least Rangers could expect to carry over as it was hit with swingeing sanctions as a consequences of Whyte leading the club into administration. To facilitate membership in the Third Division the new parent company were ordered to pay all 'oldco' debts to clubs in Scotland and Europe and did so by February 2013. They were also hit with a 12 month transfer ban and a £160,000 fine by the SFA for going into administration and bringing the game into disrepute.

Lord Nimmo's Smith's investigation may have ultimately cleared Rangers of gaining a sporting advantage in the use of EBTs but the 'oldco' were still fined £250,000 after being found guilty of failing to correctly register players. That fine is unlikely ever to be paid - but 'newco' were still hit with the SPL's legal bill of £500,000. It seems somewhat churlish to claim sanctions can pass over but honours cannot. However, doubters could always look on the UEFA website, where Rangers were ranked 92nd in Europe for season 2012/13, with co-efficient points listed for the last five years. The websites of the SFA and SPFL also link to a Rangers history section that stretches back to 1872 and lists every major honour won since then at home and abroad. Finally, never overlook the fact Rangers were first registered as a plc in 1899 to fund the development of a new Ibrox Park at a cost of £12,000. However, Rangers were formed in 1872, so did the club's first 27 years in existence not count? Try standing at the bar of the Athole Arms in the mid-1870s and spinning that line to Moses McNeil, Peter Campbell, William McBeath, Tom Vallance and Peter McNeil and see where it would have got you. Chances are those wonderful pioneers would, for once, not prove to be so gallant…

Chapter 1

The Gallant Pioneers

The magnificent Kelvingrove Art Gallery and Museum opened its doors in the summer of 2006 after a three-year refurbishment at a cost of £28 million. The beautifully restored Victorian landmark boasts 8,000 works of art and – as many Rangers fans were quick to point out – one work of fiction. In a section of the ground floor devoted to Glasgow Stories, space was given over to an exhibition of Symbols That Divide, which included flags, banners and colours, many of them associated with the city's two great clubs, Rangers and Celtic. To the annoyance of many fans of the Light Blues, the script associated with their favourites (since changed following a string of complaints) started: "Rangers began as a Protestant club…"

In an article in The Times to mark the 130th anniversary of the very first Scottish Cup tie played by Rangers in 1874, a 2–0 victory over Oxford at Queen's Park Recreation Ground on the south side of Glasgow, it was noted: "It was only thanks to large lashings of luck that Rangers were able to evolve from the primeval soup of Scottish football's prehistoric era."[1] In March 2007, as the debate on sectarianism raged back and forth in the pages of the Scottish press, one tabloid columnist took Rangers to task and in a fit of indignation declared it: "a club which has had its entire history to drive bigotry from the terraces."[2]

As an institution that has been part of the social fabric of Scotland for the best part of 137 years it is inevitable that Rangers – in particular its early years – have attracted myth, mischief-making and mis-perception on a scale to match their triumphs over the decades. This success includes a trophy haul unsurpassed in world football: 54 top flight championships, 33 Scottish Cups and 27 League Cups, not to mention the European Cup-Winners' Cup in 1972, appearances in the Final in 1961 and 1967 and a run to the UEFA Cup Final in Manchester in 2008.

Lest we forget, Rangers also won the Third Division title in 2013 as it began to claw its way back following the carnage of financial vandalism and irresponsibility by club leaders in recent years.

At a time when Rangers and its supporters are being more closely scrutinised than ever before, including some potent self-analysis, history has a vital role to play in reminding every fan (not just of Rangers) of the club's humble origins and how the Light Blues were moulded by its earliest personalities. Their fates, failures and fledgling successes may even, in turn, help redefine the future of a club they could never have dared dream would grow to become one of the biggest in the world. The early years of Rangers have been chronicled in the past, particularly by writers such as John Allan, who wrote the jubilee history in 1923 (and therein lies a story). However, much of what has been recorded on the early years has been fictionalised and regurgitated as truth to create a fog of fable as thick as any haar that rolls across the floodlit pitch at Ibrox from the Clyde during a midweek game.

So, no, Rangers were not established as a sporting front for the teachings of Knox, Calvin and Luther, even if the upbringing of the club's gallant pioneers was undeniably Protestant and the ethos of the club remains indelibly so, while still embracing fans from across the religious and social spectrum of 21st-century Scotland and beyond. If there was any criticism aimed at the club's membership list in the 1870s it was in relation to the clannish nature of its Gareloch influence, with many of the club's early members associated with a shared upbringing on the Clyde peninsula.

Questions on the importance of religion as a defining factor of the club in its formative years are as relevant as asking a survivor from the Titanic how they had otherwise enjoyed their voyage. To pin the Protestant yin to the Catholic yang of Celtic – the Parkhead club were formed in 1887 to help provide succour to the members of that religious community in the east end of Glasgow – is lazy historical shorthand. It seeks to place the debate on the Old Firm and both clubs' formations, rivalries, politics and problems into snug, pre-assembled pigeonholes, including a shared ideological birth based on religious motivation, albeit from different tenets of the Christian faith. However, the formation of Rangers does not fit. The inspiration of Peter and Moses McNeil, Peter Campbell and William McBeath as they walked through the Glasgow park in early 1872 near the spot that would later house the museum that stood and misrepresented their motives, was pure and simple. They sought nothing more than to add prowess in association football to a range of sporting interests that already included 'manly' pastimes such as shinty, rowing and athletics.

Likewise, the formation of their club and its progress throughout that decade and beyond owed absolutely nothing to good fortune and everything to solid friendships (or Gareloch clannishness), sound organisation and a firm structure. For example, within 18 months of their humble beginnings at Flesher's Haugh on Glasgow Green, Britain's oldest public park, they had already persuaded the Marquis of Lorne, future 9th Duke of Argyll, Governor of Canada and son-in-law to Queen Victoria, to become their first patron.

Finally, Rangers has not had its whole history to address and resolve affairs nowadays associated with sectarianism. Such emotive issues did not arise until at

Where it all began: West End Park, later extended and re-named Kelvingrove Park, was the inspiration for the birth of Rangers.

least 40 years after the earliest players, most of them still dressed in their street clothes, kicked the club's first, battered piece of leather around a patch of open ground, driven on by the altruistic ideal of sport for sport's sake and the dream of scoring a game-winning goal against their debut opponents, Callander (it never came, the match finished goalless). Wider debates on sectarianism are tangled in a labyrinth of landmine topics ranging from Irish nationalism, militant republicanism and the nature of Scottish, Irish and British identity at the turn of the 20th century.

In short and in truth, the story of Rangers is one of the most romantic of any of the greatest sporting clubs formed. It was born uniquely and totally out of a love for the new craze of association football that spread throughout Scotland and

England in the 1860s and 1870s. The founding fathers of the club were, in fact, no more than young boys who had come to Glasgow seeking their fortune in business and industry and who, instead, went on to develop an unintentional relationship with fame that keeps their names alive and cherishes the scale of their achievements to this very day.

Campbell and McBeath were only 15 years old, Moses McNeil was 16 and his older brother, Peter, was the senior statesman at just 17. Tom Vallance was not there at the conception but he certainly helped in the delivery of the club and was also a mere pup, barely 16 years old. The images and memories of that time are passed down through the yellowed pages of 19th-century newspapers such as the Scottish Athletic Journal, Scottish Umpire, Scottish Sport and Scottish Referee, recalling on-field successes and off-field intrigues.

Other, more personal and often harrowing stories come from the vaults and archives of museums and libraries across Britain, including long-hidden horrors of death at sea, insanity and loss of life as a result of business worries, the tag of certified imbecility, a trial for fraud and life in the poorhouse, not to mention a second marriage for one of the founding fathers that was most likely bigamous. Thankfully, there are happier tales to recollect, stories of fascinating relationships, directly and indirectly, with the growth of the steam trade on the Clyde, Charles Rennie Mackintosh, House of Fraser and a rugby club in Swindon to whom fans who cherish the name of Rangers should be forever indebted.

The pattern of Rangers' development is weaved inextricably into the rich tapestry that chronicles the growth of Glasgow, where the dominant sporting threads have been coloured blue and green for well over a century. The second city of the empire is as central to the story of the club as the River Clyde was to its earliest trade in tobacco and cotton. In 1765, a little more than 100 years before Rangers staked their first claim to a pitch at Flesher's Haugh, James Watt was walking deep in thought on Glasgow Green when a vision of an innovative use for steam power came to him and triggered one of the most important developments of the Industrial Revolution. In 1820 there were 21 steam engines operating in the city, yet within a quarter of a century that number had increased to over 300, powering operations in a range of industries including cotton and textiles, chemicals, glass, paper and soap.

Later, heavier industries came to dominate, including ironworks, locomotive construction and the aforementioned shipbuilding. In 1831 the first railway arrived in Glasgow, complementing the existing Forth and Clyde and

Monklands canals, which had been completed in the early 1790s and were vital to transport raw materials such as coal and ironstone from the bountiful fields of nearby Lanarkshire. On the Clyde, technological developments saw shipbuilding advance at such a pace from the 1820s that within 50 years more than half the British shipbuilding workforce was based on the river, including teenager Peter Campbell, producing half of Britain's tonnage of shipping – up to 500,000 a year by 1900.

It was a chaotic recipe for growth that over the course of the century absorbed hundreds of thousands of new inhabitants, the population increasing from 66,000 in 1791 to 658,000 in 1891. By the 1820s, thousands of Scots had been forcibly driven into the clutches of the new industrial age through rural depopulation and Clearances in the Highlands on the back of social reconstruction following the failed Jacobite uprisings. By 1821 the population of Glasgow had risen almost fivefold from 32,000 in 1750, much of it a result of immigration, particularly from Ireland. Many of those who settled in the city in the late 18th century were Irish Presbyterians, drawn by the common ancestry and shared sense of cultural heritage with lowland Scots. They were particularly skilled in weaving and settled in the communities in the east end of the city that traditionally nurtured the trade, such as Bridgeton and Calton. By 1820, it was estimated that up to a third of the area's weavers were of Irish origin.

In the late 1840s, further Irish immigration as a result of the potato famine also increased the city's population. The majority of those who arrived in Glasgow as a result of the famine were Catholic, although up to 25 per cent of all those who arrived in Scotland from across the water in the 19th century were Protestant. These were the best and worst of times. In the 1820s and 1830s the average life expectancy for men in Glasgow was just 37, and women fared little better at 40. By the 1880s it had increased, but only slightly, to 42 and 45. There were typhoid epidemics in 1837 and 1847 and Scotland's first cholera epidemic also hit the city, killing 10,000 people. There were further outbreaks of the deadly disease in 1849 and 1854 when over 7,500 citizens lost their lives.

Between the 1830s and the late 1850s, death rates rose to peaks not seen since the 17th century. Even 20 years later there was still a very high infant mortality rate, with up to half of all children born never seeing their fifth birthday. As late as 1906 a school board survey revealed a 14-year-old boy living in a poor area of Glasgow was, on average, four inches shorter than a similar-aged child from the city's west end. It came as only a perverse crumb of comfort that the extra inches in the city's poorer quarters would not have been welcomed, given Glasgow's status at the time as the most overcrowded population centre in Britain.

However, the west end symbolised the self-confidence of Glasgow's burgeoning mercantile classes and the two Great Exhibitions of 1881 and 1901 in Kelvingrove Park showcased its pride in its reputation as the second city of the Empire. By 1820, the development of the city westwards had reached Blythswood Square, with gridded Georgian terraces extending along Bath Street, St Vincent Street and West George Street. By the 1850s many of these buildings had been commandeered by the city's business community, which were constructed around George Square and extended up Blythswood Hill as banks, insurance houses and shipping companies expanded in size and influence.

As the city's wealth increased, so was the isolated countryside further west swallowed up from the mid-1800s, particularly with the completion of the Great Western Road and the establishment of the Botanic Gardens on the Kelvinside Estate. The relocation of

An aerial view of the park Rangers soon made their own: Glasgow Green at the turn of the 20th century.

Glasgow University from the High Street to Gilmorehill in 1870 added an academic aura still prevalent today and, all the time, the construction of handsome mansions and elegant townhouses in yellow, pink and red sandstone gathered pace, overseen by architects such as Rennie Mackintosh and Alexander 'Greek' Thomson around spacious crescents and a plethora of public parks. Glasgow has long claimed more public recreation areas per head of population than any other major European city, giving rise to its proud nickname of the Dear Green Place.

Fittingly, the story of the birth of Rangers straddles both sides of the city. Peter Campbell apart, the founding fathers and their earliest teammates could not be easily tagged as representative of either of the polar opposite communities that confidently sprang up or rose falteringly and with raspish breath in their adopted city. They represented the everyman; neither rich nor poor, privileged nor disadvantaged. They did not come from nor live in the disease-ridden wynds of the

Gallowgate, Saltmarket, Calton or High Street, but neither did their addresses declare them as young men of particular wealth or substance. Their homes, like themselves, stood on the fringes of prosperity – close to, but not part of, the affluent west end. To a man, they lived exclusively in the Sandyford area in addresses such as Berkeley Street, Kent Road, Cleveland Street, Elderslie Street and Bentinck Street. They worked, for the most part, in the service industry or white-collar occupations such as drapers, hosiers, clerks and commercial travellers.

As Moses and Peter McNeil, William McBeath and Peter Campbell walked through West End Park in March 1872, discussing their desire to form a football club, they may have looked up the hill and been similarly driven to aspire to the lifestyle of those who had just constructed their handsome and spacious homes in the Park district, with panoramic views offering a dramatic sweep across an ever-changing Glasgow cityscape. In time, their fledgling club would climb to lofty peaks in European football, but for many different reasons, personal tragedies among them, none of them would clamber from the foothills towards wealth and prosperity and all would die with their contribution to the history of Rangers virtually unheralded. Until now, their life stories have remained largely unknown and unacknowledged by all but a sympathetic few.

In those heady days their sights were set not on the west, but to the east and the public park of Glasgow Green that had been laid out over 36 acres between 1815 and 1826 by the city fathers, offering a rare opportunity for residents from the claustrophobic lanes and alleyways to sample open spaces.

The park provided a vital escape to the people of the east end who existed in appalling conditions, even after the City Improvement Trust had been established in 1866 to clear the slum dwellings and improve squalid living conditions. The park served the recreational needs of the city at the time despite, bizarrely, a bye-law introduced in 1819 prohibiting sporting and leisure pursuits. Cricket and shinty were popular pastimes, as was bowling, and there was even a huge wooden frame gymnasium on site. Rowers could be found on the Clyde and the Clydesdale Amateur Rowing Club, formed in 1857, and the Clyde Rowing Club, formed in 1865, catered for eager enthusiasts, including the McNeils, Campbell and Vallance, who had grown up participating in the pastime from a young age on the waters of the Gare Loch.

It came as no surprise that the young friends should decide to form a club of their own, inspired by the likes of Queen's Park, who were founded on 9 July 1867 when a group of young men met at No. 3 Eglinton Terrace to establish a new club, settling on their club's name only after rejecting a string of alternatives including Morayshire, The Celts and The Northern, which undoubtedly reflected the Highland roots of their founding sons. Rivals were in such short supply in the early months of Queen's Park that members were forced to find new and innovative ways to split their numbers into teams on the local recreation ground – at one point smokers played non-smokers. It must have come as some relief when, in August 1868, they finally found opponents named Thistle and rules were quickly agreed between club secretaries.

The game was a 20-a-side affair, played over two hours and Queen's Park won 2–0, setting a pattern for success that would become all too familiar over the subsequent two decades. The Spiders have lifted the Scottish Cup 10 times, which still stands as the most victories in the famous old competition by any club outwith the Old Firm.

Association football had grown increasingly popular in the public schools of England in the first half of the 19th century, although as a sport it had been around for hundreds of years and had been present in China since before the birth of Christ. Rapid advancements were made in football during the Victorian era, not least as a result of the Saturday half-day holiday. It allowed workers who toiled in industry a rare few hours of recreation time beyond the usual Sabbath observance to take part in, or look in on, various leisure activities. On the field, crucial rule changes were adopted soon after the formation of the English FA in October 1863, following a meeting of a dozen clubs from London and the surrounding areas at the Freemasons' Tavern in Great Queen Street. Until then, there had been little to distinguish the games of football and rugby.

By the mid-1860s, however, it had become forbidden for players of the association game to dart forward with the ball in hand as the focus switched to a dribbling game played on the ground. The Scots quickly adapted to new tactics and techniques, developing an early team framework far superior to anything being played south of the border. Queen's Park were among the first clubs to grasp the benefits of a more structured formation, playing a 2–2–6 formation: two full-backs, two half-backs and six forwards, with two players on the left wing, two on the right and two through the middle. The English clubs persisted with their 1–1–8, but its folly was exposed when the Spiders, playing a short, sharp passing game, saw off top English side Notts County 6–0 at Hampden. Ultimately, it prompted a demand for Scottish players by English clubs that continues to this day.

The FA Cup was instituted in 1871, two years before its Scottish equivalent, and international football also began to develop from the club game, thanks in the first instance to Charles W. Alcock, the administrator, journalist and publisher who would provide the eponymously titled football annual from which Moses McNeil took the Rangers name. It was in November 1870 when, as secretary of the FA, he wrote to the Glasgow Herald suggesting a game between players from both countries. He cajoled: "In Scotland, once essentially the land of football, there should still be a spark left of the old fire, and I confidently appeal to Scotsmen to aid to their utmost the efforts of the committee to confer success on what London hopes to be found, an annual trial of skill between the champions of England and Scotland."[3]

In total, Alcock arranged four games in London, but the Scots team was plucked from the ranks of Anglos working in the capital, as well as a couple of moonlighters, most notably W.H. Gladstone, the son of the Prime Minister. It came as no great shock when Scotland lost all the games played and the 'Alcock Internationals' have no official standing to this day.

Still, sporting history has correctly lauded Alcock as a football visionary and it came as no surprise when the first official international between Scotland and England was played in Glasgow, fittingly on St Andrew's Day 1872 (football continues to be a sport played, for the most part, from August to May each year, because cricket was the dominant summer pastime in the Victorian era, even in Scotland).

Queen's Park represented the nation that November afternoon after handing over £10 to the West of Scotland Cricket Club for the use of their ground in Hamilton Crescent, Partick, with the promise of a further £10 if takings for the game exceeded £50. In the end, 4,000 people paid £103 to watch the scoreless draw, but there was one notable absentee – the official photographer, who left the ground when players refused to promise they would purchase prints from the game. The overwhelming popularity of the game ensured the fixture's place in the fledgling football calendar and Scotland soon underlined its supremacy, winning eight and losing only two of the first 12 international matches played against the Auld Enemy.

It was against such a backdrop that Rangers had been formed in 1872, most likely towards the end of March if the earliest account of the club's history is to be taken as read. And while one or two of the facts are open to question, it carries the strong whiff of authenticity, particularly written so close to the birth itself.

One of the leading lights of the earliest Rangers team, William Dunlop, penned the history of the early years for the 1881–82 edition of the Scottish Football Annual under the pseudonym True Blue. Dunlop had joined the club in 1876 (his sister, Mary, would go on to marry Tom Vallance) and was a Scottish Cup finalist against Vale of Leven in 1877 and again in 1879; that same year he began a 12-month term as president of the club. In looking back at the game against Callander he recalled of Rangers: "Thus ended their first match, played about the latter end of May 1872, some two months after the inauguration of the club."

The idea for a football club had been discussed by the teenage pioneers during walks in West End Park, nowadays known as Kelvingrove Park, close to the residences and lodging houses of the youngsters. In the 1871 census Peter McNeil, a 16-year-old clerk, lived at No. 17 Cleveland Street with his oldest sister, Elizabeth, 30, and brothers James, 27, Henry, 21, and William, 19. Moses, a trainee clerk, made his way to join his siblings on his arrival in Glasgow, most likely towards the end of 1871, by which time Elizabeth was head of the household that had subsequently moved around the corner to No. 169 Berkeley Street. Peter Campbell, born and raised in Garelochhead, knew the Shandon brothers from childhood and he was also employed near his friends on moving to Glasgow, at the Barclay Curle shipyard at Stobcross Quay. The quartet was completed by William McBeath, an assistant salesman, who had been born in Callander but arrived in Glasgow from Perthshire with his mother, Jane, soon after the death of his father Peter in 1864. The birth of Rangers symbolised a new beginning for William, who lived in the same tenement close in Cleveland Street as the McNeils. His mother died in March 1872 of chronic bronchitis, aged just 53, with her son's youthful scrawl officially certifying her death.

Dunlop wrote: "A friend of ours, and member of the Rangers, certainly not noted for his accurate knowledge of history, used to remark that there were only two incidents in the history of Scotland specially worth remembering. Jeffrey, Brougham and Sydney Smith met in an old garret in Edinburgh and as a result of their 'crack' determined to found the Edinburgh Review. P. McNeil, W. McBeith [sic], M. McNeil and P. Campbell, as the result of a quiet chat carried on without any attempt at brilliancy in the West End Park, determined to found the Rangers FC. These old Rangers had been exercised: in fact, their feelings had been wrought upon, on seeing matches between the Queen's Park, the Vale (of Leven), and 3rd L.R.V. (Third Lanark). Viewing the interesting and exciting points of the game, even then brilliantly elucidated by the Queen's Park, had given rise to the itching

Once upon a dream: Few would have thought a walk along these paths in West End Park would result in the birth of one of the world's greatest football clubs.

toe, which could only be relieved by procuring a ball and bestowing upon it an unlimited amount of abuse."

Friends, particularly those with a Gareloch connection, were rounded up, Harry McNeil and three chums from Queen's Park agreed to second and soon Rangers were off and running (most of them in their civvies) at Flesher's Haugh. To be fair, Dunlop freely admitted that the game against Callander was considered a "terrible" spectacle and poor McBeath was so exhausted by his efforts "he was laid up for a week," although he was named Man of the Match. Nevertheless, inspired and motivated by that first encounter, office bearers were quickly elected and further games arranged.

Soon, the youthful Rangers team were the most popular draw on Glasgow Green, courtesy of their exuberant, energetic and winning brand of football. Their earliest fans would undoubtedly have included the residents of the east end of the city, many of them Irish Catholic immigrants, who would subsequently flock to watch Celtic when they were formed 15 years later. Indeed, former Celt Tom Maley, brother of legendary Parkhead manager Willie, fondly recalled going along to watch Rangers play their first Scottish Cup tie at Queen's Park Recreation

Ground in 1874 in an article for the Sunday Post in February 1927. He said: "It is a far cry, and when one, looking at the great spacious and splendidly equipped enclosure that the Rangers now possess, trace their career from Glasgow Green to Ibrox, and dwell on their vicissitudes and triumphs, one is constrained, be he even churlish, to say of them that they have a just claim to be included among those 'who have achieved greatness'."

The ghostly whispers of the founding fathers of yesteryear are now but breezes blowing on the wind, from Flesher's Haugh up and over the city centre to Great Western Road and Burnbank, swirling across the Clyde to Kinning Park before moving on towards Copland Road, the site of the first Ibrox Park. This early year history is an attempt to present the formation of a great football club against the backdrop of almighty social change in industrialised Glasgow. Rangers survived and prospered, but not all those teenagers who took it upon themselves in the spring of 1872 to form their very own club would, unfortunately, be able to say the same.

Chapter 2
The Birth of the Blues

Journalist John Allan may have had the clasp of a loyal Ranger, as Bill Struth once noted, but the strength of his grip on historical reality has always been a bone of contention to many among the Light Blues' legions. Allan was a former editor of the Daily Record and wrote the three most authoritative tomes on the club he had followed since his childhood in Kinning Park, where he was born in 1879. These days, with the aid of hindsight, The Story of the Rangers, Eleven Great Years and 18 Eventful Years, which cover much of the club's story until 1951, read like romanticised works of fiction from the empire of Mills and Boon, not Wilton and Struth. Nevertheless, they still carry significant weight, although in relation to the year that should be acknowledged as the birth of the club, The Story of the Rangers does not appear to be accurate.

Even in the 21st century, there are journalists from a bygone era who still recall Allan, who died in April 1953, less than 24 hours after attending his beloved Ibrox for the last time for a Scottish Cup semi-final replay between Aberdeen and Third Lanark. He wrote under the pen name of 'Brigadier' – literally too, for he refused to use a typewriter and filed all his copy via sports desk copy takers from notes on which his pencilled scrawl was illegible to all but himself. He joined the Daily Record as a sportswriter at the turn of the 20th century, although he also contributed a weekly column in the Athletic News and Sporting Chronicle under the name Jonathan Oldbuck.

Allan was renowned for his photographic memory, his patience – and his love of Rangers. The legendary Willie Gallagher, who wrote for decades as Waverley in the pages of the Record, noted that his colleague's "admiration for Rangers was not permitted to interfere with his written views. These were completely unprejudiced and at times he was the Ibrox team's severest critic."[1]

Others, politely, declined to agree. In his book 100 Years of Scottish Sport, written for the Record when he rode side saddle with Alex Cameron as two of the country's foremost tabloid tale gatherers, Rodger Baillie dusted down the archives to recall the famous 1928 Scottish Cup Final against Celtic, which Rangers won 4–0. Unsurprisingly, it is remembered as one of the most significant victories in the history of the club as it was the first time the Light Blues had lifted the old trophy in 25 years.

Baillie wrote: "'Brigadier' was in the Rangers dressing room at the end. It was the nom de plume of John Allan, who was later to have a spell as the editor of the paper. Other executives of that pre-war era believed he tilted the paper's coverage too much towards Ibrox. Still, he obtained a series of quotes – unusual in those times when players were seen but rarely heard, as the journalists of the day tended to give maximum space to the views of directors and other officials. 'You sunk that penalty like an icicle, man,' I told Davie Meiklejohn. 'Icicle!' he said. 'Why, I never felt so anxious in all my life. It was the most terrible minute of my football career. I hadn't time to think what it would have meant if I had missed and I can tell you I was relieved when I saw the ball in the back of the net.'"[2]

Allan's respect for Meiklejohn (who, incidentally, went on to write for the Record) was absolute and that is not surprising as the Govan-born right-half, who also operated in the centre of defence, was an Ibrox giant who played 635 games between 1919 and 1936 and won 12 Championship medals, in addition to 15 caps for Scotland. He was one of the club's greatest captains and his strength of character was never better illustrated than in that Scottish Cup final when he stepped up to slot the vital first goal past Celtic keeper John Thomson from the spot, opening the floodgates for his team to go on and secure one of their most emphatic Cup Final victories.

Nevertheless, Allan's love of football in general and Rangers in particular did cause unrest on the editorial floor of the Record in the 1930s, as former Record and Scotsman editor Alastair Dunnett admitted. He recalled: "John McCall…who became editor of the Sunday Mail, told me once how he had been in charge of the Record on the night when the news broke of King Edward VIII and Mrs Wallis Simpson.

"He had rushed in with it to John Allan's room, where the editor was sitting with his cronies, drinking and talking about football. Allan interrupted his discourse to look at the story and hear John McCall saying: 'This is very important Mr Allan. It must be front page.' Allan looked over the pages briefly, puffed his pipe and handed the pages back, saying: 'Aye. Two columns down the page.' And turned to his visitors with '…as I was saying, Davie Meiklejohn is always at his best when he's in defence…' This was a man who knew little in life except football and he was a rabid Rangers supporter, which did not do the paper any good at all."[3]

Allan's influence stretched beyond the written page to the very corridors of power at Ibrox itself, where he was recognised as a confidant of Struth in particular. The legendary Rangers boss was effusive in his praise in an obituary for Allan that appeared under his byline in the Rangers' Supporters Association Annual of 1954, his last year as Ibrox boss. In all likelihood, it would have been written by Allan's nephew Willie Allison, who succeeded the man he affectionately referred to as 'Muncle' as club historian and public relations official.

Struth recalled of Allan: "I still see him walk into my room with the smile of the kindly heart and the clasp of a loyal Ranger. He knew many of my secrets. They were sacred to him. No confidence was ever in danger when given to John. Our success was his success, yet in his role of critic he was a forthright, honest chronicler who sought no favours and gave none in the line of duty."

Struth added: "I have known him to leave his office after many hours of exacting work in putting away his morning paper, slip quietly into his home and pen the deeds of our great teams of the past until roused from his labours by the dawn breaking in on his thoughts. A few hours sleep and he was back at his desk. So brilliant a pen as his could have told an absorbing story without the necessity of detail. But as he said to me: 'Without the facts to prove the greatness of the club, my task would be incomplete.' It meant days of research – yes, months if measured in the hours he spent among his unique record books and in the old files that took him back to the beginning of the game."[+]

There's the rub. Allan may have boasted files that went back to the beginning of the game, but it appears his records relating to the rise of Rangers were 12 months out. He insisted the birth of the club came in 1873, a year still celebrated on the intricate mosaics on either side of the Ibrox Main Stand (opened in 1929) and a date which the club has been happy to accept since the publication of Allan's The Story of the Rangers in 1923, the first great book on the club's history. It was published to celebrate its jubilee and opened with: "In the summer evenings of 1873 a number of lusty, laughing lads, mere boys some of them, flushed and happy from the exhilaration of a finishing dash with the oars, could be seen hauling their craft ashore on the upper reaches of the River Clyde at Glasgow Green."

Further evidence for the 1873 inception was provided by Moses McNeil himself, in the only ever newspaper interview with the co-founder which research has uncovered. Significantly, however, his first-person piece was printed in Allan's own Daily Record in April 1935, 48 hours after Rangers had won the Scottish Cup against Hamilton Accies. The influence of Allan loomed large over the copy, which appeared under McNeil's byline and a headline stating: 'When Rangers First

Reached the Final.' McNeil, reminiscing on his career three years before his death at the age of 82, wrote: "In the summer of 1873 my brothers Peter and Willie and myself, along with some Gareloch lads, banded together on Glasgow Green with the object of forming a football club."[5]

Allan went further and categorically stated in The Story of the Rangers that the club was born from a match played at Flesher's Haugh on 15 July 1873 between two teams, Argyle and Clyde. He added: "These names did not represent organised clubs. The two sides were selected for the purpose of providing a game and names were chosen to give the event some individuality." He then goes on to list the names of the players from the two competing teams including, for Argyle, Moses and Peter McNeil, William McBeath, Tom Vallance and Peter Campbell. He continued: "It is recorded in a news print of the period that the game was very exciting and ended in a draw." Despite extensive research enquiries, the news print of the period has never been unearthed.

However, that is not to say the match did not take place. If it was played, it was likely the game between Argyle and Clyde featured players all attached to Rangers and who were split on geography based on upbringing to give a practice match a sharper edge. Games were not always easy to arrange in the early 1870s and there was fluidity around player movement that seems quaint in comparison to the watertight contracts of the modern era. Moses McNeil, for example, took a spell away from Rangers for four months between October 1875 and February 1876 to represent brother Harry's Queen's Park in games against London cracks the Wanderers, while Tom Vallance returned to his home village for the festive holidays and turned out for Garelochhead on 3 January 1882 when a touring Queen's Park select won 2–0.[6]

Queen's Park players regularly played against each other using the flimsiest of defining factors to differentiate between sides (smokers against non-smokers, for example, lightweights against heavyweights and even north against south of Eglinton Toll). Certainly, at least two names in the Clyde line up mentioned by Allan, Rankine and Hill, were associated with Rangers as players. Remember too, Allan also had access to a primary source of information in McNeil himself who, by the early 1920s, stood with Tom Vallance as the only survivor from the club's formative years. If history is written by winners then McNeil was best placed to occupy the podium from which he could oversee a selective narrative, even if it was arguably as flawed as the memory trying to recollect events from 50 years in the past.

Further evidence which suggests Allan's ability to recall incidents with historical accuracy was not to be trusted came in 'Brigadier's' obituary of Vallance, which appeared in the Daily Record on 18 February 1935, two days after the death of the club's former skipper and president from a stroke at the age of 78. Brigadier noted: "Tom was in the Rangers team that competed in the English Cup and got to the semi-final, only to be beaten by Aston Villa." In actual fact, by that time in 1887 Vallance had long since hung up his boots – his career was compromised by ill-health following a short spell working in the tea plantations of Assam in the early 1880s – and he was at that time focused on building his business career and behind-the-scenes duties at Kinning Park.

It would be mean-spirited to pin the inaccuracy of 1873 solely on Moses McNeil or John Allan, and the club's date of formation was a source of debate around Ibrox in the early 1920s as its jubilee loomed. A celebratory dinner hosted by chairman Sir John Ure Primrose and attended by the greats of the Scottish game took place at the restaurant Ferguson and Forrester's on Buchanan Street on 9 April 1923 and received widespread coverage in all newspapers the following day. The Evening Times recorded: "There has been some difference of opinion as to the year in which the Rangers Football Club originated, but it has been settled to the satisfaction of the gentlemen who at present control the club that the foundation was laid in 1873."[7]

Nevertheless, a stronger body of evidence exists to suggest 1872 was much more probable. Firstly, the Scottish Football Association Annuals, published as early as season 1875–76, carried details of every club operating in the game at that time, with information provided by each club secretary. Rangers, with their background most likely recorded by Peter McNeil, were acknowledged from the very first edition as being instituted in 1872. Their entry in one of the earliest editions of the respected handbook even gives a brief, potted history of that period and states: "This club has been one of the most successful of our Scottish football clubs, having played on Glasgow Green as a junior club from 1872 to 1874. The rapid increase of members necessitated the committee to get private grounds and being successful in securing Clydesdale's old cricket ground at Kinning Park, the club at once placed itself in the first rank of senior clubs."[8]

One of the earliest and most respected histories of the British game, published in 1905, also declared 1872 to be the year. Furthermore, the article on 'The Game in Scotland', part of a four-volume series Association Football And The Men Who Made It was penned by Robert Livingstone, the former president of the SFA. He wrote: "The seed sown by Queen's Park did not all fall on stony ground, however, for in 1872 there sprang into life two clubs which today stand at the very forefront. These were Rangers and Third Lanark and they were accompanied before the footlights of the world by Vale of Leven, destined for a chequered existence, but a still plucky survival."[9]

The official Rangers handbook – known affectionately to generations of Ibrox followers as the Wee Blue Book – was published every year from the turn of the 20th century until the 1980s. From its first edition, Rangers were acknowledged as having been formed in 1872. As late as the edition for season 1920–21, under a page section listing historical data, the club's birth was given as 1872. Significantly, the section of historical data did not appear in the following year's edition, or in the handbook published for 1922–23. However, it returned for season 1923–24 when, lo and behold, the club's birth was listed as 1873. Perhaps surprisingly, no explanation was ever offered by the handbook's editor – John Allan. A theory has surfaced over the years that Allan was under such pressure to publish a jubilee history that he altered the year of formation to suit his own punishing deadline – and historical ends. Allan certainly appears in a literary rush as he gallops through the very early years of Rangers in his book.

Further weight to the claim it was expedient for Allan to overlook 1872 as the year of formation comes from the fact that the earlier date does not even merit a mention at all. Surely Allan, with a reputation for such fastidious research, would have at least attempted to explain, in the first great history of the club, why the formation of 1872 that had been universally recognised up to that point was actually wrong? The fact that Allan failed to devote even a sentence to it suggests he was happy to alter history for purposes that suited himself and the club at that time, more than likely related to the constraints of time in organising a programme of events for a milestone few clubs had reached.

Furthermore, that first written review of Rangers, by William 'True Blue' Dunlop in 1881, is also adamant the club was formed in 1872 – late March to be precise – by the three lads from the Gareloch and William McBeath as they strolled in Glasgow's West End Park. Naturally, Dunlop was writing closer to the club's birth date than anyone, so his evidence carries more authority, although, intriguingly, he claimed the young Rangers were inspired to form their club by watching the exploits of other teams at the time, including Queen's Park, Vale of Leven and Third Lanark, yet the latter club, who survived until 1967, were not formed until December 1872. Likewise, Vale of Leven did not appear on the scene until the second half of 1872, when Queen's Park accepted an invite to teach locals

A S I watched the crowd assemble at Ibrox Park my memory turned back its pages, and I envisaged a Cup tie in which Rangers were engaged some years ago.

As a matter of fact, I believe it was their very first venture in the Scottish Cup competition. It was played on what we as youths termed the Cricket Park—Queen's Park recreation ground.

Their opponents were a team known as Oxford, and if memory hasn't tricked me Rangers won two-nil.

That match placed Tom Vallance in a niche in my temple of famous players. Picture it if you can, you who may not know what the surroundings were. The playing area was marked out by means of boundary flags. The goalposts had no crossbars, tapes did duty, and umpires and referee conducted the service.

Lined around the playing area were spectators. My view of the proceedings was obtained through the legs of one who, having brought me there to see, considerately enough ensured me vision.

It was a duel—a sort of man beat man. Concerted play came mostly from Rangers' left wing. I haven't a reference handy, but I do remember there were M'Neills as well as a Vallance, and to the Rangers' members they were giants.

It is a far cry, and when one, looking at the great spacious and splendidly-equipped enclosure that the Rangers now possess, trace their career from Glasgow Green to Ibrox, and dwell on their vicissitudes and triumphs, one is constrained, be he even churlish, to say of them that they have a just claim to be included amongst those " who have achieved greatness."

TOM MALEY.

Tom Maley, of that great Celtic family, paid a warm tribute as he recalled watching Rangers in their earliest days.

in the Dunbartonshire town of Alexandria the rudiments of the new game of association football, luring them away from their previous and long love affair with shinty.

If Moses McNeil, writing in the 1920s and 1930s under the influence of Allan, was convinced the club was formed in 1873 then Vallance, speaking much earlier in 1887, believed otherwise. At the grand opening of the first Ibrox Park in August of that year, at the Copland Road End of today's stadium, he toasted the future of the club. In his speech, printed in the press at the time, he stated: "Well, about 15 years ago, a few lads who came from Gareloch to Glasgow met and endeavoured to scrape together as much as would buy a football and we went to the Glasgow Green, where we played for a year or two. That, gentlemen, was the foundation of the Rangers Football Club."[10]

Former player Archibald Steel, who played for the club in the 1870s before moving to Bolton, wrote one of the first authoritative histories of Scottish football in 1896 under the pen name of Old International. His book 25 Years Football mines a rich seam of anecdote and first-hand experiences of playing against almost all the major clubs in the early years of the game in Scotland. Steel named 1872 as the year of Rangers' foundation as he recalled: "In the west, particularly, the game quickly took root and any spare ground where football could be followed was seized upon with avidity by the eager aspirants to dribbling proficiency. Two of the earliest I may mention were the Queen's Park juniors and the Parkgrove, besides which a year later – in 1871 – the Dumbreck and in the 12 months afterwards the Clydesdale, Rangers, Rovers and Third Lanark."[11]

If the formation date of the club has caused confusion down the years there is less ambiguity about the origins of the Rangers name. Allan's early Rangers' history, while largely sanitised, contains more than just kernels of truth. A flattering profile of Harry McNeil, the great Queen's Park winger and occasional Ranger, in the Scottish Athletic Journal of 27 October 1885 reads like a Victorian version of Hello magazine and credits him with naming the club. Likewise, True Blue claimed the club was named Rangers as rudimentary rhyming slang after the fact so many of its earliest players were strangers to Glasgow.

Neither tale rings as true as Allan's account in his book that "Moses McNeil proposed that it should be called the Rangers Association Football Club and to the young minds the name had an alluring appeal. It was adopted unanimously. Mr McNeil has related that he had been reading C. W. Alcock's English Football Annual and had been attracted by the name he had seen belonging to an English rugby club."[12] McNeil's claims, made through Allan and again in the pages of the Daily Record in 1935, hold water. Alcock's annuals were elementary guides to the newly formed clubs across Britain and their preference for the various codes of football, including association and rugby. They were first published in 1868 and are so rare that even the British Library does not boast any copies dating from before 1873. The RFU Museum at Twickenham does, however, and their issues make for fascinating reading.

Before 1870 no rugby team in England featured the Rangers name, although other wonderful handles included the Mohicans, Owls, Pirates and Red

The Rangers Football Club Ltd.
IBROX PARK, GLASGOW.

Season - 1920 - 1921.

Directors.
Sir JOHN URE PRIMROSE, Bart., *Chairman.*
Ex-Bailie JOSEPH BUCHANAN, J.P.
Ex-Bailie DUNCAN GRAHAM, J.P.
WILLIAM CRAIG, J.P.   JOHN MACPHERSON.
W. R. DANSKIN.   GEO. SMALL.

Manager—WM. STRUTH.
Secretary—W. ROGERS SIMPSON, C.A.
Trainer—G. T. LIVINGSTONE.
Groundsman—ANDREW WOODROW.

The Rangers Club was founded in 1872, and was incorporated 27th May, 1899.

Kinning Park ground was closed on 26th February, 1887; Old Ibrox Park was opened on 20th August, 1887; Ibrox Park was opened on 30th December, 1899.

The total extent of the enclosure at Ibrox Park is 14·140 acres. The playing pitch measures 115 yards by 72 yards. The size of the running track is one quarter of a mile, measuring at one foot from edge of grass.

In 1898-99 the "Light Blues" made the record of winning every match in the course of the League competition, scoring 79 goals and losing only 18.

In League and Cup-tie matches last season, Rangers scored 144 goals and lost 34. This was the best record of any Scottish club.

Alex. Smith is Rangers record Internationalist —having been "capped" 33 times.

J. Gordon, J. Bowie, T. Cairns, A. Cunningham, and R. Manderson were called upon last season to uphold the honour of the country of their birth.

Another Scottish League flag will be unfurled at Ibrox this season.

24

CLUB RECORDS, DATES, AND DATA.

The Rangers Club was founded in 1873 and incorporated 27th May, 1899.

Kinning Park ground was closed on 26th February, 1887; Old Ibrox Park was opened on 20th August, 1887; Ibrox Park was opened on 30th December, 1899.

The total extent of the enclosure at Ibrox Park is 14·140 acres. The playing pitch measures 115 yards by 72 yards. The size of the running track is one quarter of a mile, measuring at one foot from edge of grass.

Rangers have won the Scottish Cup four times, the Glasgow Cup fifteen times, the Glasgow Charity Cup eleven times, and the Scottish League Championship twelve times, and once joint with Dumbarton F.C.

In 1898-9 the "Light Blues" made the record of winning every match in the course of the League competition, scoring 79 goals and losing only 18.

The beginning of great things :—Total drawings at first Rangers v. Celtic Glasgow Cup Tie, £89 17s. 6d. Rangers' first League cheque from Celtic, ½ share of gate, £34 3s. 10d. Compare this with the record attendance at Rangers v. Celtic Cup Tie Match, played at Ibrox on 6th March, 1920—80,493 spectators.

Last year Rangers finished first in League Table—five points ahead of the nearest challengers, Airdrieonians.

Since formation of Scottish League, 33 years ago, Rangers have never been lower than fourth on the League table, except in 1891-92, when they finished fifth.

On September 8th, 1888, Rangers played Canada on Old Ibrox Park; result was a draw, 1 goal each.

Alex. Smith is Rangers' record Internationalist, having a total of 34 caps.

The Wee Blue Book of season 1920-21 acknowledged the year of the club's formation as 1872. No reference was made in the club publication in either of the following two years, but by 1923-24 the date had been changed to 1873, without explanation.

Rovers. However, in the 1870 edition of Alcock's annuals a team called Rangers does appear, based in Swindon, with a kit that included white trousers, white jersey with a blue star on the breast, and a white cap. The Rangers football team that lost the Scottish Cup to Vale of Leven after three games in 1877 were pictured in the photographer's studio shortly afterwards in a very similar kit, including the blue star on the breast of their shirts, but it can be no more than a coincidence as the blue star arguably owed more to their connection with Clyde Rowing Club, who used it then (and still do now) as their club emblem.

In Alcock's 1871 edition Rangers are again mentioned, still at Gorse Hill in Swindon, but with the additional information that they had been formed in 1868 and played a form of rugby known as Marlborough. If it is accepted that Rangers were formed in the spring of 1872, as the weight of evidence suggests, and Moses McNeil named the club immediately, then the Swindon rugby team are the club from whom the Glasgow side took its name. Still, as always, there is scope for debate, because by the publication of the next edition, in the autumn of 1872, the Swindon club had disappeared and another club named Rangers (formed in 1870, but making its first appearance in Alcock's annual) had taken its place. This second club played rugby union and were based on Clapham Common in London. They were listed next to a club named Old Paulines – from Battersea Park to the south of the Thames, not Walford in the east. Another rugby union rival, from Stamford Hill near Stoke Newington, was named Red, White and Blue. Now, would that not have been a name for Moses to have contemplated?

The origins of the club name still inspire debate more than 140 years later, but Rangers have now embraced 1872 as their year of birth and marked their 140th anniversary celebrations in December 2012 with an on-field parade of club greats and legends before the league game with Stirling Albion. The sign atop the Govan Stand, which looks over the pitch, has also been changed and the year 1872 now book ends Rangers FC. The club have even established and marketed a range of clothing labelled the 1872 collection, including replicas of the shirts in which the Scottish Cup final team of 1877 were once pictured.

Rangers were also able to boast a royal connection in its very infancy, as a membership card from season 1874–75 announced the patron of the club as the Most Noble, the Marquis of Lorne, who would go on to become the 9th Duke of Argyll. Unfortunately, the reasons behind his formal relationship with Rangers have been lost in the mists of time as the minutes of the club from that era no longer exist, while the archives from the Duke's ancestral seat at Inverary Castle sadly, for the most part, are closed to the general public and have yet to undergo indexing.

However, it is clear that the new association football clubs saw patronage by the aristocracy as lending authority to their new ventures – not to forget, of course, the financial support that often came with the acceptance of an honorary position at the fledgling clubs. Queen's Park, for example, charged captain William Ker with finding a patron in 1873 and he immediately set his sights on the Prince of Wales, who politely declined. The Earl of Glasgow, however, agreed and quickly forwarded a donation of £5 to his new found favourites. In all likelihood the Marquis of Lorne, John Douglas Sutherland Campbell, better known as Ian, would have donated a similar sum to his fellow lads from Argyll to boost their new enterprise.

The Marquis was 27 years old when Rangers were formed and clearly had a level of interest in the association game as he was also an honorary president of the SFA at the time and was still listed as a patron of the association in the 1890s. It was something of a coup for the Rangers committee to persuade him to patronise their infant venture, not least because only a year earlier he had married Princess Louise, daughter of Queen Victoria, at Windsor, and had become one of the most high profile figures in British public life even if, as a Liberal member of parliament, he was regarded as something of a political plodder on the back benches at Westminster.

As future Clan Campbell chief, the Marquis of Lorne is likely to have been acquainted with John Campbell, his namesake and father of Peter, who would have enjoyed a position of standing in the Argyll community as a result of his successful steamboat enterprises. The McNeils would also surely have had access to high society, even if indirectly, through their father's position as head gardener at Belmore House on the shores of the Gare Loch. The Marquis, or Lorne as he was best known, was also a keen supporter of sporting pastimes, particularly those with an Argyll connection. The landed gentry viewed patronage of such healthy pastimes as an extension of their traditional responsibilities as clan chiefs, even in the latter half of the 19th century. In many instances, they would make prizes available or give financial support through an annual subscription to cover the cost of hosting get-togethers in sports such as shinty, cricket, curling, bowls and football. In addition to

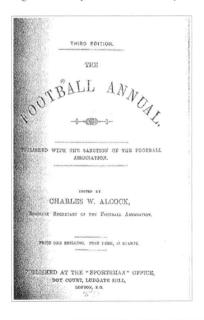

The Alcock Annual of 1870: The Rangers name appears for the first time, belonging to a club in Swindon (not specified as a rugby team until the 1871 edition) and with a design of kit similar to the one in which their Glasgow namesakes were pictured in the aftermath of their Scottish Cup final appearance in 1877.

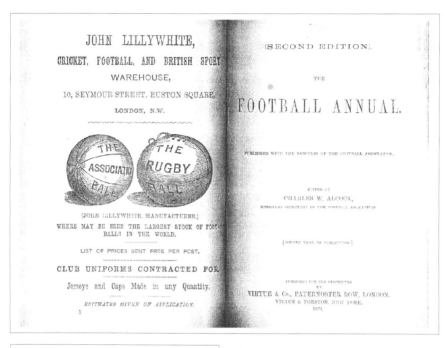

Rangers.
1. 1868.
2. 30.
3. Gorse Hill.
4. About quarter-mile from Swindon
   Station, on Great Western Railway.
5. Marlborough (modified Rugby).
6. W. H. Shepherd, Hon. Sec., 8, Bath
   Buildings, Swindon.
7. White trowsers, white jersey bound
   with blue, white cap.

The Charles W Alcock Football Annual from 1871. Rangers, from Swindon, are listed and confirmation is given of their preference for the Marlborough rugby code of football, as opposed to the association game.

Rangers and the SFA, Lorne was also a patron of the Inverary shinty club and the local curling club.[13]

It is unlikely Lorne ever watched Rangers play in the early years – there is no record of it – as his life in London and Argyll was demanding, not to mention the fact that in 1878 he left British shores to become Governor General of Canada. He and Louise made a massive contribution to Canadian life at the time and their patronage of the arts and letters was underlined with the establishment of institutions such as the Royal Canadian Academy of Arts and the National Gallery of Canada. Lorne and Louise returned to Britain in 1883 and he became ninth Duke of Argyll following the death of his father in April 1900. Lorne died of pneumonia on the Isle of Wight in May 1914, aged 68 and was buried at Kilmun – not the first

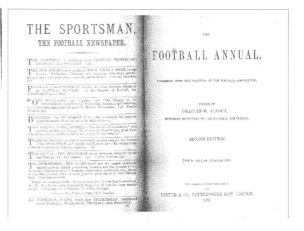

Rangers.
1. 1870.
2. Limited to 40.
3. Clapham Common.
4. Ten minutes from Clapham and North Stockwell Station on L.C. & D.R.
5. Rugby Union.
6. A.F. Browne, Milton Road, Dulwich Road, S.E.
7. Crimson and white in bars.

Alcock's annual in 1872 – Rangers from Swindon were no longer listed, but a Rangers from London were, with the Clapham Common club formed for fans of rugby union in the area.

with a Rangers connection to be buried at that peaceful graveyard by the shores of the Holy Loch. Louise, his wife of 43 years, lived out the rest of her long life at Rosneath Castle, although she died at Kensington Palace in 1939, aged 91. In her latter years she thought nothing of using her royal status to walk into any house in Rosneath unannounced to ensure all within were well. She shared the village for many years with Moses McNeil, who lived out his latter years in the close-knit community where he had been raised for part of his younger life. History has not recorded if they were ever on speaking terms. They may have led two very different existences, but they could claim without fear of contradiction membership of special institutions that still mean so much to so many.

It is to the credit of the founding fathers that they quickly attracted supporters of means and substance, not just financially, that would give their infant club the best chance of survival beyond a few short years – it was a feat few teams would manage in those chaotic times of the game's development. In addition to the Marquis of Lorne, the McNeils also used their family connections at Gare Loch to secure the backing of the two most important families in the Glasgow retail trade, who built a palace for high-class shoppers that is still in use in the city in the 21st century.

John McNeil, father of Moses, was a master gardener at Belmore House which still stands as

The Marquis of Lorne, first honorary president of Rangers, before his wedding to Louise, daughter of Queen Victoria.

One of the first members' cards, from season 1874-1875. The names of all the founding fathers are to the fore, along with the patron, The Most Noble The Marquis of Lorne.

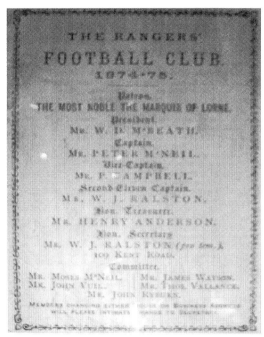

THE RANGERS'
FOOTBALL CLUB
1874-75.

Patron.
THE MOST NOBLE THE MARQUIS OF LORNE.

President.
Mr. W. P. M'BEATH.

Captain.
Mr. PETER M'NEIL.

Vice-Captain.
Mr. P. CAMPBELL.

Second Eleven Captain.
Mr. W. J. RALSTON.

Hon. Treasurer.
Mr. HENRY ANDERSON.

Hon. Secretary.
Mr. W. J. RALSTON (pro tem.),
100 Kent Road.

Committee.
Mr. Moses M'Neil.   Mr. James Watson.
Mr. John Yuill.   Mr. Thos. Vallance.
              Mr. John Keiden.

part of the Faslane Naval Base. In 1856, within 12 months of the birth of Moses, the house was sold by corn merchant John Honeyman to a family of impeccable merchant class who would, with one small gesture, have Rangers off and running 16 years later. The McDonald family had been significant players in the Glasgow retail industry since 1826 when John McDonald, a tailor from Vale of Leven, joined forces with Robertson Buchanan Stewart, a soldier from Rothesay. Their company, Stewart and McDonald, would become such giants of the industry that by 1866 it was turning over a colossal £1 million a year.

Stewart and McDonald opened a wholesale drapery business in the upstairs of a tenement building at No. 5 Buchanan Street, taking a bold risk on the expansion of the city centre westwards from its main thoroughfare on Argyle Street. It was a calculated gamble that paid off within three years when the Argyll Arcade, a glass-covered thoroughfare of jewellers and upper-class outfitters, which retains much of its elegance to this day, was opened and lured more and more shoppers to an area of the town that had hitherto been under-developed for the fashionistas of the age. Stewart and McDonald expanded to meet the demand from the growing population and by 1866 it occupied a massive 4,000 square yards and its huge warehouses dominated Argyle Street, Buchanan Street and Mitchell Street.

The first Hugh Fraser was a lace buyer to the company and rose to become a manager in 1849. A series of buyouts and mergers over the next 100 years finally led to it becoming known as House of Fraser. The current Fraser's department store on the west side of Buchanan Street still occupies the building that was first constructed for Stewart and McDonald.

John McDonald died in May 1860 aged just 51 and the debt of gratitude Rangers owe is to his sons, Alexander or, most probably, John junior. Alexander had been made a director of Stewart and McDonald in 1859 but passed away in his prime, dying of consumption during a tour of the Upper Nile in March 1869, aged only 31. The family fortune, including Belmore, passed in trust to John, then aged only 18, but the McDonald family would help develop a football legacy with one act of kindness, revealed by John Allan in his early history of Rangers. He wrote: "To

The memorial at Garelochhead Parish Church to John McDonald of Belmore, credited with gifting the first football to Rangers. He was also an early patron of the Clydesdale Harriers, who had close links with the Kinning Park club. The inscription at the base of the monument reads: 'This cross was erected by the earliest and most intimate friends of John McDonald of Belmore and Torlochan in affectionate remembrance of his many excellent qualities and the noble example of his manly and blameless life. He died at St Leonard's Windsor, 17th June 1891, aged 40 years, and rests in Clewer Churchyard.'

William (McNeil) there fell the rare gift of a football from the son of a gentleman by whom his father was employed in the Gareloch. The generous donor was a Mr McDonald of the firm Stewart and McDonald, in Buchanan Street."[14]

It was the same ball Willie would stuff under his arm before storming off in a huff at the prospect of being refused permission to play for the newly formed Rangers, telling his brother and their pals: "If you can't have me, you can't have my ball."[15] He was not allowed to wander far, as Moses admitted in later years: "Willie was the proud possessor of a ball so, although he was the veteran of the little company, it was indispensable that he should be a member of our team."[16]

A 12ft tall Celtic cross still stands in honour of John McDonald junior at Garelochhead Parish Church. He lived long enough to see the club flourish from birth into one of renown but he did not survive into old age and died, after complications arising from flu, in June 1891, aged just 40.

The influence of Stewart and McDonald on the early years of Rangers was more than just an accidental donation of the club's first football and it is entirely reasonable to conclude that it was through the relationship with the McDonalds that Rangers also secured the support from their business partners, the Stewarts. John Stevenson Stewart was another notable patron of the club and was listed as honorary president of Rangers in the Scottish Football Annuals across various seasons between 1878–85. Born in 1862, he was still a teenager at the time, but would no doubt have been encouraged by his father, Alexander Bannatyne Stewart, to take an active role in public life and choose an association with the Light Blues, perhaps on the back of the growing reputation of the club as a result of their appearance in the 1877 Scottish Cup Final. The title passed to his younger brother Ninian at the Rangers annual meeting in May 1885 and he also gave good service. Certainly, it would not have harmed the reputation of the club to be so closely associated with two of the leading business figures in the city at the time.

Setting the record straight: In the earliest SFA annuals the year of the formation of Rangers was clearly recognised as 1872.

Their father Alexander, born in 1836, had a residence in Langside on Glasgow's south side known as Rawcliffe, as well as a country retreat, Ascog House on the Isle of Bute, and was a man of substantial means. He died in the Midland Hotel in London during a trip to the capital in 1880 and left an estate worth a staggering £350,000. Alexander had become a partner in the family firm in 1866, six years after the death of his father, and while the business continued to prosper under his command he also had a strong charitable nature. For example, the Robertson-Stewart Hospital in Rothesay was established and supported financially by the family, while the local parish church also benefited from his largesse.

Alexander was a financial backer of the construction of the aquarium and esplanade in the seaside town and many other good causes locally received substantial donations. Indeed, Rangers opened their season in 1879–80 with a game on a public park in Rothesay to raise funds for charities on the Isle of Bute, undoubtedly at the request of John Stevenson Stewart and his father. The Light Blues lost the game 1–0 against Queen's Park. Clearly, even in those days, charity never extended onto the field of play.

Chapter 3
Moses McNeil

Moses McNeil has led Rangers historians a merry dance for decades, matching any trickery he ever showed with the ball at his feet on the left wing for his beloved club. Finally, however, we can picture this giant of Scottish football. The will-o'-the-wisp forward dashed past opposition defences with ease in the 1870s and 1880s but has finally been given up to the Rangers support. That mischievous glint in his eye suggests he wouldn't mind one little bit.

There are still those of a certain vintage around today who can remember Moses McNeil living out his latter years in the village of Rosneath on his beloved Clyde peninsula, where he was born on 29 October 1855. He lived modestly for much of the final part of his life before his death from heart disease at the age of 82 on 9 April 1938 at Townend Hospital in Dumbarton. The house he shared latterly with his sister Isabella, Craig Cottage, is still standing, tucked up off the main road leading into the village, away from prying eyes. It is somehow fitting because this giant of Scottish football appeared to withdraw gradually in his latter years from all he had helped create, including Rangers.

Even in death, Moses continues to play hide and seek with those keen to acknowledge the enormous role he played in establishing Rangers as a club of stature and also pay tribute to the former Scottish international for his contribution to the game in general. He is buried in the nearby Rosneath graveyard, for sure – his death notice in the Glasgow Herald and records at Cardross Cemetery confirm it – but only recently has the paperwork from the time been uncovered to confirm his interment in a double plot with Isabella and her husband, former sea captain Duncan Gray, and the McNeils' eldest sister, Elizabeth. As the last of his family line, it is unsurprising that the name of Moses is missing from the gravestone under which he lies. For decades he has given Rangers historians the slip, in the same way he dashed past opposition defences in the 1870s and 1880s as a will-o'-the-wisp left-winger.

A couple of miles beyond Rosneath, in the village of Kilcreggan, Ian and Ronnie MacGrowther potter around the boatyard they own and which has provided them with a living for more years than they care to remember. The sheds in which they work may be beginning to show signs of age, but the recollections of the brothers from yesteryear in the community in which they were born and raised remain as sharp and mischievous as ever. If Ronnie, born in 1932, closes his eyes he can still picture Moses McNeil, a small man with a navy blue suit and walking stick and very rarely without his bowler hat. "He always looked respectable, but I don't think there was a lot of money around," he recalled. "A lot of people in the community didn't know about his connection with Rangers, but my father did. Moses was a nice old man, but he could also be a wee bit prickly on occasions."

Another former neighbour recalls Moses leaving for Glasgow once a month, they believed to pick up a pension from Rangers. More often than not, there was a spring in his step, a glint in his eye and a slight slur in his speech by the time he returned home much later in the day.

Time, thankfully, was not playing tricks with the memories of Ian and Ronnie as the rich mosaic of Rangers history was coloured still further with the delightful discovery of a new picture of founding father Moses. The family snap was taken at Rosneath in the early 1930s, shortly before his death, and only came to light in the aftermath of the publication of The Gallant Pioneers in 2009.

The picture shows a dapper Moses with nieces Mary Margaret Stewart and Isabel Scott and Mary Margaret's husband, Archie. Mary Margaret and Isabel were grand-daughters of Harry McNeil, Moses' brother - the great Queen's Park and

Scotland winger who guested for Rangers in their first game, that 0-0 draw against Callander at Flesher's Haugh in May 1872. The snap is significant as it is the only picture of Moses from the 20th century research has unearthed. It came from the family scrapbook of Anne Law, great granddaughter of Harry. Anne, from Glasgow, said: "Mary Margaret was my

Moses, pictured in the 1930s, with nieces Mary Margaret Stewart (left), Isabel Scott and Mary Margaret's husband, Archie. Mary Margaret and Isabel were grand-daughters of Harry McNeil.

mother and Moses was very fond of her. My mother and father used to visit Moses and his sister Bella in Rosneath quite often in the 1930s and my own middle name is McNeil. I didn't realise the significance of the photograph until recently, but I was delighted to share it with Rangers fans because I'm also a big supporter of the club."

The jigsaw was completed still further when club historian David Mason put Founders Trail organisers Iain McColl and Gordon Bell in touch with Elizabeth Pirie. David had worked with her son several years previously and believed there may have been a connection with Moses. Iain said: "Very nervously I rang Elizabeth and, incredibly, within a couple of days Gordon and I found ourselves sitting in her Glasgow home for what was a jaw-dropping experience. Elizabeth's grandfather was James McNeil, brother of Moses and Peter, and became very successful in the drapery and lace trade, working for Stewart and MacDonald's in Buchanan Street. He is buried at Craigton, which Elizabeth didn't know, so Gordon and I arranged to take her on the Founders Trail. We visited many locations, including four homes where her grandfather once lived, and she was able to pay her respects at the final resting place of James and some of her great uncles. To top it all, we contacted the club and she was invited to join the 140th anniversary celebrations at Ibrox in December 2012. She watched the match from the directors' box with her son and daughter."

The memory of that special day will live long in Elizabeth's memory. She said: "It was a joy to sit at Ibrox with so many people. I was treated like royalty in the Blue Room before the match and it was all a bit of a shock because I never realised how much Uncle Moses meant to so many people. I can still vividly recall travelling from our home in Prestwick as a child with my mother and aunt to visit him in Clynder. We would take the train to Helensburgh and then a small boat across the loch and walk along the coast to his home, where we'd spend many a weekend. He was a happy, kind man who would often take me for walks around the village and down to the local shops."

Moses, like most of the children of John and Jean McNeil, was raised in a world of wealth and privilege which, unfortunately, was not their own. John McNeil was born in Comrie, Perthshire, in 1809, the son of a farmer, also named John, and mother Catherine Drummond. He came to Glasgow in the early part of the 19th century where he met Jean Loudon Bain, born in around 1815, the daughter of Henry Bain, a grocer and general merchant from County Down. They married in Glasgow on 31 December 1839 and although little is known about their early years, religion was clearly important in their lives judging by the grand

Moses McNeil in a family snapshot – the bowler hat was to remain a feature throughout his life.

standing of the minister who conducted their wedding service. The very reverend Duncan McFarlan had been named principal of Glasgow University in 1823 and minister for Glasgow Cathedral in 1824. At the time of the marriage of John and Jean, he had already been Moderator of the General Assembly of the Church of Scotland in 1819, and was appointed for his second spell in 1843.

According to census records of 1841, John was a gardener at rural Hogganfield Farm, in the north-east of the fledgling city, which only expanded to swallow well-known districts of today such as Anderston, Bridgeton, North Kelvinside and the Gorbals into its boundaries as late as 1846. The young couple's joy continued when daughter Elizabeth was born the year after they wed and they remained in Glasgow until 1842, celebrating the birth of their first son, John junior. In total, the couple had 11 children, including footballers Moses, Henry, William and Peter, but two boys did not survive infancy, a sad but all too common aspect of childhood at the time.

By the time second son James was born in 1843 the family were living in Rhu and had begun a relationship with the Gareloch that would continue until the death of Moses almost a century later. John, who was now a master gardener, had accepted an offer of employment from John Honeyman at Belmore House near Shandon, on the east side of the Gare Loch now occupied by the Faslane Naval Base. The house, which still stands, had been built to modest dimensions in around 1830 by a local fishing family, the MacFarlanes, but Honeyman, showing an eye for architectural design that would later earn his son his fame and fortune, subsequently bought the house and set about remodelling it, as John took control of its sizeable gardens and brought to fruition his own landscape design skills and vision.

Honeyman was a corn merchant with a principal residence off Glasgow Green, but had bought Belmore as a weekend and summer retreat. The new steamer routes from Glasgow to the coast and, from 1857, the introduction of the railway to the nearby town of Helensburgh, had made the area more easily accessible for the growing business class. Finance was clearly not an issue for

Belmore House, birthplace of Moses McNeil and where his father John lived with his family and worked as a master gardener under the Honeymans and McDonalds. It is now part of the Faslane Naval base.

Honeyman, with no expense spared on Belmore. The education of his son, John junior, was also the very best. He boarded at Merchiston Castle in Edinburgh and attended Glasgow University, before setting up an architectural practice in the city in 1854. Honeyman junior joined forces with another designer, John Keppie, in 1888 and within 12 months a young, up-and-coming architect joined the firm's

Row from the Bay, Gareloch

Rhu from the bay at Gare Loch, a village and stretch of water the Gallant Pioneers, William McBeath apart, knew intimately.

offices at No. 140 Bath Street in Glasgow city centre – Charles Rennie Mackintosh.

Back at Belmore, the McNeil family continued to expand with the birth of Alexander in 1845, Henry in 1848 and Isabella Honeyman McNeil in 1850 – the latter named in honour of the wife of John's employer. William McNeil was born in 1852, followed by Peter in 1854 and, finally, in 1855, Moses. Not only was the family of John and Jean growing, so too was the community in which they were living as Glasgow's new, prosperous, middle classes sought a release from the city and the smog by building second homes on the coast, in towns and villages such as

Shandon, Garelochhead, Rhu, Rosneath and Kilcreggan.

Iain McColl, Neil Stobie and Gordon Bell outside Belmore House in Faslane with Royal Navy representatives, leading seaman McFadden (left) and warrant officer Craig Campbell MBE (right).

In 1856, Belmore House was sold to the McDonalds, that family of impeccable merchant class. By 1871 John, Jean and Moses, then 14, had moved across the Gare Loch to a cottage named Flower Bank, which still stands today above Rosneath. It is possible that John was still in employment at Belmore as it was an easy commute across the loch to the pier at Shandon. The gardens in which John worked no longer stand in their past glory. At their peak, the grounds extended to 33 acres. The house left the McDonald family in 1919 and was sold on again in 1926 to biscuit manufacturer George McFarlane, before eventually passing into government control following his death in 1938. Faslane was developed as a military port from 1942, a role it continues to fill to this day as the home of the UK's Trident nuclear defence programme.

The Royal Navy had no inkling of the connection between Belmore House and Rangers and, intrigued to find out more, they invited organisers of the Founders Trail to Faslane in September 2011. Iain McColl said: "We couldn't have been made to feel more welcome. Their interest in our research and their hospitality was overwhelming. After giving the background to the link with Belmore House, the McNeil family and the story behind The Founders Trail, we were presented with a plaque from The First Mine Countermeasures Squadron as a token of their friendship. We, in turn, presented them with copies of The Gallant Pioneers. I thought we'd be viewed as nothing more than geeky enthusiasts who would be allowed to take a few pics and then ushered back off the base quick style. I couldn't have been more wrong. It was a wonderful day and a chance to connect still further with the story of our wonderful club."

Warrant Officer Craig Campbell MBE of Faslane's First Mine Countermeasures Squadron hosted the visitors - and was thrilled to do so. He said: "As a life-long fan of Rangers I was delighted to show the group around. I've worked in Belmore House for a number of years but had no idea of the historic links to the football club. It was fascinating to speak with the guys and learn about the connections. I don't think I'll look at my workplace the same way again."

Undoubtedly, growing up in the area Moses had access to one of the best backyards in Scotland and he and his brothers clearly took advantage of the leisure spaces the Gareloch and its surrounding countryside had to offer. Shinty was a popular sport – his brother Harry was credited as a player – while Moses also found enjoyment in rowing and athletics. A memento to his prowess as an athlete is to be found in the Ibrox trophy room still, an eight-inch silver goblet he won for finishing first in a half-mile race at the Garelochhead annual sports in 1876. It is the oldest trophy on display, but he had been setting the pace at the village sports meeting, held every New Year's Day, for several years before.

In 1873, for example, the Dumbarton Herald reported on him pipping close friend and fellow Ranger Peter Campbell in a quarter-mile race for the Under-16s. Moses made it a double when he teamed up with Tom Vallance to win the three-legged race, but there was no old pals' act in the 200 yards when Tom held off the youngest McNeil for first prize. Undeterred, on 1 January 1874 Moses returned home and this time triumphed in the half-mile race for the Under-20s. He then followed it up with success in the hurdles and 200 yards and repeated his three-legged feat from 12 months earlier with Tom.

The entrants' list at the Garelochhead sports read like a who's who of Rangers in the 1870s, with the Campbell, McNeil and Vallance brothers all to the fore. Despite his escapades on the track that year, Moses still had more to offer 24 hours later on Friday 2 January when he, brother Peter and William McBeath scored the goals for Rangers in a 3–0 challenge match victory against wonderfully named local select side the Garelochhead Dollopers.

Still, despite the pleasures on offer at home, it came as no surprise when Moses followed the well-worn path of his brothers and sisters to Glasgow, most likely towards the end of 1871. Employment was plentiful and his siblings, under matriarch Elizabeth, had established themselves in the Sandyford district, first at No. 17 Cleveland Street and then around the corner at No. 169 Berkeley Street. Elizabeth, listed in the census as housekeeper, effectively operated a home from home for her younger brothers and their friends from the Gareloch, including John and James Campbell, two great Rangers and brothers of founding father Peter. Indeed, Berkeley Street would remain a base for the McNeils for at least the next two decades under the watchful eye of Elizabeth, who never married and died in 1915 in Rosneath.

By 1881 their father and mother were being lured back towards Glasgow and lived at Old Kilpatrick with their other daughter, Isabella. John may have been 71, but even in his eighth decade he was still listed as a master gardener and employed three men. By the end of the decade, John and Jean had moved back into the city, to the family hub at Berkeley Street. Jean died at the house in September 1890 aged 76, just five months after John had passed away in the same place at the age of 82.

Fittingly, they were buried together at Craigton Cemetery in a lair that had been purchased 15 years earlier by their son Alex. Unfortunately, their graves lay unmarked and untended until recently when Rangers fans stepped in to mark and tend the plots. It was appropriate, not just in honouring the family, but in giving consideration to the pleasure a well maintained garden gave John McNeil through his long working life.

Moses, on the other hand, restricted his design skills to the football field – and what pretty

Harry McNeil, pictured with his grand-daughters in his garden at Rutherglen, circa 1920. He was still a regular at Ibrox, with the children, at this time.

patterns he could weave. However, he was almost lost to the club he helped to form within three years when he was seduced by the covetous glances of Queen's Park, no doubt prompted by his brother Harry, who was already a Hampden stalwart. Moses joined Queen's Park on 5 October 1875 and it is surely no coincidence that it was just four days before his new club were due to face Wanderers at Hampden Park.

Wanderers were the first great powerhouses of English football; they were winners of the first FA Cup in 1872, once again in 1873 and triumphant in another three straight finals from 1876–78. The Glasgow club had met Wanderers once before – in the semi-final of the English competition that first season – and their willingness to travel to London to face such mighty foes was considered a remarkable show of courage. In actual fact the visitors' play was a revelation. Not for them a series of aimless dribbles up the park, more in hope than expectation, but an accurate passing game that had rarely before been seen outside of Glasgow. The game finished goalless but Queen's Park were forced to scratch as they could not afford to stay in London for the replay, especially as their fares to the capital had been paid from a public subscription in the first place.

Moses and Harry played starring roles on 9 October 1875 as Queen's destroyed Wanderers 5–0 in front of 11,000 at Hampden Park. Opposition players such as C. W. Alcock and Lord Kinnaird, the first president of the FA, a Scotland cap and veteran of nine FA Cup Finals, could not get close to them. One report read:

Did James forget that Chairman Bowie was also a Queen's Park boy,

they still are wandering in the forest of relegation, for St. Mirren, Dunferm-

M'Killop and Winning; Brownlie, Macauley, Fiddes, Latif and Roberts.

WHEN RANGERS FIRST REACHED FINAL

By MOSES McNEIL

IN the summer of 1873, my brothers, Peter and Willie, and myself, along with some other Gareloch lads, banded together on Glasgow Green with the object of forming a football club. Willie was the proud possessor of a ball, so, although he was the veteran of the little company, it was indispensable that he should be a member of our team. Discussion arose as to what the club should be called, and finally, at my suggestion, it was decided to call it Rangers Association Football Club. Little did we think, in those far-off days, that we were forming a club whose fame was to become world-wide.

It was in season 1876-77 that Rangers played in their first Scottish Cup Final. Vale of Leven were our opponents, and on their way to the final they had defeated Queen's Park. This was the first defeat inflicted on the Queen's since their inception nine years previously.

The football public naturally considered our chances to be extremely slender. However, we were confident, and went into special training in preparation for our first Cup Final. No trips to Turnberry in those days, but a glorious " tuck-in " of ham and

Moses McNeil is the sole survivor of the original Rangers team. He played for them, at outside-left, from 1875 till 1883, and was capped for Scotland against England 1 and Wales in 1876.

eggs and steak after each morning's training.

When the great day arrived, the following team faced Vale of Leven at Hamilton Crescent, Partick:—

J. M. Watt; George Gillespie and Tom Vallance; Wm. M'Neil and Sam Ricketts; D. Hill, W. Dunlop, A. Marshall, Jas Watson, Peter Campbell, and Moses M'Neil.

Third Game

The result was a draw, neither side scoring. The replay was staged at the same ground; at the end of the regulation time the score stood at one goal each, and extra time had to be played. Excitement ran high as both sides strove for victory. Only a few minutes remained when a melee occurred in the Vale goal. The 'keeper, W. C. Wood, cleared his lines, but we claimed that the ball had passed over the goal-line. The referee disallowed our claim, but I still maintain to this day that it was a perfectly good goal, and that

Rangers' name should have been inscribed on the Cup that season.

However, as we were still equal at the end of the extra half-hour, a third game had to be played. This time, the venue was Hampden (the old ground, now Cathkin, occupied by Third Lanark).

This replay tie fairly aroused the public interest, and one report states, " cabs, 'buses, etc., swarmed to Hampden, and before the start *there would be nearly 7000 or 8000 present.*" It certainly was the biggest crowd before which we had ever played. I do not think, however, that we were affected by the crowd. It was the strong physique of our opponents that told in the end. At half-time we were down 1-0, but soon after the change-round Peter Campbell equalised. Then I scored to put Rangers on the lead. The Vale, however, put on the screw, and soon drew level, and shortly afterwards Watt came out of his goal and made a faulty clearance. The ball went to the feet of R. Paton, of the Vale, who had nothing to do but guide the ball through an empty goal. This ended the scoring, the final result being—Vale of Leven, 3; Rangers, 2. So for the first, but by no means the last time, the Cup eluded us, after we had battled our way to the final.

Players were seen and not heard in the first decades of the game. Here, Moses McNeil takes a very rare, on the record stroll down memory lane for readers of the Daily Record in 1935. His first person piece would almost certainly have been ghost-written by the paper's editor and Rangers historian, John Allan.

"The brothers McNeil – Harry well backed up by Moses – made some beautiful runs, nor were they, in fact, ever away from the ball when it was in their part of the ground. Their English opponents too found it was no use knocking them over as they just rolled on to their feet again."[1]

Moses returned to the arms of Rangers immediately after the return match in London, which was held on 5 February 1876. Wanderers took their revenge, winning 2–0, to inflict on Queen's their first defeat since their formation in 1867. Moses was scarcely mentioned in the match reports, although the correspondent of the North British Daily Mail lamented on the poor turnout of spectators: "The number, I believe, did not reach any more than 1,000. Londoners will not and do not crowd to see a football match."[2] His crystal ball was as defective as the Queen's Park performance.

Still just 20, Moses came increasingly to the fore in the mid-1870s and he was confirmed as a Rangers player again on 19 February 1876 when Glasgow travelled to Sheffield for their annual inter-city match, almost as important and high profile at the time as the yearly meetings between Scotland and England. Moses and teammate Peter Campbell (the latter a last minute call-up) became the first Light Blues to earn representative honours as they helped their new city to a 2–0 win in front of 7,000 fans at Bramall Lane.

Moses also represented Glasgow against Sheffield in 1878 and 1880 and won two full caps for Scotland, the first in a 4–0 win over Wales at Hamilton Crescent in 1876, while the second came during a 5–4 victory over England at the first Hampden Park in 1880. As a left-winger, he played with something of a dash for club and country – the SFA Annual in 1881 considered him: "an excellent forward, possessing great determination and pluck…a good dodger and dribbler, his long passing is at times very effective."

His brief hiatus at Hampden apart, Moses played for Rangers for a full decade from the birth of the club, playing somewhere in the region of 135 matches and scoring approximately 40 goals until he bowed out in a goalless draw at home to South Western on 5 April 1882. In contrast to his brother Peter, the politics and internal structures of football seemed to hold little interest for him. Peter undoubtedly compensated for his lack of skill and ability on the park by concentrating on the contribution he could make as an administrator off-field. The opposite applied to Moses, who seemed to find fulfilment enough in playing the game at the very highest level possible. Certainly, the running of the club appeared to hold limited appeal – the most senior position he was awarded in office was the post of honorary treasurer in 1876–77. Moses was a committee member of the club throughout the 1870s, but this appeared to be an honour bestowed on most first-team players, courtesy of the high regard in which they were held for their footballing skills. Membership numbers would rarely climb above 70 in the early years, so founders and stalwarts from the early seasons would have been at an immediate advantage when it came to drawing up the club's portfolio of office bearers.

That his dynamism was reserved for the football field is also suggested in Moses' employment record throughout the latter half of the 19th and into the 20th century. Moses, who never married or had children, spent most of his professional career in the employ of Hugh Lang junior, a commission agent who was based at No. 70 Union Street in Glasgow, not far from H. and P. McNeil's sports outfitters at No. 91. Lang came from a famous family whose name has long been synonymous with Scotch whisky. Hugh Lang senior was a Broomielaw innkeeper in the first half of the 19th century, famed among sailors for the quality of his blends, which were sold in his bar, as well as in five gallon jars around the local area. In 1861 three of his

Homeward bound: The village of Rosneath, where Moses returned to live out his final years with sister, Isabella.

five sons – Gavin, Alexander and William – decided to take their father's whisky and market it more widely and the Lang Brothers brand proved so successful that by 1876 they bought over the Glengoyne Distillery at Killearn, which remained in the family's hands for over a century.

Hugh Lang junior was clearly close to his siblings and became a director of Lang Brothers when it was incorporated in 1897. He undoubtedly shared their passion for their popular brand but, in actual fact, census records between 1871 and 1901 clarify that the nature of his business was as a wholesale hosier. Moses started working for him as a clerk and later became a commercial traveller – in effect, a travelling salesman, with a contact book of buyers that most likely included his brothers' shop along the road.

Moses worked for Lang for around two decades but by 1901 was living in a lodging house in Stanley Street (now known as Baliol Street, just off Woodlands Road in the West End) and still working as a commercial traveller, this time as a brush and oils salesman. The specific nature of his employment is not known, but it is possible he had been found his new position by his nephew John McNeil, son of older brother Alex. John started work as a commercial traveller with Craig and Rose, the renowned Edinburgh paint merchant who provided the paint for the Forth Bridge when it was constructed between 1883–1890. John was promoted through the ranks of the company after many years of distinguished service and eventually became managing director.

It is tempting to suggest that Moses distanced himself from the club he helped to create as his life progressed, but the evidence is too flimsy, its weight not heavy enough to sustain an argument for any length of time. However, it is surprising, for example, that Moses, so recognised as an influential figure in the early years of the game, did not participate in the trailblazer reunions for up to 80 ex-players organised by Vale of Leven benefactor James Ferguson up and down Loch Lomond throughout the 1920s.

More intriguing was the decision by Moses to send an apology to excuse his presence from the gala dinner at Ferguson and Forrester's in April 1923 to mark the 50th anniversary of the club he helped create. The Evening Times reported: "Tom Vallance, one of the two sole survivors of the original team, was present. The other, Moses McNeil, wrote regretting that he was unable to participate in the reunion." Teammate James 'Tuck' McIntyre, by then approaching his 80th birthday, was there to help lower Tom Vallance into his grave following the death of the club's first great captain in 1935, but Moses was not mentioned as being present at the funeral of one his closest childhood friends.

The other side of the argument is that Moses still played an active role in and around the club in the years immediately following his departure from first-team football, even if he chose not to participate politically behind the scenes. He was regular enough for the Rangers ancients and was listed in a team of Kinning Park old boys that took on the Cameronians at Maryhill Barracks in November 1885. He did not play in the ancients against modern game in February 1887 that marked the closure of the old Kinning Park ground, but was pictured in the souvenir photograph taken on the day in a position of prominence in the second row, his trusty cane at hand and that dapper bowler on his head.

Brother Harry bowed out of football in September 1888 when a team of Queen's Park old boys took on a side of Rangers veterans at the exhibition showgrounds at Kelvingrove Park and beat them 2–1. 'Mosie' had been tipped to play by the Scottish Umpire but prematurely, although he was not alone in the no-shows. Another McNeil brother, Willie, also failed to trap but the likes of Harry, William 'Daddy' Dunlop, George Gillespie, the Vallance brothers and 'Tuck' McIntyre kept the sizeable crowd entertained.

Of course, Moses was the source of much of John Allan's material in his 1923 jubilee history of Rangers and was also quoted at length in the Daily Record of 1935, talking about how he had helped form the club so many years before. He was arguably still in contact with Rangers (if, as his neighbour suspected, he was drawing a pension) or at the very least with people such as Allan, who were close to the Ibrox powerbrokers at the time. However, as life moved on he possibly preferred the pace of a quieter existence, especially after moving to Rosneath around 1930. Few people in the community knew of his connection with Rangers and he was able to live quietly with his sister Isabella at Craig Cottage (before then he had been living in a flat at West Graham Street in the Garnethill district of Glasgow).

Moses was certainly company for his sister Isabella, who died in 1935 and whose own life had been touched with terrible sadness. She married master mariner Duncan Gray in 1884, but his life ended at Rosneath in 1907, with his death certificate ominously recording his passing as a result of a gunshot injury to the head. Those still around today with an intimate knowledge of the Grays' former marital home confirm his suicide.

Perhaps it is inevitable, given the size of the family and the time in which they lived, that untimely deaths and tragic passings would so affect the McNeils. Harry also knew his share of grief and lost his second wife, Margaret, in bizarre circumstances in November 1895 at the Royal Hotel, the establishment they had run together in Bangor, County Down, from May 1892 until Margaret's death on 2 November 1895.

The Belfast Newsletter of Tuesday, 5 November told the sad story in grisly terms, reporting on the coroner's inquest that established Margaret's death was a result of an accidental overdose. The court was told she had been struggling mentally after the loss of her first child in infancy following his birth in March 1893 and the hotel had even been put up for sale 12 months earlier, before a change of mind from the couple. The Newsletter quoted the attending physician, a Dr Bolton, revealing how Margaret was left broken hearted at the death of her son and "grief, worry, anxiety and chloral were the sequence."

She had been put to bed that Saturday afternoon by Harry, as was her habit, and had taken a nip of brandy, some soup and a narcotic draught to help her sleep but unfortunately - and not for the first time - had taken twice the prescribed level of the drug, which she had been using for 18 months. Harry checked on her at 5pm and all was well but two hours later, when he next looked into the room, she was struggling for breath and appeared to be choking on her false teeth. Dr Bolton was called, but could do nothing to prevent her untimely death at the age of just 32.

Rosneath old cemetery, burial place of Moses McNeil, who rests with sisters Isabella and Elizabeth and his brother-in-law, Captain Duncan Gray.

The coroner passed no blame and ruled her death was a result of narcotic poisoning, leading to paralysis of the heart.

Moses, the youngest McNeil child and the longest surviving, eventually succumbed to cardiac disease on 9 April 1938 and while someone loved him enough to send a short notice recording his death to the Glasgow Herald and the Evening Times, his name was never added to the gravestone in Rosneath graveyard that includes the inscriptions, faint now after so many decades, in memory of his sisters and brother-in-law. At the time of his death, the sports pages were dominated by the forthcoming Scotland versus England clash at Wembley. Scotland won the match 1–0, courtesy of a goal from Hearts ace Tommy Walker. Rangers also played that afternoon, with a solitary strike from Bob McPhail securing a slender win over Clyde in the League at Ibrox.

The passing of Moses did not merit a mention in the press that week. He was buried on Tuesday 12 April but it was not until six days later that 'Waverley' penned an obituary of sorts in the Record. He wrote: "A famous player of a long past era in Moses McNeil has also departed. Moses was one of several brothers who helped to form the Rangers clubs [sic] in 1873 and he was the last of the old originals. He played against England in 1880. It is wonderful to think that one who was at the start of the Rangers 65 years ago should have been with us until a few days ago."[4]

In recent years, as the final resting place of Moses has become more widely known among the community of Rangers fans, many have made a pilgrimage to Rosneath to pay their respects to easily the best-known name among the club's founding fathers. The Founders Trail have also organised hugely popular days out to the village to walk in the footsteps of the gallant pioneers. A few years ago Rangers awarded Moses one of the first inaugurations in the club's Hall of Fame and discussions are still ongoing for a more lasting memorial to him in or around the local burial ground.

He gave us all the slip for too many years, left us trailing in his wake like a bemused 19th-century back trying to tackle him on the wing. Little by little, Moses McNeil is finally being pinned down. For all his achievements, he deserves nothing less than the widest public acknowledgement.

Chapter 4

Valiant, Virtuous — and Vale of Leven

It says much for the camaraderie and friendships formed in the early years of Scottish football that reunions of its earliest pioneers were still being held half a century after they had first kicked leather. Old scars were put on display and old scores playfully settled on a day cruise up and down Loch Lomond, held annually throughout the 1920s. The host was one of Vale of Leven's most fanatical supporters, James Ferguson, a successful colour and dye making merchant who built a thriving business in Merton, South London, that survived well into the 1960s, two decades after his death in 1941.

Those in attendance included former Vale skipper John Ferguson, no relation to James, a skilful forward who won six caps for Scotland, scoring five

The pavilion at Tarbet, Loch Lomond, in 1923 as the old boys of Scottish football gathered for a sail down memory lane - Tom Vallance is seated in the front row, far left.

goals, and was an equally proficient athlete and former winner of the Powderhall Sprint. The group, typically around 80 strong, "their tongues going like 'haun guns',"1 would gather on Balloch Pier at noon before boarding the steamer for a trip to a hotel where a lavish lunch was served.

Drink flowed as freely as the anecdotes and on the journey back to Balloch

The above photo was taken at Rowardennan, Lochlomond, on the occasion of the annual outing of the survivors of the 1876 Vale of Leven team which won the Scottish Cup that year and were the first provincial club to win it. The aggregate number of caps won by the International players in the group is 77.

Back row (from left to right)—John M'Pherson (Vale of Leven)—E., 1879, 1880, 1883, 1884; W., 1879, 1881, 1883; I., 1885. A. M'Intyre (Vale of Leven)—E., 1878, 1882. Jas. Kelly (Celtic)—E., 1888, 1889, 1890, 1892, 1893; Wales, 1894; I., 1886, 1893, 1896. Walter Arnott (Queen's Park)—E., 1884, 1885, 1886, 1887, 1888, 1889, 1890, 1891, 1892, 1893; W., 1883, 1885, 1887; I., 1884; Canada, 1891. James M'Auley (Dumbarton)—E., 1883, 1884, 1885, 1886, 1887; W., 1882, 1883, 1885, 1887. A. Hamilton (Queen's Park)—E., 1885, 1886, 1888; W., 1885. Peter Logan (Vale of Leven)—A noted sprinter. Colin Macrae (Vale of Leven)—Played for the Vale in the seventies. A. Lamont—Played for the Vale before they ever took part in a Scottish Cup tie. Bailie Jas. A. Crerar, ex-president Scottish Football Association.

Sitting (left to right)—J. Lindsay, one of the forwards in the Vale 1876 Scottish Cup winning team. A. M'Lintock (Vale of Leven)—E., 1875, 1876, 1880. J. Ferguson (Vale of Leven)—E., 1874, 1876, 1877; W., 1876, 1877, 1878. The first provincial forward to play for Scotland v. England. J. M'Gregor (Vale of Leven)—E., 1877, 1878, 1880; W., 1877. W M'Kinnon (Queen's Park)—E., 1872, 1873, 1874, 1875, 1876, 1877, 1878, 1879; W., 1876. T. Vallance (Rangers)—E., 1877, 1878, 1879, 1881; W., 1877, 1879; 1881—One of the pioneers of the Rangers F.C.

The Evening Times captured 'the old contemptibles' in front of the Rowardennan Hotel during their day out at Loch Lomond in September 1928, shortly before Tom Vallance (seated, front row, far right) jokingly revealed he was considering a comeback.

speeches were delivered to the assembled throng. On the last get-together organised by James Ferguson, on Saturday 1 September 1928, a year before the death of John at the age of 81, a familiar old foe stepped forward to speak – former Rangers president Tom Vallance. Amazingly, video footage of the gathering exists on the news website, www.itnsource.com. It gives a remarkable glimpse into the close knit relationships that existed between players in those days, with pioneer Tom very much to the fore.

Opposite Tarbet, the signal had been given for the vessel, the Prince

Edward, to cut its engines in order that the speakers might be more distinctly heard as Vallance, by then in his early seventies, stood up to propose the toast. His jovial address[2] to the throng was a touching and heart-warming tribute that underlined just how highly respect and friendship were valued in the very earliest years of the

Rangers played at Burnbank for a season between 1875-76. The image on the left shows the view north from Park Quadrant circa 1867 across Burnbank to the new tenements on Great Western Road. The road to the left, next to Lansdowne UP Church is Park Road, while the houses in the foreground belonged to the Woodside cotton mill and stand on what we know today as Woodlands Road. The other image is looking west across Burnbank in the 1870s. Who knows, that may even be a Rangers game going on in the foreground. The land has been dominated by tenements for well over a century. Pictures courtesy of Mitchell Library.

game.

Vallance started by saying to those whom had played football that the years spent kicking a ball were the most pleasant of their lives. To loud applause he went on to say he never regretted the decade he committed to Rangers as a player. "In fact," he revealed, "I mentioned this to my good wife, indeed more than once, and she had replied: 'You should be playing football yet,' and I did not know whether that was sarcasm or not, but thinking over what she had said, I went to the manager of Rangers and asked if he could find a place for me in the team."

There was laughter as Vallance admitted Bill Struth had asked him for a fortnight to consider his request and that several months on he was still waiting for his reply. Vallance said it was a great joy to meet with old friends again and added:

"The other day I read in a spiritualist paper that games were played in heaven and I earnestly hope that is the case, for a heaven without games would have little attraction for me. And if there was football beyond, then assuredly I would get the old Rangers team together and we would challenge the old Vale – and I could tell them the result beforehand; the Vale wouldn't be on the winning side."

Vallance reflected on a period soon after their formation during which the youthful nomads of Rangers finally established themselves on the map of the burgeoning Scottish football scene. They were helped to a huge extent by the three games it took to settle the 1877 Scottish Cup Final, and even if they eventually went down to the men from Leven's shores, they attracted an audience they have never lost since as "thousands of the working classes rushed out to the field of battle in their labouring garb, after crossing the workshop gate when the whistle sounded at five o'clock."[3] Rangers have played countless crucial Championship, Cup and European matches in their long and successful history but, even now, few games have been as important to the development of the club as those three encounters, two played on the West of Scotland Cricket Ground at Hamilton Crescent in Partick and the third and decisive head-to-head at the first Hampden Park.

As a fledgling club, effectively a youth team with no 'home' to call their own, Rangers were not invited and nor did they apply for membership of the Scottish Football Association in March 1873 when eight clubs came together at the Dewar's Temperance Hotel in Bridge Street, Glasgow, to form a sporting alliance. Each club – including, of course, the mighty Queen's Park – contributed £1 towards the purchase of a trophy for a newly established Cup competition – the Scottish Cup. Rangers secured membership in season 1874–75 and in their first Scottish Cup tie, on 12 October 1874, saw off a team called Oxford (from the east end of Glasgow) 2–0 on the Queen's Park Recreation Ground, with goals from Moses McNeil and David Gibb. In the second round, played at Glasgow Green on

Queen's Park Recreation Ground, a line drawing from The Bailie magazine in 1890. Football captured the attention of Glasgow in the Victorian era like no other city. The earliest Rangers players would not have been unfamiliar with the scenario as depicted here – they played their first Scottish Cup tie on Queen's Park Rec, a 2-0 win over Oxford, from the east end of Glasgow, in 1874.
Picture courtesy of Glasgow City Archives.

28 November, Rangers drew 0–0 with Dumbarton but lost the replay a fortnight later 1–0 to a controversial winner. The consensus of opinion in an era when goal nets were still a brainwave for the future was that the Dumbarton 'goal' had gone over the string bar, rather than under. However, the umpires and referee signalled the goal to stand and Rangers were out of the tournament – for the first time, but certainly not the last – in controversial circumstances.

The backbone of the team in the early years, of course, came from the Gareloch connection – Moses, Willie and Peter McNeil, Peter, James and John Campbell, Alex and Tom Vallance, as well as other friends including William McBeath, James Watson (who became president of the club in 1890), John Yuil and George Phillips. Queen's Park were regarded as visionaries and pioneers and regularly undertook tours across Scotland to teach the new game to interested participants.

However, the great Hampden outfit initially refused to face Rangers in its infancy, citing the new club's lack of a permanent home as the principal reason. They agreed instead to send their second side, known as the Strollers, but Rangers wanted all or nothing and refused their offer. They wrote again to Queen's Park in July 1875, and this time the standard-bearers slotted in a game against them on 20 November, with the £28 proceeds from the fixture, a 2-0 victory for the more senior club, distributed to the Bridgeton fire fund.

The charity pot had been established to help the eight families left homeless and the 700 workers left idle following a blaze at a spinning mill in Greenhead Street, which was recognised as the biggest ever seen in the city to that date. Amazingly, there were no casualties. An official publication on the history of Queen's Park, from 1920, was adamant the big boys of the Scottish game were acting not out of malice in refusing a game, but out of concern for the well-being of the youthful club, fearful of crushing its spirit so early in its development.[4]

The third season of Rangers' existence had offered glimpses of better to come, with 15 matches played in 1874–75 against sides long since gone, such as Havelock Star, Helensburgh and the 23rd Renfrewshire Rifles Volunteers. Rangers won 12 games, losing only once. The issue of a more permanent base was addressed in time for the start of the 1875–76 season, when the club moved to recreational space at Burnbank, a site on the south side of Great Western Road near St George's Cross, today bordered by Park Road and Woodlands Road. A move to Shawfield had been briefly considered and then rejected, no doubt as Burnbank was much closer to the homes of the founding fathers around the Sandyford and Charing Cross districts of the city. Initially, Rangers shared the space with Glasgow Accies, the rugby club who were formed in 1866, although they later moved to North Kelvinside. In addition, the Caledonian Cricket Club, who also had a short-lived football team, played on the site, which was later swallowed by developers for tenement housing which still stands today.

Burnbank did its damnedest to stand as an oasis in an increasing desert of red sandstone and was also the home of the First Lanarkshire Rifle Volunteers, who were raised in 1859 by the amalgamation of several existing Glasgow corps as a

The Rangers ground at tranquil Kinning Park, captured on canvas in 1851 as a Glasgow select takes on England at cricket. The Grapes, The Red Lion and The District Bar would come later.

forerunner to the modern territorial army. Among the members of the First Lanarkshire Rifle Volunteers and the Glasgow Accies was William Alexander Smith, who founded the Boys Brigade in Glasgow in October 1883. Smith was moved to form his Christian organisation in frustration at his difficulty inspiring members of the Sunday School where he taught at the Mission Hall in nearby North Woodside Road.

The youngsters were bored and restless, in stark contrast to the enthusiasm he came across as a young officer among the Volunteers on the Burnbank drill ground every Saturday afternoon. Smith, who was born in 1854, would have been no stranger to Burnbank at the time Rangers were playing there: more than likely, at the same time, he was fermenting his ideas for an organisation that still boasts more than half a million members worldwide.

Rangers played their first fixture at Burnbank on 11 September 1875 against Vale of Leven, who had quickly established themselves as the second force in the Scottish game behind Queen's Park. The match finished in a 1–1 draw, but

The dressing rooms at Kinning Park were so small the players washed themselves outside, using buckets of water.

Rangers were beginning to cause a stir. Previously a draw among fans at Glasgow Green, their youthful endeavour and skill at the infant game was starting to attract strong and admiring glances in the west end of the city.

A Scottish Athletic Journal rugby columnist, The Lounger, looked back over a decade in 1887 and charted the growth of the fledgling club as he recalled: "When I used to go to Burnbank witnessing the rugby games that were played there I always strolled over to the easternmost end of that capacious enclosure to see the Rangers play, and I was never disappointed. They were a much finer team then than they are now. The Vallances were in their prime, Peter McNeil was at half-back, Moses – the dashing, clever dribbler of those days – was a forward and Peter Campbell and David Gibb – both dead, I am sorry to say – were also in the team."[5]

However, a lengthy run in the Scottish Cup, the principal tournament, was to elude Rangers for a second successive season. In the second round, Rangers defeated Third Lanark 1–0 at Cathkin Park, but their opponents protested that the visitors had kicked-off both halves. The appeal was duly upheld and the game was ordered to be replayed at Burnbank, with Third Lanark winning 2–1. This time it was Rangers' turn to appeal on the grounds that the opposition keeper wore everyday clothing and could not be distinguished from the crowd, that the winning goal was scored by the hand and that the game had been ended seven minutes early as a result of fans encroaching on the field of play. Their pleas fell on deaf ears. The result stood and Rangers were out.

Nevertheless, there was further cause for optimism as Rangers headed into season 1876–77 and a campaign that would not only underline their new-found reputation as a club of substance, but would also earn them their 'Light Blues' moniker that stays with them to this day. Firstly, they secured a 10-year lease on a ground at Kinning Park that had recently been vacated by the Clydesdale club, who had first played cricket on the site in 1849. The cricketers originally rented fields next door from a Mr Tweedie for up to £9 per annum but they were evicted within a year (after playing only two matches) when they literally refused to allow the grass to grow under their feet, thus denying his herds valuable nutrition.

The Clydesdale lads had better luck when they approached a Mr Meikelwham for permission to build a club on the fields he was leasing in Kinning Park and the precious acres were to remain dedicated to sport until Rangers moved to the first Ibrox Park in 1887. Land which, less than 125 years ago, was given over for agricultural use and sporting prowess now forms part of the M8. It is something for present day fans to think about as they crawl towards the Kingston Bridge from Ibrox in their cars and supporters' buses at the end of every matchday.

Rangers' move to Kinning Park in the summer of 1876 took them to the south of the city for the first time and it has remained their spiritual home ever since. For their part, Clydesdale had located to a new ground for their favourite pastimes of football and cricket further south at Titwood. Memories of football at Clydesdale have long since faded, although they boast the honour of playing in the first Scottish Cup Final in 1874, a 2–0 defeat to Queen's Park.

The crack of willow on leather can be heard at Titwood still. The reasons behind Clydesdale's desire for a new home away from Kinning Park have never been recorded, but the creep of industrialism and demand for space across the south side of the city in the period is likely to have been a factor. As late as the 1860s, the eminent Scottish sportswriter D.D. Bone reckoned: "Kinning Park was…a beautiful meadow surrounded by stately trees and green hedges, a pleasant spot of resort for the town athletes, away from the din of hammers and free from the heavy pall of city smoke."[6]

In 1872 it sat in splendid isolation, but within 12 months the Clutha Ironworks had been constructed on its doorstep and by 1878 a depot for the Caledonian Railway had been built across the street. The dimensions of a cricket field being considerably larger than a football pitch, maps of the time show that

Rangers occupied only a portion of the land originally allocated to Clydesdale.

Rangers had been boosted in the summer of 1876 by the arrival of several new players, most notably George Gillespie. A former player with the Rosslyn club based in Whiteinch, he was a back who later converted to goalkeeper and went on to win seven caps for Scotland between the sticks with the Light Blues and Queen's Park. He was never on the losing side in an international and luck appeared to be on his side in his debut season with his new club.

Rangers also strengthened their youthful squad with the addition of goalkeeper James Watt and forward David Hill and there were also two new additions to the forward line, William 'Daddy' Dunlop (of True Blue fame) and Sandy Marshall. Watt and Dunlop came from the Sandyford club (Gillespie is also credited with once being a member). Players at Sandyford were well-known to founders of Rangers as they were part of the same community on the western fringes of the city centre.

The prospects for Rangers never looked better, particularly when they opened the new ground on 2 September in front of 1,500 fans, again with a match against Vale of Leven, and this time the boys from Dunbartonshire were defeated 2–1. Of the 16 challenge matches Rangers were acknowledged as playing that season they lost only three and their form in the Scottish Cup won them a new army of admirers among the Glaswegian labour class that they still maintain to this day.

Rangers could certainly not be accused of lacking enthusiasm, which endeared them to an audience that had been growing since those early kickabouts on Glasgow Green. Scottish football was frightfully territorial in the 1870s. The club with greatest mass appeal, Queen's Park, had secured a fan base on the back of their all-conquering success of previous seasons, but at heart they were considered a club for the wealthy and their cloak of on-field invincibility was also beginning to slip from their shoulders as the decade drew to a close.

The time was right for a new challenger. Other clubs drew their audience from the immediate areas in which they played – Pollokshields Athletic, Govan, Whiteinch, Parkgrove, Partick and Battlefield to name just a few. To some extent, the nomadic status of Rangers in their early years worked to their benefit, as they moved from the east of the city to the west and then on to Kinning Park, representing no particular district but winning an audience with their exuberance on the pitch.

Such was the dedication of the players to their new home that stories abounded in the local community of eerie sounds and peculiar sights coming from the ground during the night. Soon, there were whisperings the place was haunted. In fact, it was the zealous Light Blues, whose dedication to the new game and their new environment saw them consult astronomy charts to train late into the night under the full moon, leading to the nickname the 'Moonlighters.' It highlighted the tremendous commitment to their new club and the new sport by the young amateurs.

The picture that emerges of the time is of football as a thrilling new adventure for young men on the cusp of adult life. Moses McNeil fondly recalled 'tuck-ins' of ham and eggs and steak at a local eating house every morning after a 6am rise for a 10-mile training walk or a 90-minute session with the football in the build up to the 1877 Cup Final. Up to 11 plates were laid out for the famished players, with John Allan poetically recalling in his jubilee history: "It happened frequently that only six or seven players were able to sit down to the feast; still, the waiter never took anything back on the plates except the pattern."[7]

Rangers were fortunate to have huge personalities in their squad to match their appetites. Gillespie, for one, was a renowned practical joker. In April 1879 Rangers accepted an invite to play a match at Dunoon to celebrate the birthday of Queen Victoria, but the players were ordered back to the city on the Thursday evening to prepare for a Glasgow Merchants' Charity Cup semi-final tie against Dumbarton at Hampden 48 hours later.

All the players took the last steamer home, with the exception of Gillespie, Archie Steel and Hugh McIntyre. Blatantly breaking curfew, they booked into the Royal Hotel for the night instead. Steel and McIntyre, who were sharing a room, were awakened from their slumbers by a loud banging on the door and the frantic order from Gillespie to follow him to the pier as they had overslept and were about to miss the first boat across the Firth of Clyde. Steel and McIntyre dressed at speed and dashed along the pavement outside their lodgings before they realised it was still the middle of the night. Gillespie had earlier returned to bed, where no doubt he chuckled himself back to sleep. The rude awakening did not perturb Steel too much, as he scored on the Saturday afternoon in a 3–1 victory.

Steel, writing in 1896 as Old International in one of the first in-depth histories of the Scottish game, 25 Years Football, also fondly recalled Rangers teammate Sandy Marshall. He was tall and thin as a rake and it was claimed John Ferguson ran under his legs during one of the games in the 1877 Final when the Light Blues player took a fresh air swipe at the ball. Training at Kinning Park frequently ended with a one-mile run around the ground, after which the players were treated to a 'bath' of a bucket of cold water poured over their heads by the trainer as they stooped double, their fingers touching their toes. One evening Marshall took up his usual angular pose and jokingly warned the bucket holder "see and no' miss me," and his comments induced such fits of giggles the water went everywhere except over the player's head.[8]

The majority of the Rangers team were barely out of their teens when they kicked off the Scottish Cup, hoping for third time lucky, with a 4–1 defeat of Queen's Park Juniors at Kinning Park on 20 September 1876. Defender George Gillespie was just 17, while James Campbell, the only goalscorer from that match to be officially recorded, was 18. His older brother Peter and friends Moses McNeil and Tom Vallance were all 20 years old and William Dunlop was the oldest at 22. Towerhill were swept aside in the next round 8–0 and Rangers also travelled to Mauchline and Lennox and won comfortably 3–0 on each occasion. Surprisingly, even though fixture scheduling can charitably be described in the 1870s as haphazard, Rangers were given a bye at the semi-final stage. The kids from Kinning Park had made the Scottish Cup Final for the first time in their short history – and Vale of Leven lay in wait.

The club from Alexandria is long gone as a senior outfit – they withdrew from the Scottish League in 1892 and limped on at various levels until 1929 – but Rangers still owe them a debt of gratitude, in part for their Light Blues nickname, which first came to the fore around the time of the Final. In his history of Rangers, written for the SFA's annual in 1894, a scribe operating under the name of 'Obo' claimed Rangers had been known as the Light Blues for the first 22 years of their existence as a result of the colour of their shirts. However, his claims do not stand up to scrutiny when compared against the evidence provided by club officials for the earliest SFA annuals. All teams were required to list their colours and Rangers' shirts were frequently listed as blue (1876 and 1878) or, more commonly, royal blue (from 1879 onwards). Light blue was never mentioned. They also wore white knickerbockers and blue and white hooped socks.

It has been argued, with some merit, that the Light Blues refers not to the colour of the shirts but the dash of performers such as Moses McNeil and Peter Campbell when they pulled the cotton kit, most likely provided by H. and P. McNeil, over their youthful shoulders around the time of the 1877 Final. The Glasgow News of Monday 19 March references the "light and speedy" Rangers, while Archie Steel makes a compelling case for the Light Blues to be considered in the context of the tradition of Oxford and Cambridge universities. Vale's colours were a very dark blue, almost black (although they wore plain white in the second of the three epic matches) and he claimed Vale were similar to the Dark Blues of Oxford in their appearance, while Rangers, in a hue of kit not as powerful, resembled the Light Blues of Cambridge.

To describe Vale of Leven as favourites to win the Scottish Cup on Saturday 17 March 1877 is as much an understatement as saying football had caught the imagination of the general public ever so slightly. True, the Vale had never lifted the trophy, but the previous season they had been considered unfortunate to be knocked out of the competition at the semi-final stages following a narrow 2–1 loss to Queen's Park, prompting the editors of the Scottish Football Annual that summer to conclude that the rest of the Scottish game, in particular Vale of Leven and Third Lanark, were quickly catching up with the Hampden giants.

The men from Alexandria had caused a sensation in the fifth round by handing Queen's Park their first defeat on Scottish soil after a decade of existence. Furthermore, experienced players such as Alex McLintock, John McGregor, John Ferguson, John McDougall and John Baird had already been capped for their country – Moses McNeil and Tom Vallance were the only two Scotland players in the Rangers team at that time and the latter had only won his first two caps in the fortnight before the Final. Vale of Leven had age and physical presence on their side, not to mention that morale-boosting win over the greatest club of them all.

The rain had fallen ankle deep on the Hampden playing surface that historic Saturday afternoon of 30 December 1876 as the visitors celebrated their 2–1 win over Queen's Park to take them into the semi-final. However, subsequent events threatened to dampen the feelgood factor of their sensational victory.

The following Tuesday, several Queen's Park members were strolling over the playing surface and noticed suspicious marks in the turf that looked as if they had come from spiked boots, which were strictly forbidden at the time. As a result, Queen's Park wasted no time in dispatching a delegation of two men to the lodgings of various Vale players with a request to see the footwear worn three days earlier. They first called upon the home of John Ferguson and although he was out, his wife invited the visitors into their home and produced her husband's boot bag.

As luck would have it – or, from the point of view of Queen's Park, bad fortune – the bag also contained the boots of teammate Bobby Paton and there was not a spike in sight. Undeterred, they marched on to the home of another player, John McGregor. Initially, he mistook their arrival as a show of bonhomie to welcome the New Year and uncorked a bottle as the three men toasted the arrival of

The Gallant Pioneers: The Rangers team that played in the Scottish Cup final in 1877. Back row (left to right): George Gillespie, William McNeil, James Watt, Sam Ricketts. Middle row (left to right): William Dunlop, David Hill, Tom Vallance, Peter Campbell, Moses McNeil. Front row (left to right): James Watson, Sandy Marshall. Tom Vallance wore a lion rampant on his chest to symbolise the two international appearances he made that season, against England and Wales.

1877. However, when the true nature of their business became clear McGregor threw his unspiked boots at their feet in disgust and swore bitterly that he regretted ever proffering a dram in the first place.

He was not alone in being incensed. The Vale committee pointed out that the holes on the Hampden pitch were various sizes and more consistent with marks from the tip of a shooting stick or umbrella, which had been carried by at least one umpire. One newspaper correspondent mischievously suggested the markings were made by crows, which thrived in the district, and the game was forever after known as the 'Crows' Feet' match. There was no replay and Vale went on to meet Rangers following a 9–0 demolition of Ayr Thistle in the semi-final, adding to victories in the earlier rounds against Third Lanark, Vale of Leven Rovers, Helensburgh and Busby.

On the morning of Monday 19 March 1877 newspapers went into overdrive to describe the Final that had taken place at the West of Scotland Cricket Club in Partick 48 hours earlier. One declared the game as "decidedly the finest match that has ever been played since the dribbling game was introduced to Scotland."[9]

The teams lined up as follows and did not change over the course of the next three games – Rangers: J. Watt, goal; G. Gillespie and T. Vallance, backs; W. McNeil and S. Ricketts, half-backs; W. Dunlop, A. Marshall, P. Campbell, D. Hill, J. Watson and M. McNeil, forwards. Vale of Leven: W.O. Wood, goal; A. Michie and A. McIntyre, backs; W. Jamieson and A. McLintock, half-backs; R. Paton, J. McGregor, J. McDougall, J. Ferguson, D. Lindsay and J.C. Baird, forwards.

Headlines had been dominated that week by the acceptance of William Gladstone, who would soon become Prime Minister for his second of four terms, of the candidacy to become Lord Rector of Glasgow University; a New Kilpatrick farmer was fined five guineas in the Glasgow courts for selling sour milk to the public, which contained 38 per cent added water; while in Dumbarton, the council turned on local MP Sir Archibald Orr Ewing and called on him to retract or disown statements he had made alleging excessive drunkenness in the district.

However, Vale of Leven players had other things on their minds than the slating of their neighbours by the man charged with representing their interests at Westminster because they knew, despite their tag as favourites, that their rivals from Kinning Park would be no pushovers. Tradition dictated that a Scottish terrier, known as the 'Derby dog', was brought out before kick-off at 3.30pm to parade up and down in front of the fans in the pavilion at Hamilton Crescent. Snow, rain and sleet had fallen all week, although the weather had improved slightly in time for the kick-off and a crowd estimated at 8,000 was present.

In a breathless encounter, Vale took the lead when Paton nodded home from a McLintock cross early in the second half and the crowd awaited the inevitable onslaught. However, even with the wind in their faces the plucky youngsters from Kinning Park, inspired by skipper Tom Vallance, refused to be cowed and drew level with 20 minutes remaining when McDougall put through his own net.

A draw was acceptable to neither team as the action swung from one end of the field to the next, the air punctured with cries such as: 'Time to win the Cup yet, Rangers!' and 'Waken up and run through them, Vale of Leven.' Eventually, time was called with the score still locked at 1–1 and while a replay was scheduled it was the underdog Rangers who claimed the moral victory as their players were carried off the field shoulder high by their excited fans. Both sides came together again later that evening, this time at the Athole Arms in Dundas Street, where every kick, pass and opportunity was examined over a glass of beer.

Three weeks passed between the Final and the first replay, but time had

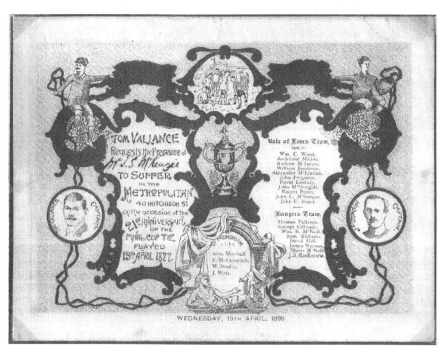

The captain's table: Tom Vallance invited all survivors from the 1877 Scottish Cup final to a 21st anniversary dinner at his Metropolitan Restaurant on April 13 1898. Each invite was intricately and individually drawn by the talented artist, with tribute paid to the four Rangers who had passed in the previous two decades – Sandy Marshall, Peter Campbell, William Dunlop and James Watt.

neither dulled nor dampened the enthusiasm for the second match. If anything, a fevered excitement and anticipation hung in the air with the grey clouds above Partick that Saturday afternoon, 7 April, and even the rainfall would not keep the supporters away. Inside the ground, more than 8,000 fans huddled together against the weather, with just as many outside trying desperately to sneak a look over the fence at the action.

The Glasgow News of 9 April reported that "an enormous crowd assembled within the well known cricket enclosure of the West of Scotland Club and outside the railings and on the high ground to the north thousands of spectators took up positions. A dozen omnibuses, numerous cabs and other conveyances collected in the roads and from the top of these vehicles a large number of people enjoyed a much better view of the game than many who had paid for admission – the crowd around the ropes standing three and four deep. An estimate of the numbers present will be gathered from the fact – officially announced afterwards – that the receipts exceeded any previous amounts collected at any match in Scotland and it may be asserted without hesitation that Saturday's assembly was the largest ever seen on any football rendezvous in Britain."[10]

The game kicked off at 3.30pm and within seven minutes Rangers had opened the scoring after William 'Daddy' Dunlop struck a well-placed shot between the posts. Vale, kicking downhill and with the wind at their backs, immediately searched for an equaliser but their attacks were repelled time and again by the ever reliable Tom Vallance and keeper James Watt. Rangers enjoyed the advantage of the conditions as the second half kicked off but Vale scored within two minutes of the restart, although the roar of the crowd was muffled by peals of loud thunder as the heavens opened. Moses McNeil passed up a couple of opportunities late on, while Vale also went close before the game swept into an extra-time period of 30 minutes. However, it was never completed as five minutes into the second period a shot from Dunlop caused chaos and sparked fierce debate among fans that lasted for years afterwards.

Rangers argued passionately that the ball had crossed the line from Dunlop's shot and bounced off a spectator before landing safely back in the arms of Wood, but the referee, SFA honorary secretary William Dick, was too far from the action to make a balanced call. To add to the confusion, one of his umpires insisted the ball had crossed the line, while the other debated just as vigorously that no goal had been scored.

The spectator the ball was alleged to have struck was Sir George H.B. McLeod, regius professor of surgery at Glasgow University, who later offered to swear on oath a goal had been scored, but his offer was not accepted by the football authorities. In the time it took to discuss the incident many fans, who had been craning their necks all afternoon for a closer glimpse of the action, burst on to the field and arguments broke out between them about the validity of Dunlop's 'goal'. It was a scene of utter bedlam and when the pitch could not be cleared the final whistle was blown 10 minutes early and another replay arranged for the following week at Hampden.

In the 21st century, football administrators are often criticised for arranging times and dates for matches that do not always suit the paying public but, as ever, the only thing new in life is the history not already known. The third and final game between Rangers and Vale of Leven in the Scottish Cup kicked-off at the unusual time of 5.30pm at Hampden on Friday 12 April (rumours of a Rangers no-show in disgust at Dunlop's disallowed goal in the previous match proved unfounded).

The attendance and gate receipt record from six days earlier was smashed again as 10,000 fans crammed into the first Hampden Park, sited at Crosshill, next to Hampden Terrace. It was estimated that a similar number again sought every height advantage outside the ground to watch the match from the tops of cabs, buses and trees. The majority of the crowd were Rangers fans, although they were hardly partisan.

The Scottish Football Annual recalled: "In justice to the great majority of the people it is only fair to add that when a bit of brilliant play was shown on the Vale of Leven side it did not pass uncheered, and when the goals were taken on each side the scene baffled description. The hum of human voices was heard far and near and caps, hats, and sticks were waved overhead in thousands."[11]

Among the crowd were two youngsters from Alexandria, presumably Vale of Leven fans, who would pay a heavy price for their attendance. The following Tuesday, 17 April, the Glasgow Herald told how Hugh McArthur, 12, John Slowan, 11, had rushed to the final from their home town, but only after McArthur had stolen the princely sum of £3 10s from a chest belonging to his uncle to fund the adventure. The two youngsters lived high on the hog during their trip to Glasgow and purchased, among other things, pipes, tobacco and "several luxuries". They duly appeared at Glasgow Sheriff Court and pleaded guilty to theft. McArthur was sent to prison for 30 days, his sidekick Slowan for 20.

If Rangers had the better of the first game and Vale of Leven showed their strength in the second then the third was more evenly balanced although not, according to match reports of the time, as much of a football spectacle, despite five goals being scored. Vale of Leven netted through McDougall after only 15 minutes, making amends for his own-goal in the first tie. However, Rangers equalised in the second half when a tame Peter Campbell shot was missed by Wood, who made a feeble and unsuccessful attempt to kick it clear, and the Glasgow youngsters took a grip on the game 10 minutes later when Willie McNeil slotted home the second.

The mental strength of Vale came to the fore as John Baird snatched an equaliser only three minutes after McNeil had given Rangers hope that it might be their year. There was clearly little appetite among both groups of players for a fourth match as the game reached an exciting climax, swinging from one end to the other. Sam Ricketts and Tom Vallance went close with shots for Rangers, while Watt was a sterling performer between the sticks. However, it was Baird who had the final say when he knocked in the winner with 10 minutes remaining to give his side a 3–2 victory. Unsurprisingly, the game was more bad-tempered than the previous two fixtures and one unnamed Vale player was chastised for kicking out at Moses McNeil.

This time, the informalities of the Athole Arms were dispensed with as Vale of Leven headed to Alexandria to celebrate with their families, friends and fans, who had waited patiently at the post office in the town for news of the result, which finally arrived at 7.30pm. The Vale of Leven players descended from the Glasgow train two hours later, by which time a crowd of 3,000 were waiting to greet them. The players were lifted shoulder high onto an open-top wagon and paraded around the town, with the Bonhill band leading the way. Amid joyous scenes at the departure of the Cup from Glasgow for the first time, "cannons were fired, pipers were discoursing Highland music and all the dogs of the district barked their part in the chorus of rejoicing over the famous football victory."[12]

Rangers players, who had practised so long and hard at Kinning Park under the light of the winter moon, could only howl in frustration. However, these pups would soon have their day.

Chapter 5
Peter McNeil

Peter McNeil long had the back of Rangers in the early years and so it was entirely fitting when the club's support decided to look after their own when the story of his sad plight came to light for the first time in the pages of The Gallant Pioneers.

Death casts a shadow: The gravesite of Peter McNeil, who lies buried with his brother, fellow pioneer Willie, and their parents John and Jean.

Peter was one of the founding four of Rangers and, while his temperament may have been even and his judgement as a football administrator regarded as sober, his personality was clearly underpinned by a tenacious streak of stubbornness. It was to stand the club in good stead during its first season at Flesher's Haugh as he fought – no doubt, sometimes even literally – to preserve for Rangers the most favourable playing corner of Glasgow Green, thus allowing the club to forge its early reputation among the casual observer as one worth watching.

There is no escaping the high regard with which early pioneer William 'True Blue' Dunlop held the contribution of Peter to the formation and growth of the club in its infancy. He wrote: "Peter McNeil, with characteristic self-denial and zeal for the best interests of the club, used to journey to the most desirable part of the Green about twelve noon, and set up the now noted standards (early goalposts). But it was not enough to set them up. He had, at first, either to watch them himself or pay a boy for doing so until the classic hour in the afternoon was reached."[1]

Time fades, however, and as the 20th century gave way to the 21st, Peter's selflessness in establishing the club that would go on to scale such great heights was in danger of being overlooked. His final resting place at Craigton Cemetery was a sad metaphor - unmarked, unheralded, overgrown, consumed by the passage of time. Subsequent events indicated this should come as no great surprise - even Peter's two grand-daughters, sprightly eighty-somethings Heather Lang and Doreen Holland, knew nothing about their grandfather's greatest achievement until contacted about their stories for the book.

However, Peter's contribution to the club has now been fully recognised, thanks to the sterling effort of fans and the support of the Founders Trail. It was the Light Blues legions who raised the funds to commission a portrait of Peter and his friends by renowned Scottish artist Helen Runciman. It was presented to the club at a Founders Dinner at Ibrox in October 2009 with Heather and Doreen in attendance as guests of honour, alongside club legend Davie Wilson and a capacity crowd of more than 300 supporters. The portrait now has pride of place at the top of the Marble Staircase, where it has since been admired by thousands of visitors to the club. A month previously, Heather had also unveiled a plaque at Flesher's Haugh in honour of her grandfather as Sandy Jardine, club historian David Mason, fan liaison officer Jim Hannah and John MacMillan of the Rangers Supporters Association looked on.

The sorry state of Peter's final resting place was also put right by fans, again led by Iain McColl and Gordon Bell of the Founders Trail. There was a

Founding father Peter McNeil, former SFA treasurer and player, honorary match secretary and vice president of Rangers.
Picture courtesy of Scottish Football Museum.

poignancy about the occasion in June 2013 when new memorial headstones were unveiled during one of the visits by fans as part of the hugely popular Trail experience around Glasgow and Ibrox Stadium. Two young lads, part of the tour with their families, were asked, instinctively, to place a wreath on the graves of Peter and his brother James as the other supporters looked on. The boys, only a couple of years shy of the age of Peter when he helped form the club, immediately stepped up to the challenge - just as Peter had done at Glasgow Green on behalf of the club 141 years previously.

Iain McColl said: "At the Founders Trail we felt strongly for some time the incredible contribution made by the McNeil brothers in first forming Rangers and guiding it through our turbulent early years should be recognised by the club by way of the restoration and the placing of memorial stones at these plots at Craigton."

Peter is laid to rest in one of two previously unmarked plots that also include his mother Jean, father John and brothers William, James and Alexander. Iain added: "We have taken thousands of fans on the Founders Trail since 2009 and the state of the McNeil graves at Craigton was always a source of dismay to supporters. We liaised closely with Peter's grand-daughters Heather and Doreen and James' grand-daughter Elizabeth Pirie, who is the legal owner of both plots. They were fully supportive and we handed a lengthy document into the club for approval. Jim Hannah very kindly submitted it to the board on our behalf and they responded by saying: 'We are delighted to back this project that honours the men who formed our club.' No-one present at Craigton that June afternoon when the two boys stepped forward to lay the wreath will forget the humility and pride we all felt for our club."

Fittingly, a fine view is afforded from Craigton Cemetery towards Ibrox Stadium and on sunny days its famous red-brick facade glows ruby rich in the brilliant bright light. For those with an interest in Rangers' history Craigton Cemetery has, until now, been better known as the final resting place of legendary manager Bill Struth, the Ibrox colossus who led the club from 1920–54, winning 18

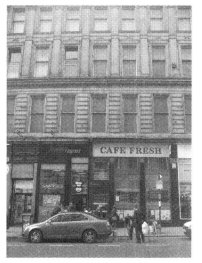

The site of H and P McNeil at 21-23 Renfield Street in the 21st century. No longer a premier sports outfitters, but the coffees and baguettes are highly recommended.

League Championships, 10 Scottish Cups and two League Cup Finals. Until recently his grave lay badly neglected too as dozens of headstones, including his own, were toppled over or dislodged by a cruel juvenile demolition squad fuelled by a warped sense of adventure and, sadly, too much alcohol.

Admirably, the neglect of Struth's grave was raised by fans at a club AGM and Rangers quickly agreed to assume responsibility for the restoration of the headstone and future upkeep of the plot. The only problem, cemetery staff point out with a smile, is that Mr Struth lies with his back to the club he helped establish as one of the most famous in the world.

Sadly, however, there are few moments of humour in the story of Peter, who was shredded of his dignity in the latter stages of his life by the tragedy of mental illness.

Peter McNeil was listed as aged 42 or 43 at the time of his death on 30 March 1901, although earlier census records indicate his date of birth was more likely to have been around 1854, making him four years older. He was a small man, standing a little over five feet four inches tall, but he possibly had bigger vanities as his wife, Janet, was at least eight years his junior and may have been reluctant, in his eyes, to enter into a courtship with a man of more advanced years. Birth records were less stringently kept before 1855, allowing those born before that date to play fast and loose with their age. McNeil clearly had no such qualms about clutching on to his youth a few years longer than most for the best of intentions, love and eventual marriage, even if his attempt at holding back time was strictly unauthorised.

The picture that emerges of McNeil is of a man of modesty, order and principle, characteristics that would serve his fledgling club well as it grew in power and influence in the Scottish game throughout the 1870s and early 1880s. He arrived in Glasgow from the Gareloch, where he was born, around 1870 and was in his mid-teens when he made his way to the city. He lived at No. 17 Cleveland Street and No. 169 Berkeley Street in Charing Cross with oldest sister Elizabeth, among other family members, and quickly set up with brother Harry in the business of H. and P. McNeil, listed as "hatters, hosiers, glovers and shirtmakers" but better known as the "leading athletic outfitters in Scotland."

They had premises at No. 21 and No. 23 Renfield Street before moving to a new shop at No. 91 Union Street in Glasgow city centre in 1883. They were regular advertisers in the sporting press at the time, including the Scottish Football Annuals. Their banner displays called out "to all the principal clubs in Scotland, also to the Scottish, Sheffield, Ayrshire and Welsh football associations" and they were "outfitters for all amateur athletic sports" and promised "association footballs specially made."

Football quickly became the McNeils' sporting obsession and any early disputes on the right of Rangers to play in their preferred corner of Glasgow Green were, according to Dunlop, soon replaced by a widespread acceptance that this was a special team of young players, as worthy of their right to indisputably own a patch of public ground for a few hours every week as they were the support of football fans for whom a trip to Hampden Park to watch Queen's Park was either too far or too expensive for average wage-earners.

Dunlop added: "Peter's commendable zeal was not taxed to the utmost… the rapid strides with which Rangers had acquired (their) reputation constrained the followers of the ball to look, wonder and admire. As a consequence, the desirable part of the Green was, with something like mutual agreement, regarded

Heather unveiled a plaque to her grandfather, Peter McNeil, and his friends at Glasgow Green in September 2009 watched by VIPs including Rangers legend Sandy Jardine

by all as sacred to the Rangers. And if players looked, didn't spectators come and stare? The sacred spot became the Mecca of the Green, the god Football being there worshipped by thousands of devotees whose piety would not bear either a journey to Hampden Park, or the necessary subscription...Football was their Allah and the Rangers, if not at that time the prophet, were at least their prophet."

Peter played alongside brothers Moses, William and, occasionally, Queen's Park stalwart Harry, and was one of the club's early captains, a reflection of the respect with which he was held at the new club for his powers of organisation. As a player he featured regularly early on for the Light Blues and took part in the club's first match against Callander in May 1872. He held down a regular first-team place until 1876, when the position of honorary secretary would have at least lessened the blow of being overlooked in favour of more capable performers on the pitch. He served the committee well and was secretary from 1876 to 1883, the equivalent position of the modern team manager, and vice-president of the club from 1886–88.

In addition, he was one of the earliest treasurers of the SFA, beating off several other candidates to win the vote of football's governing body in April 1879, a further reflection of the admiration in which he was held, not only at Rangers but throughout the infant game. After he stepped down in April 1883, the Scottish Athletic Journal noted: "The meeting expressed their sense of the worth of the

The new headstones were dedicated during the Founders Trail tour in June 2009 - and two youngsters present placed a wreath to mark the resting place of the McNeils.

'genial Peter' and he must have felt proud at the reception accorded him when he stood up to acknowledge the vote of thanks awarded him."[2]

However, his tenure as treasurer at the SFA was not without it challenges, as the new regulatory body struggled to find its feet financially in the early years of the game. Peter resigned as treasurer at the association's AGM in 1883 to concentrate on his own business affairs, but it was a time of frustration at the inability of the SFA to balance its books.

Nevertheless, his contribution was noted in the minutes of the time and Peter also received a formal vote of thanks for his efforts. The minutes stated "that the association regret that Mr McNeil has resigned the office of treasurer and that this association feels deeply indebted to him for his great services in the past."[3]

Andrew Carnegie himself would have struggled to make sense of the game's financial figures, which relied heavily on the money raised at the gate every second year from the fixture against England. By October 1883 the SFA's debt had

The Glasgow team from 1880 that defeated Sheffield 1-0, in Sheffield. Committee man Peter McNeil is seated on the floor, far right, next to brother Moses, on the chair. Rangers were also represented by William 'Daddy' Dunlop, third from right in the bottom row and goalkeeper George Gillespie, back row, far left.
Picture courtesy of Scottish Football Museum.

risen to a daunting £120, secretary John K. McDowall had not been paid for nine months and was owed £80 and even Scottish Cup winners Dumbarton had still to be reimbursed for the £15 they had spent on medals for their players. However, the situation improved as the decade progressed, in part as a result of a move from premises at well-to-do Carlton Place into Waterloo Street, halving the SFA's rent at a stroke (the SFA returned in September 1889 and bought the Carlton Place premises outright, moving in after refurbishment by 1892).

For much of the 1870s and 1880s, and even into the early 1890s, McNeil appeared to lead a prosperous life. He had married Janet, who came from Cathcart, in March 1885 and within five years they had two children, John Fraser and Gertrude Grace. At that time, H. and P. McNeil were still regular fixtures in the Post Office Guide, an early Yellow Pages in which relatively well-to-do citizens paid

Union Street, Glasgow, circa 1896. The H and P McNeil store was towards the top of the street, on the left hand side. Moses also worked here for Hugh Lang junior, a commercial agent involved in the hosiery business.
Picture courtesy of Mitchell Library.

to advertise their business and home addresses. By 1891, according to the census, Peter, 34, (but probably 37 or 38) and Janet, 29, had moved with John Fraser (5) and Gertrude Grace (1) and a domestic servant to No. 37 Bentinck Street in Glasgow, a stone's throw from the West End Park, later renamed Kelvingrove, where the idea of forming a club had first been mooted in 1872.

From the outside, the family clearly boasted trimmings of wealth, but it was a veneer masking the grim reality of Peter's slow decline in mental health, although his psychological sensitivities were hinted at in earlier newspaper articles. The 'Echoes' columnist of the Scottish Athletic Journal noted in February 1883: "I am sorry to learn that Mr P. McNeil, through pressure of business, has been compelled to resign his position as match-secretary of the Rangers."[4] Three weeks later the same columnist wrote: "Publicity is given to a rumour that Mr Peter McNeil will, at the coming general meeting of the Scottish Football Association, retire from the position of treasurer. The cares of an increasing business, I know, have been weighing somewhat heavily on him for some time past and for that and other reasons he would, I believe, like to relinquish all connection with the Association. The idea to get up a testimonial is a splendid one and I hope it will be taken up heartily by all the clubs."[5]

No testimonial was ever granted, but it was not without further promptings from 'Echoes', as the Scottish Athletic Journal columnist clearly felt that Peter could have done with a financial boost as he prepared for his marriage. Writing a month before Peter's wedding in March 1885, he implored: "I would like to revive a little matter that should never have been allowed to drop. When Mr P. McNeil resigned the treasurership of the Scottish Football Association there was a universal feeling that he should be the recipient of some mark of respect for the great service he had rendered that body. At the time the Association was in financial difficulties and it was thought advisable to wait for a little while. Well, three years [it was actually two] have

H and P McNeil occupied 91 Union Street from 1883. Today, number 91 is an eat-all-you-can Chinese buffet. The 1877 squad, renowned for their ham and egg tuck-ins, would surely have put them out of business.

gone and nothing has yet been done, which I think is a little ungrateful. But what has remained so long undone can now be done and I call upon the present committee of the SFA to move in the matter. Mr McNeil is to be a conspicuous figure in a very interesting ceremony which is to take place shortly [his wedding] and it has occurred to me that the present would be the most fitting time to honour one who devoted ungrudgingly so much labour to devising means that would result in enriching the Association."[6]

There was to be no SFA dowry, however, and by 1896 H. and P. McNeil's had disappeared completely from the Post Office Guides, their business premises at No. 91 Union Street taken over by a seedsman, William Leighton. Peter was also a member of the Clydesdale Harriers for at least five years in the 1890s and was a regular advertiser in their annual handbook. By the 1896–97 edition he was no longer listed as a member and H. and P. McNeil's were no longer advertising.

Significantly, their place as official outfitters to the Harriers had been taken by a Robert Scott ("late with H. and P. McNeil"), who had premises at No. 232 Buchanan Street. Clearly, Peter's business or personal life had taken a wrong turn with devastating consequences – bankruptcy, perhaps, or a family feud that dissolved the partnership?

Certainly, he would never again be in business with Harry – his older brother left Scotland in the mid-1890s to take over the running of the Royal Hotel in Bangor, County Down, where their mother had been born. Peter's character may have been stubborn (witness his determination to secure a sacred acre of Glasgow Green on which he and his friends could play games in the early years of the club) but it probably acted as camouflage for a more sensitive soul (the Scottish Athletic Journal referred to him as the 'genial' Peter).[7]

Irrespective, soon Peter's mental health issues could no longer be ignored and, not unnaturally, his decline into insanity caused such anguish in the immediate family that even his granddaughters, still alive and in their eighties, knew nothing of him or his mental state when traced as part of the research for this book. Thankfully, their story comes with a happier ending and acts as a fitting epilogue.

The day before Victoria's death two doctors, Gilbert Campbell and James Hamilton Campbell, certified the insanity of Peter McNeil as a result of financial worries after his wife, Janet Fraser McNeil, had applied under a sheriff's order to have him sectioned at Hawkhead Asylum in Paisley. The Govan District Asylum at Hawkhead was built for the Govan District Lunacy Board – the brutal, callous language was typical of the time – and opened in 1895, with a capacity for 400

WE would call special attention of Clubs to our CELEBRATED No. 5 ASSOCIATION HAND-SEWN WATERPROOF FOOT-BALLS, for lightness and durability, are unsurpassed in the trade ; specially manufactured for ourselves ; thoroughly tested and measured before leaving the premises. Clubs can rely on getting the right article ; every ball guaranteed, made of the best leather.

Price, 10s. 6d.
PARCELS POST FREE.

This ball we supply to all the leading Clubs in England, Ireland, Scotland, and Canada. One trial solicited.

Hand-Sewn Football Boots, - - - - 10/6.
Leg Guards (Patent), - - - 2/6, 3/6, and 4/6.
Knickerbockers, - - - - from 4/6.
Boys' Jerseys, all Colours, - - - ,, 2/6.
Men's ,, - - - ,, 3/6.
Men's Racing Knickers, all Colours, - - 6/6 each.
Football Travelling Bags, - - - from 7/6.

H. & P. M'NEIL,
Hatters, Hosiers, Glovers, and Shirtmakers,
LEADING ATHLETIC OUTFITTERS IN SCOTLAND,
91 UNION STREET, GLASGOW.
PRICE LISTS ON APPLICATION.

An advertisement for H and P McNeil in Union Street, Glasgow. Their store stood next door to where the side entrance of Central Station is found today.

patients. The story of Peter McNeil's hospitalisation unfolds more than 100 years later using information from public records gleaned from sources such as the NHS and National Archives and also the Govan Poor Law Relief applications of the time, held at the Mitchell Library in Glasgow.

The official cause of McNeil's death on Saturday 30 March 1901 was given as "general paralysis", as the certifying doctor, typical of the time, spared his family from the heartache of having their husband and father publicly cast as mentally ill. His two-line death notice, which appeared in the Evening Times and Glasgow Herald, made reference only to his name, address and cause of passing as "a lingering illness".[8]

In the same week, smallpox outbreaks were reported in the press, along with regular bulletins on the ailing health of the Prime Minister, Lord Salisbury, and the news that a new railway had opened, taking passengers along one of the most scenic routes in the world, from Fort William to Mallaig. In football, a preview of the Partick Thistle AGM showed that the Firhill club had spent £360 on

H and P McNeil were prolific advertisers in the Scottish press from the early 1870s until they went out of business in 1896. The advert to the right is taken from the SFA Annual of 1878-79.

HARRY & PETER M'NEIL,
Outfitters
TO ALL THE PRINCIPAL CLUBS IN SCOTLAND,
ALSO TO THE
SCOTTISH, SHEFFIELD, AYRSHIRE, & WELSH
FOOTBALL ASSOCIATIONS.

OUTFITTERS
FOR ALL
AMATEUR ATHLETIC SPORTS

ASSOCIATION FOOTBALLS
SPECIALLY MADE.

H. & P. M'NEIL,
Hatters, Hosiers, Glovers & Shirtmakers
CRICKET & FOOTBALL OUTFITTERS,
21 & 23 RENFIELD STREET,
GLASGOW.

A public subscription and the success of the Founders Trail helped pay for headstones to mark the final resting place of Peter and his family members, including brother Willie, at Craigton Cemetery.

player transfers the year before.

The decline in the quality of life of the McNeil family could no longer be hidden from the wider world. By May 1897 they had downsized through necessity, from Bentinck Street to a four-apartment flat at No. 32 Gibson Street in Hillhead ("three up, first door, name on door")[9] and Peter began to display the signs of the mental distress that would kill him within four years. In his health records of January 1901 from Hawkhead, which was renamed Leverndale in 1964, it states he had suffered "growing (mental) paralysis for three years."

By the time he was sectioned he had been insane for six months and although he was not listed as suicidal or epileptic, he was considered dangerous. [10]

He weighed only eight stones 13 pounds, stood five feet four and a half inches tall and had grey hair, brown eyes and a pale complexion. He was listed as being in fair nutritional state and his first check-up at the asylum disclosed "a large scar on the front of the left leg." An old reminder of the rough and tumble from his playing career with Rangers, perhaps?

McNeil was admitted to the Hawkhead Asylum only after being granted Poor Law Relief by the Govan Parish, of which Hillhead was a part in the early 20th century. He was described as "wholly" disabled as a result of "insanity" and his wife was struggling so badly to pay the rent of £25 a year she had resorted to keeping lodgers. Fraser, 14 by this time, had already been put to work as a clerk earning five shillings a week, while Gertrude was approaching her 11th birthday and still at school. The family was described as having "no means, no society" and, unsurprisingly, their application for relief was approved.

On arrival at Hawkhead, it was recorded that none of McNeil's relatives were known to be insane and the reason for his admittance, as stated earlier, was "paralysis induced by financial worries."The records states his "speech was thick and hesitant and incoherent. Tongue tremulous, gait uncertain and pupils pin-point." Furthermore, it noted: "Wife says he is very irritable and at times excited. He has no idea of where he is or what time of year it is."The records added: "On admission, patient was somewhat excited and resisted when his clothes were being removed, but he soon became quiet and went to bed without further trouble. Patient has a difficulty in his speech. His words are pronounced in a thick and hesitating manner."

The following day, 22 January, McNeil seemed to have calmed and adapted to his new situation. The records noted: "Patient…submits readily to examination. His pupils are contracted and there is a suspicion of cardiac disease."The next entry from doctors, on 6 February, reads: "Patient is up every day. He is very happy and contented and thinks that he is staying in Dunbartonshire. He takes his food well and sleeps well." On 12 February: "Patient now recognises that he is staying in a hospital. He is able to be up every day. He takes his food well and sleeps well. Patient appears to be very contented and happy." A fortnight later, on 26 February: "Patient remains in much the same condition. He answers questions readily but does not know very well where he is or what he is talking [about]. He is happy and contented and eats and sleeps well." The following week, 4 March: "Patient continues in the same happy and contented condition."

However, within four weeks McNeil's condition had changed dramatically as his life drew to a close. On 30 March his records stated bluntly: "Patient became much worse since last night and gradually sank, dying at 6.20pm today. No PM (post mortem) allowed."

Janet Fraser McNeil married again two years later to potato merchant James Fulton. She died on 18 April 1932, her age listed as 74, at a Glasgow nursing home, having outlived both her husbands. Gertrude Grace married in 1925 to a William Stewart Chapman at Pollokshields, who worked as a trader in East India. Until recently, little was known of the life of Peter's son, John Fraser McNeil.

Four days after his death, on Wednesday 3 April 1901, Peter was laid to rest at Craigton Cemetery, where he was buried in the family plot with his parents John and Jane McNeil. The plot, in the name of James N.B. (Neil Brodie) McNeil, the second-oldest McNeil brother, was opened for the last time on 19 August 1908 when brother William, who gave sterling service as a Rangers player until 1878, was buried following his death aged 53. In plot 1502, again unmarked, lie the bodies of James Neil Brodie McNeil, listed as aged 64 when he died in November 1909, his first wife Lucy Ann McNeil, aged 42 when she passed away in March 1895 (James remarried, to a Jane McAllister MacHaffie, in April 1899) and also a Brodie McNeil, most likely the son of James and Lucy Ann, who died aged 32 in May 1914. In plot I500, marked with a handsome headstone, lies Alexander McNeil, the third oldest brother of Peter and Moses, who died in 1914 aged 66, and three of his family members.

The records of Craigton Cemetery show the cost of Peter McNeil's Class C burial was 12 shillings and sixpence. Extensive as the records are, they do not state how the bill was settled. Peter's death went virtually unnoticed in the press, although the Scottish Referee conceded: "Mr McNeil has long been ailing and his death, even in life's primal age of the forties, was not unexpected."[11]

Heather Lang reflected on the grandfather she never knew in an interview at the Mitchell Library in the summer of 2008. Appropriately, she was sitting in the cafe that overlooks Cleveland Street, where Peter first lived when he moved to the city from Garelochhead around 1870, as she spoke. She said: "The news came as an absolute shock, a bolt from the blue. My sister Doreen was speechless on the telephone when I told her about our connection with Rangers. We didn't know a thing about it."

Beyond the formation of a great football club, the personal stories surrounding the four founding fathers cry out for a happy ending, and they find one in the shape of Heather and Doreen and the happy, prosperous families they have raised and whose branches have, in turn, spread out fruitfully across the UK, the US and even the Caribbean. The two daughters of Gertrude Grace and her husband William Chapman are the closest descendants of the founding four. It quickly becomes clear that the lineage of Peter and Janet McNeil has been in strong, firm hands these last 100 years.

Sadly, their uncle John Fraser – Peter's son, known in the family as Fraser – did not survive World War One. A second lieutenant with the Royal Field Artillery Regiment, he made it to within two months and two days of the Armistice before he died in France on 9 September 1918, aged 31. He is buried at the Ligny-St Flochel British cemetery in the town of Averdoingt, near Arras. Fraser was a keen golfer and his name is still acknowledged on the memorial board for fallen heroes at the local club where he was a member, Ranfurly Castle in Bridge of Weir. He is also remembered on the memorial board at the Western Baths in the west end of Glasgow, a swimming and fitness club, where he was a member with Harold Vallance, son of Tom.

Heather said: "We knew about Uncle Fraser and his death in World War One, although little about his background and employment until that point. I'm rather pleased, knowing what we do now about the sad circumstances of my grandfather's death, that Fraser did not seem to be affected by his father's financial worries as he moved into adulthood. My mother didn't inform us about any details of her father's death. The only explanation I can think of is she must have been very distressed and upset about the whole thing and not wanted to talk about it. Of course, we knew about Fraser and also my grandmother's second marriage – my mother was 13 when grandmother remarried.

"I never even asked my mother how she got on with her stepfather and in what ways, if any, the marriage affected her at that time in her life. I'm interested now, of course – back then we were so wrapped up in what was going on in our own, busy lives. Peter was never, ever discussed and maybe, in many ways, it was a result of the 'shame' they felt at his mental decline. Mother lived until the age of 93 and was always very guilty, when asked about her father and other events of her family past, of saying: 'Och, I can't remember.' We were absolutely never aware of a football connection in the family, though maybe that was because there were no boys, only Doreen and me. The favourite sport in our family was tennis – mother became quite a star at her club in Pollokshields and also played with my father when he came back on leave from his job in the east."

Gertrude Grace and

Ibrox aristocracy . . . Heather Lang (left) and Doreen Holland are a direct link to the formation of Rangers in 1872. They were guests of honours at a Founders' Tribute dinner held at Ibrox in October 2009

husband-to-be William (better known by his nickname 'Chappie') met, Heather recalls, in 1922 at a dance in the Glenburn Hydro Hotel in Rothesay. Chappie, who was originally from Kirkcaldy and born in 1893, was the son of a shipping captain. The family moved to the west of Scotland when Chappie was a young man and he began his career in a junior position at a Glasgow merchant. By coincidence, the Chapmans regularly holidayed at Garelochhead, the village so associated with the McNeils and Peter Campbell. William, who lived to the age of 83, became a general

The stunning protrait of Peter and his friends, by artist Helen Runciman, now has pride of place at the top of the Marble Staircase.

Iain McColl of the Founders Trail officially presented the commissioned picture of the founding fathers to Rangers skipper David Weir at Murray Park.

manager with Steel Brothers, East India merchant traders in commodities such as rice and teak, and the nature of his employment ensured a long courtship with Gertrude Grace.

They may have met in 1922, but William worked a pattern of three years on and six months off, so it was not until 1925 and after many letters sent back and forth that they could finally declare their love officially through marriage. Heather and Doreen, three years her junior, were born in Burma and also lived the early part of their lives in Bangkok before moving to boarding school at Westcliff-on-Sea in Essex. They returned to Scotland in 1940 and Heather became a home economics teacher until she married and Doreen a speech therapist.

Heather said: "Mother never once said to us: 'Let's go and have a look at where I used to live,' even though we moved back to the west of Scotland in 1940. I vaguely remember the death of my grandmother Janet, Peter's wife, in April 1932. I was only five and mother must have been upset at losing her own mother, but she couldn't make it home because their two leave periods at that time were in 1931 and 1934. When Moses died in 1938 I don't even think mother knew anything about it. By that time, father was still out east and mother was with us at Westcliff-on-Sea.

"As far as I know, we were never in touch with any other members of the McNeil family and, to be honest, didn't even know they existed. It's amazing to think both sides of the family had a connection with Garelochhead and we didn't even know about one another. My father's mother ended her days at Whistlefield, which is a stone's throw from Garelochhead, and I still have pictures from a holiday there in 1934. It's incredible to think my great-uncle Moses was still alive then and living only a few miles along the road in Rosneath.

"I'm sure Peter would be very pleased with the way his family has turned out. I was glad to see his decline and eventual death came over a very short period of time. It all happened so quickly in the end, only a few months, and that's at least a crumb of comfort. It's such a pity we didn't know more about the McNeils before now, but I'm very proud of my grandfather's achievements, even though his life ended so sadly. Rangers Football Club is quite a legacy to leave behind."

Doreen, who lives in Surrey, shares another pleasant connection with the club, this time indirectly. Her husband Michael is the nephew of former Arsenal player and manager Tom Whittaker, who was coach under the great Herbert Chapman in the 1920s and 30s before taking over at the club after World War Two. The Gunners and Bill Struth's Rangers battled for supremacy in a series of annual challenge matches throughout the 1930s at Ibrox and Highbury that determined, arguably, the best club side in the world at the time – and Rangers lost only once in six head-to-heads.

Doreen reflected on her grandfather's life and achievements ahead of the game against Stirling Albion in December 2012 to mark the club's 140th anniversary and admitted it was happy coincidence the game was against the senior side closest to the roots of the Callander team Rangers faced in its first game in May 1872.

She said: "Our grandfather would walk from his home in the Sandyford district on a Saturday morning and stake out a pitch at Glasgow Green, 'holding the fort' before the rest of the players arrived for kick-off by mid-afternoon. Peter, his brother Moses, Peter Campbell and William McBeath had no money, no ball and not even a home in those fledgling months of the club. I'm absolutely thrilled to hear that very line has now become a staple of one of the most popular Rangers songs!

"Heather and I were thrilled to be invited to Ibrox by Iain McColl, Gordon Bell and Neil Stobie of the Rangers Founders Trail in October 2009 to be guests of honour at a dinner for the 'Gallant Pioneers'. The artist Helen Runciman painted a beautiful picture of the boys and it is deeply humbling to know it is now on display at the top of the Marble Staircase.

"Helen kindly gave us a very limited print of her canvas and mine now has pride of place at the home of my son, Rory, in Barbados. A new generation of fans has been inspired among the ranks of our families. We didn't know about our grandfather's contribution to the formation of Rangers until recently and it's a fantastic achievement we have happily shared with everyone we know. Their amazement is matched only by our pride and delight.

"We know the last couple of years have been the most difficult in the history of the club, but the trials have been overcome, thanks to the support of the best fans in the world. They have responded magnificently to these testing times and good times will surely come again in future. Peter and Moses McNeil and their wonderful group of friends would be so proud of the loyalty shown by Rangers fans to the club."

Chapter 6
Sweet Charity

If charity begins at home then good causes in and around Glasgow never had to stray far for support in the early years of Scottish football. The game echoed the benevolent paternalism of Victorian society at large and Rangers were never found wanting, with their generosity of time and spirit to boost fundraising efforts for a whole range of groups. They asked for nothing in return, but received thanks of a kind in 1879 in the shape of the fledgling club's first piece of silverware – the Glasgow Merchants' Charity Cup, which made some amends for the loss of the Scottish Cup Final that same year following another controversial final against Vale of Leven.

Since its formation in 2002, the Rangers Charity Foundation has given £3 million in financial support and assistance to a range of grateful groups, but the Light Blues have been willing contributors to a host of good causes from their very earliest days. Their first game against Queen's Park, played in November 1875, raised £28 for the Bridgeton Fire Fund. They played on a public park on Rothesay in August 1879, once more against Queen's Park, in support of local good causes, then followed it up early the following year with another benefit game aimed at swelling the coffers of a group of players who hoped to represent Scotland on a tour of Canada.

They moved swiftly to set up a benefit game against Scottish Cup holders Dumbarton in July 1883 when the Daphne went down following its launch at Alexander Stephen's Linthouse shipyard on the Clyde with the loss of 124 lives. They regularly played fundraisers at Kinning Park to boost the coffers of the local unemployed in days long before the safety net of social security was available to protect the most vulnerable. One such match, against a Glasgow select side known as the Crusaders, raised £18 in 1886. Those who have carelessly linked Rangers to uber-Protestantism since its formation in 1872 may be surprised to learn that the club fought out a 2–2 draw against Hibs at Easter Road in May 1903, in a game played to raise funds for the Leith Roman Catholic School Building Fund. The Star of the Sea RC School was built in the grounds of the Stella Maris Church in Constitution Street in Leith as a result.

The Glasgow Merchants' Charity Cup, which survived as a competition until 1961, raised over £10,000 between 1877 and 1890 for various good causes and its formation came as a result of the interminable squabbles that characterised the early years of the sport, this time between Queen's Park and Vale of Leven. The Glasgow giants had taught the men from Alexandria how to play the new game in 1872 and initially relations between the clubs were good, but things soured when the SFA, under influence from Queen's Park, refused to give Vale of Leven permission to compete in the first two Scottish Cup tournaments.

Cancellation of subsequent fixtures between the clubs led to a claim from Vale of Leven that the trailblazers of the Scottish game were running scared. They seemed to have a point, as Vale of Leven handed Queen's Park their first defeat by a Scottish side, 2–1 in the quarter-final of the Scottish Cup, in season 1876–77. The victory, in turn, led to those contentious allegations from the Hampden club that the Vale of Leven players had used forbidden spikes on the soles of their boots. Glasgow merchants put up the new trophy in the hope it would heal the gaping wounds between the clubs, but Vale of Leven refused to enter the competition in its first year. Rangers did play, however, as defeated Scottish Cup finalists, but were dismissed 4–0 at Hampden by Queen's Park. They fared little better the following year when they were knocked out by Third Lanark in the early stages, 2–1 at Hampden. However, season 1877–78 was memorable in many other ways. It was during this campaign that Rangers played their first game in Edinburgh, against Brunswick (a 2–1 win), in England, against Nottingham Forest (a 4–2 victory), and also secured their record victory, twice (13–0 against Possilpark and repeated against Uddingston, with both games in the Scottish Cup).

Nevertheless, the charitable work on the football field paled into insignificance in comparison to the fundraising efforts that had been undertaken off it in Glasgow as Rangers set off on a season that would yield their first success after seven years in existence. In October 1878 the failure of the City of Glasgow bank was considered to be the greatest disaster ever to hit the business community in Britain and would find echoes in the credit crunch of the modern era. At its annual general meeting in June 1878 the bank, a haven for small investors, revealed the number of branches had risen to 133 and deposits stood at £8 million. All appeared well, and although rumours of its instability had been expressed as early as 1857, there was still genuine shock and dismay when the directors announced they were closing its doors.

The business community of the city was paralysed and many merchants faced ruin as auditors estimated the bank's losses to total £6.2 million. One business after another went to the wall, while the 1,200 shareholders had a call made on them by liquidators of £500 for every £100 of stock owned in a bid to raise £5 million. Civil unrest was predicted, but Lord Provost William Collins raised a fund of £400,000, primarily from big-hearted Glaswegians and, astonishingly, within two years creditors were paid 18 shillings in the pound. The directors of the bank did not escape punishment and were sent for trial at the High Court in Edinburgh in January 1879. It was revealed that large unsecured loans had been made to insolvent companies with which some of the directors were involved. Two directors were imprisoned for 18 months and others were sent to jail for eight months with the public, unsurprisingly, unsympathetic to their plight.

The debate on the financial uncertainty of the city that dominated the front pages was vigorous, and if worried investors hoped they would escape controversy in their leisure time by following their favourites from Kinning Park they would be sadly mistaken. For the second time in three years Rangers made the Scottish Cup final, conceding only three goals in six games en route to a rematch with Vale of Leven. The Alexandria club had won the Cup for the first time in 1877 and also knocked Rangers out of the tournament in the fourth round in 1878 with a comfortable 5–0 replay win in Dunbartonshire following a goalless draw at Kinning Park. They subsequently went on to win the trophy for the second season in a row with a 1–0 victory over Third Lanark.

However, Rangers fancied their chances this time, not least because Queen's Park had been conquered by the Kinning Park squad for the first time in the semi-final. Previously, the Spiders had won all four Cup ties against the Light Blues and had not conceded a goal in the process, but that all changed at Hampden in March 1879. Rangers forward William Dunlop had placed a sovereign (then worth the considerable sum of 21 shillings) on Queen's to win the trophy that season in a move that would earn him the wrath of administrators were he playing in the 21st century. However, when the ball landed at his feet in the last minute, and with the goal gaping, he paused only to poetically reflect: "There goes my sov," as he rammed the winner between the posts.

Another record crowd was attracted to Hampden on Saturday 19 April 1879 to see Rangers play Vale of Leven. Included in the throng, one newspaper was delighted to note, were "a number of ladies."[1] Not all fans were happy, however, and in a letter to the North British Daily Mail on the Tuesday after the Cup Final a reader by the name JMW championed the advent of all-seater stadia over a century before the Hillsborough disaster was a catalyst for such a move. JMW wrote: "It is anything but fair that the public should be asked to pay such a sum as a shilling each to be allowed to roll on each other as we are compelled to do, if at all inclined to see the game as it goes on. It is not to be wondered that thousands of the people prefer to stand outside rather than be crushed as we were on Saturday last, not to say one word of the inconvenience to the traffic and annoyance to the people of the district. I am sure it cannot be for the want of funds that better accommodation is not provided as three or four hundred pounds, I think, would go a long way in providing seats all round, which would add not only to the comfort to the sightseers but profit to the coffers of the club."[2]

Rangers had six survivors from the side that had lost over the epic three games only two years earlier – Tom Vallance, Moses McNeil, William Dunlop, Peter Campbell, David Hill and George Gillespie, although the latter had switched position from back to goalkeeper in the interim period, while Vale of Leven contained five of the team that took part in the Final in 1877. The 1879 line ups were: Rangers – Gillespie, goal; T. Vallance (captain) and A. Vallance, backs; H. McIntyre and J. Drinnan, half-backs; W. Dunlop, D. Hill, W. Struthers, A. Steel, M. McNeil, P. Campbell, forwards. Vale of Leven – R. Parlane, goal; A. McLintock and A. McIntyre, backs; J. McIntyre and J. McPherson, half-backs; J. Ferguson, J. McFarlane, P. McGregor, J. Baird, J.C. Baird, J. McDougall (captain), forwards.

The match kicked off at 3.30pm and as Rangers had the better of the early exchanges it came as no surprise when William Struthers opened the scoring with a shot from close range after only 12 minutes. However, then came the moment on which subsequent events centred. Peter Campbell and Moses McNeil worked the ball down the wing and when it was sent into the middle an exchange of headers resulted in Struthers knocking another effort between the Vale posts. Vale appealed against the goal for offside and the referee R.B. Colquhoun from the Havelock club disallowed the effort. According to one report it was "a decision which, as might be expected from the strong partisanship displayed by the crowd, evoked a storm of hisses and counter-cheering."[3]

Vale immediately pressed for the equaliser, but Rangers maintained their lead to half-time and looked as if they would hold out as the clock ticked down on the second-half action, despite pressure from the Cup holders. Vale fans had all but given up hope of three-in-a-row when, with only two minutes remaining, a shot from Ferguson squirmed inside the post, with Gillespie mistakenly believing the ball was heading past.

The crowd had no sooner dispersed from Hampden anticipating a replay than Rangers announced they were appealing the result on the basis that the second 'goal' from Struthers should have stood. They were given short shrift at an SFA committee meeting on the Monday evening. Astonishingly, Colquhoun chaired the discussion in his position as vice-president of the SFA, which ruled an appeal could not be heard. He argued that Rangers' claim was being made against a decision of the referee, whose word was final, so the argument was invalid. Rangers were ordered to play the replay at Hampden the following Saturday.

Rangers dug in their heels and 24 hours before the replay was due to go ahead at Hampden the Glasgow News announced the game would not be played as the Kinning Park club were refusing to take to the field until their appeal had been heard. It further revealed that Rangers were happy to play a replay if the decision of the appeal went against them. Queen's Park, fearing lost revenue, quickly arranged a game at Hampden against Glasgow University. Vale of Leven duly arrived at the ground in time for kick-off the next day, along with the referee and his two umpires but, as expected, Rangers were nowhere to be seen. Vale pulled on their kit and remained on the pitch for several minutes before the officials declared them Cup winners by default, a decision ratified by the SFA at a committee meeting the following Monday. Meanwhile, a telegram was sent to Alexandria informing the eager public of the news. There was general feeling of satisfaction, mingled with disappointment.

Rangers officials were persistent, and in the week after the replay that never was Tom Vallance, in his position as club captain, and former goalkeeper James Watt, the ex-president who was by then honorary treasurer, demanded to address the AGM of the SFA at the Trades' Hall in Glasgow on Tuesday 30 April. Some of the exchanges were pointed and personal, but Vallance and Watt clearly had their supporters from other clubs in the assembled throng as Colquhoun was forced to defend himself against one of the earliest recorded allegations of match-fixing[+]:

> **Vallance:** Why, in face of precedents, was the Rangers protest not opened for discussion at the last committee meeting? Last year, Vale of Leven lodged a dispute following our Cup tie with them and it was heard, even though it related to nothing but a question of the play. (Shouts of 'hear hear'.)
> **Colquhoun:** Stick to the facts.
> **Vallance:** If the Vale of Leven's protest was given consideration, so

ought to have the one from Rangers. (Applause.) We are entitled to have our case heard.

Watt: The Vale of Leven team did not, after having claimed and received from the umpire the offside allowance, take the free-kick from where the offside took place. This is becoming personal, but there has been a lot of personal talk in the matter. One of the judges informed a Vale of Leven player near the end of the game he had five minutes left to save his team's honour. (Applause.) Is it possible for judges to be neutral in such circumstances? (Cheers.)

(Rangers then demanded the protest should be considered by the meeting, but Colquhoun refused, claiming it was out of order as the SFA committee had already disposed of the matter the week previously.)

Watt: How can Vale take possession of the Scottish Cup when they haven't won it?

Colquhoun: Because Rangers did not appear when the committee of the association ordered them to play.

Watt: Well, it was impossible that the game could be played anyway when a match between Queen's Park and the University had been arranged on the Hampden pitch that day. (Laughter.)

Colquhoun: Our secretary, Mr Dick, had secured the ground for the Cup tie and had Rangers turned up they would have played at the hour advertised. On the issue of precedent on the grounds of the Vale protest last year, it was actually considered because the incident related to an interpretation of the rules. Rangers have received the utmost fair play. I'd also like to address rumours that I had money on the game but I declare on behalf of myself, the other umpire and referee there were no bets placed on the match whatsoever. As for telling players how much time was left to play, I informed members of both sides when asked. This has been my practice in the past and will continue to be my practice in future.

Colquhoun sat down to a burst of applause and following further discussion Watt was told to make any proposal to play the match again to another committee meeting which, unsurprisingly given the time that would have then elapsed, he never did. However, Rangers clearly had the goodwill of the majority of the Glasgow public on their side if the letters to the News in the weeks that followed were anything to go by. There was anger that the SFA had ratified the decision of the referee and umpires to award the trophy to Vale of Leven when Rangers refused to show on point of principle. One particularly irate reader, named only as J.C., thundered: "With respect to this match there is only one conclusion to which anyone present at the association meeting can come – namely, that, come what may, the committee were determined that the Rangers should not get the Cup."[5]

A writer named 'Olive Branch' called on Vale of Leven the same day to offer to play the game again in a gesture of true sporting spirit. He said: "As a witness of the contest on Hampden Park, I have followed the progress of the dispute along its devious course to the present point, and deplore the depth to which the game of football has sunk in the estimation of those who are its exponents…It is difficult to see how the Vale of Leven club can enjoy possession of the Cup even under the plea that it has been awarded them by the association, and I think it would be a magnanimous act on their part, and help to raise them in the good opinion of all who like fair play, were they to say to one another, 'Well, we don't want to lie under the stigma of holding a Cup we have not won and, although the association have vindicated our legal title to it, we are ready to play the Rangers afresh and abide by the result.'"

No more than 24 hours later, reader 'Mackenzie' went straight to what many considered the nub of the issue when he asked: "Why did the Vale kick from goal instead of from offside? And the decision of committee not to consider the protest, while they had considered similar ones? It was apparent to disinterested spectators of the match that the umpires and referee had 'lost their heads,' and I am afraid this opinion will gain ground in regard to the association also."[6]

Immediately 'An Old Half Back,' surely with leanings towards Vale of Leven, took J.C. and Olive Branch to task for their points of view. He hit out: "J.C.'s remarks in today's Glasgow News seem to me to be the outcome of disappointed spleen. The Rangers, by their high-handed and unjustifiable proceedings in regard to the decision of the committee, have debarred themselves from any and all chances they had to secure the Cup and the committee, in handing it over to the Vale of Leven, adopted the only course open to them. The childlike statements of Olive Branch are also, to say the least, very nonsensical. To expect the Vale of Leven club to offer to play the Rangers for possession of the Cup is absurd."[7]

That argument cut no ice with the wonderfully named 'Hard Nut', who cracked in a fiery letter to the News on the Saturday morning and demanded his favourites resign from the SFA all together. He wrote: "Before An Old Half Back assumes such a bold tone against the Rangers let him answer the following pertinent questions: Can the disputed goal be proved a 'no goal' when the umpires and referee could not tell which player was offside? Assuming it was 'no goal', is it fact that in resuming play the Vale men did not kick from the offside, but kicked from goal, thereby infringing the rule? Is it the case that one of the umpires at the match, Mr. R.B. Colquhoun, occupied and retained the chair when the Rangers protest was decided in committee, and, if so, when a man sits in judgement upon his own action what is the usual result? Let Old Half Back crack these nuts and then supporters of the game can decide as to the justice or injustice of the committee's decision. If this cannot be done satisfactorily (which I fear it cannot) then the Rangers have certainly not had justice afforded them, and they would do right, as suggested, in withdrawing from an association that sanctions such questionable proceedings."[8]

Things were bubbling up nicely for the Charity Cup Final on 20 May, which Rangers had reached following a 4–1 defeat over Third Lanark two weeks earlier. Preparations were underway throughout Scotland on the day of the Final to celebrate the birthday of Queen Victoria 24 hours later, with many shops and businesses preparing to close for the day. In Kilmarnock, for example, excursions were being arranged to places such as Carlisle, Greenock and Arran, although the Evening Citizen reported that "as usual, the Provost issued a caution to those likely to be outrageous in their methods of celebrating the holiday."[9]

In the pavilion at Hampden the atmosphere was more sober as the two captains turned to face one another. Vale of Leven's John McDougall looked Tom Vallance in the eye and said: "Well Tom, this is the conqueror." Tom replied, "It is." In total, 10,000 fans crammed into Hampden to watch teams so evenly balanced they had each also claimed a win at home against the other earlier in the season, 2–0 at Vale of Leven and 3–0 to Rangers at Kinning Park. Vale stunned Rangers after only two minutes of the Final when McDougall, playing the skipper's role to perfection, nodded his side in front. However, the game was level on 15 minutes when Struthers, repeating his scoring feat of the Final, headed home an equaliser that could not be disputed. Rangers pressed after the interval for the winner and the ball was finally scrambled over the line for a clincher so ugly the scorer has never been recorded. Still, it was a thing of beauty to Rangers as they celebrated lifting silverware at last.

With so much tension hanging in the air for several weeks it is hardly surprising the game ended in a bad-tempered fashion. Players traded punches and even the Rangers fans jostled their rivals as they left the pitch. Bob Parlane, the Vale of Leven keeper, was accused by the North British Daily Mail of deliberately kicking an unnamed Rangers player as he lay on the ground, sparking the furious reaction from the crowd. Parlane, however, vehemently denied any wrongdoing and wrote to the paper claiming he travelled home on the bus with the player he was alleged to have assaulted. It seemed all the best battles took place off the field that season, rather than on it.

Chapter 7
Peter Campbell

The family of Peter Campbell undoubtedly reflected on fate as a fickle mistress when the Rangers founder was forced to give up his life to the sea in the spring of 1883 at the tender age of 25. It was a cruel end to a life robbed short. Perhaps it was a gnawing guilt that finally led Dame Fortune to deliver one of Peter's most prized possessions back into the safe hands of the Rangers support after more than 125 years.

In 1967, 11 year-old Stephen McCafferty was walking from his home in West Mains, East Kilbride, to Duncanrig Secondary School. Dragging his heels, as schoolboys are wont do do at the thought of double maths and science, his head was down as he tried instead to focus on the thought of a game of football with his pals later in the day. Suddenly, as he trudged across a piece of waste ground in the district of Westwood, his eye caught a sliver of gold glistening off the sun through the weeds and grass. Reaching

Blues Brothers: Stephen McCafferty (left) helped with research from his friend William Mason, is keen to solve the mystery of Peter Campbell's Charity Cup medal.

down to pick it up, he turned it over gently in his hands, hardly believing what he had found. It was an old, gold medal - and not just any medal, but one awarded to a player from his favourite team, Rangers.

Almost half a century later, Stephen is still amazed at the combination of fate and good luck that led him to find and cherish the first medal any Rangers player ever won. It came from the Glasgow Merchants' Charity Cup final of 1879, the club's first trophy success following its formation

The gold may have worn after so many years, but there is no doubting the authenticity of the winner's badge.

seven years previously. More than that, the winner's badge from the 2-1 victory over old foes Vale of Leven at the first Hampden Park belonged to Peter Campbell, one of the club's founding fathers.

Stephen said: "I struggled to come to terms with what I had found at first. I thought: 'This must be a fake,' but quickly realised it was so well made it had to be an original. There was no way I could keep it so my parents and I contacted the police and handed it over in the hope it could be returned to its rightful owner. What was it doing there on that piece of waste ground? I wonder still. There was a link attached to the medal, as if it had been on a chain, and it was quite worn. Initially, I thought it must have been lost but 12 months later the police made contact again. No-one had claimed the medal and so, legally, it now belonged to me. I was invited to the station to pick it up. I can only think it must have been stolen at some point in time past and therefore couldn't be claimed. Why else would anyone abandon it?"

It quickly became one of Stephen's most prized possessions, but the issue of ownership continued to gnaw at him and he even contacted then Rangers boss David White in the hope it could be returned to Peter's family. Stephen added: "I still have the letter from Mr White. He replied on official Rangers notepaper, admitting he knew only brief details about the life of Peter Campbell and wasn't aware of any relatives we could contact, so the medal stayed in my family for many years, in a box at my mother's home.

"I actually took it to Christie's twice, in the 1970s and 1980s, with the thought of putting it up for auction. They quickly verified its authenticity and calibre of gold, 24 carat, and it was of such high quality I barely needed to shine it. All those years and it wasn't even tarnished. They couldn't believe it had survived a couple of major depressions, because players often cashed in on their medals by melting them down at times of financial difficulty. However, they couldn't put a value on it as they had never seen anything with which which to compare it.

"I admit there have been times in my life when the money from a sale would have come in handy, especially the early years of my marriage when finances were tight. But on both occasions I pulled back from putting it up for auction. Something at the back of my mind told me not to sell it, that fate would take its course. The medal was never mine, I only found it. Deep in my heart I knew it belonged within the Rangers family and that it had to be shared and not kept hidden away in a box at my home."

Stephen told the story a few years ago to workmate and fellow Bluenose William Mason, who took it upon himself to find out more about Peter's life. The details were fleshed out still further in the pages of The Gallant Pioneers and soon Stephen was in touch with Sandy Jardine and presented the medal to Rangers, who framed it to hang proudly in the Blue Room. Stephen said: "The medal deserves more than just a select few to take enjoyment from it. It is unique and the story on how it came to be in

Peter Campbell's winning medal from the 1879 Glasgow Merchants' Charity Cup now hangs proudly at the top of the Marble Staircase

my possession is surreal. Believe it or not, I still haven't been to see it on display inside Ibrox, but I'm glad it's on general view. I'd love to find out more. Perhaps now it's on show people will see it and start to talk about it and we can clear up the mystery of how it came to be in East Kilbride that morning in 1967. It would be good to know."

The story of Peter's death was tragic as the ship on which he was a seaman, the St Columba, capsized and sank in the Bay of Biscay, south of Nantes in 1883. The news was confirmed on 2 March 1883 with a message to the Registrar General of Shipping and Seamen in Cardiff, which was blunt and to the point. It read: "Reliable information received here direct from Marennes stated some wreckage from steamer St Columba washed ashore near Marennes, Bay of Biscay. She left Penarth Dock, January 28, for Bombay."[1] Tears were shed up and down the country for loved ones lost, particularly at Glasgow and Garelochhead as relatives and friends of Peter came to terms with his untimely passing.

Peter McGregor Campbell was born at Craigellan, a villa in Garelochhead, on 6 March 1857, the son of John McLeod Campbell, a steamboat master, and Mary Campbell, who came from Kirkconnell near Dumfries. Of all the gallant pioneers, Campbell's early life was easily the most privileged. He was raised in a substantial sandstone property his father had built on land feued from the Clan Campbell chief, the Duke of Argyll, in 1850. It still stands today on the shores of the Gare Loch, next to an almost identical home constructed at the same time by Peter's uncle, Alexander. The houses were built after the Duke began to allocate lucrative parcels of his extensive land holdings to allow the construction of sizeable properties, many of them weekend and summer retreats for the Glasgow mercantile classes. John McLeod Campbell became a man of means and influence throughout a life spent mostly on the Clyde, where he thrived as a successful steamboat captain and shipping entrepreneur.

Captain John Campbell, father of Peter Campbell, Firth of Clyde pioneer and steamship entrepreneur.

He married into a family of substance when he wed Mary Jenkins at Rhu in 1846 – her brother, Sir James Jenkins, was honorary surgeon to the Queen and a graduate of medicine from Glasgow University who had entered the Royal Navy in 1841. He went on to

Garelochhead. The birthplace of Peter Campbell, whose family home lay around the sweep of the bay to the left.

become a staff surgeon, then Inspector General of Hospitals, in a fulfilling career littered with honours before his retirement in 1878. The Jenkins family, as the name suggests, hailed originally from Wales, but settled in Upper Nithsdale in the latter half of the 18th century, where they were widely respected for the benevolence shown to the poor at the family farm, Nivinston, at Kirkconnel.

A local history, The Folklore and Genealogies of Uppermost Nithsdale, almost beatifies the family for their charitable disposition, which included turning over one of the farm buildings to vagrants and itinerants. Their country hospitality

Garelochhead West, circa 1912. The house on the extreme right is Ellangowan, originally the home of Captain Alex Campbell, uncle of Peter. Next door is the house where Peter was born, Craigellan, built by his father, Captain John McLeod Campbell on land feued from the Duke of Argyll. Both handsome sandstone properties still stand today.

The pier at Garelochhead, a landmark that would have been more than familiar to Peter Campbell and his father, John.

even extended to setting up a makeshift infirmary for the homeless wanderers who fell ill "so that among the outcast, the name of Jenkins became the synonym of all that was good."[2]

Peter Campbell had two sisters, Jessie, five years his senior, and Mary, five years his junior. In the 1871 census, taken when he was 14, the family also included older brothers Alex, 23, and William, 22, both engineers, and John, 15, James, 12, and Allan, 11. Sadly, the lives of the three oldest sons would prove tragically short, as was the life of another daughter, Margaret, who died within a year of her birth in 1852. Two years before Peter's death, William drowned in an accident in the harbour of the German port of Geestemunde. Alex also died young, aged just 28 when he passed away in October 1876 of tuberculosis. The story of the Campbells is the story of the Clyde itself, as the family's history and fortunes flowed with the tides of time, lapping the banks of the river at Govan long before the legacy left by Peter and his friends on Edmiston Drive came to compete with the cranes of the shipyards for dominance on the skyline of the city's south side.

John McLeod Campbell, born in 1815, and his brother Alexander came from a line of ferrymen and fishermen who made their living on the waters of Argyll, from the west side of the Gare Loch through to Loch Goil, Loch Long and the Holy Loch. It was inevitable that their careers would intertwine with the new

Garelochhead . . . a village the McNeil, Campbell and Vallance brothers knew intimately.

steamship industry, which began to flourish from 1812 when the paddle steamer Comet was commissioned and built at Port Glasgow and became the first successful commercial vessel of its type, running daily services between Greenock and Glasgow.

Astonishingly, before then, the shallow nature of the Clyde allowed journeys along the river only at the top of each tide and, depending on the vagaries of the wind, it took up to 12 hours to complete a trip – miss the high water and an overnight stay at Bowling became a hastily scripted part of any traveller's itinerary.

John became a ship captain as early as 1835 when he took charge of a vessel named the James Dennistoun, followed by the St Mungo the following year. Soon he was a regular on the Glasgow-Gareloch route in command of ships such as the Sovereign, the Monarch and the Fire Queen. He served his apprenticeship working for ship owners such as Henderson and McKellar and James and John Napier but, time-served, by the mid-1850s he and Alexander began to set out on their own lucrative journey.

The expansion of Glasgow as an industrial centre gathered pace throughout the 1850s and the Gareloch was to feel its benefits in many different ways. For a start, the wealthy urban elite began to look for weekend retreats away from the grey backdrop of the Industrial Revolution and suddenly picturesque corners of the Argyll countryside became accessible by steamship and affordable through the rapid economic advancement of the lucky few merchants and industrialists.

However, the working classes also derived benefits from the advance of the steamship trade. The Glasgow tradition of going 'Doon the Watter' began in the 1850s and the Campbells were at the forefront of transporting the poorer citizens back and forth from often wretched living environments to resorts where the lungs could be cleared of the gritty reality of industrial living, even if only for a few short hours. The regular commuters may have looked down their noses at the passengers they disparagingly referred to as 'excursionists', but they were to play a vital part in the economic success story of the Campbells.

Unsurprisingly, perhaps, passenger motives for a trip on the steam ships were not always so well intentioned. The Forbes McKenzie Act of 1853 had forbidden pubs from opening on a Sunday, but pleasure craft were conveniently excluded from the legislation and so began the trend for booze cruises, leading to the popular west of Scotland slang term for overindulgence as 'steaming'.

The Campbells clearly had an entrepreneurial bent that allowed them to trade successfully in ships and develop new markets. Amazingly, this included an important role in the American Civil War for one of their vessels, the Mail, built in 1860 but sold three years later for the princely sum of £7,000 after its speed attracted the attention of Confederate agents looking for blockade runners in the Bahamas port of Nassau. The US Navy had been ordered to halt all maritime traffic in and out of Confederate ports, which caused the armies of the south considerable hardship. As an economy based mostly on agriculture, the southern states relied heavily on Europe for their essential military and medical supplies. As a result, Nassau and ports in Havana and Bermuda were used as staging posts, where supplies were loaded on to blockade runners such as the Mail and taken to the Gulf of Mexico, where they were distributed to those areas most in need. The Mail had been guided across the Atlantic in June 1863 by the Confederate conspirators and although she was captured by Union forces in 1864, dismissed as a prize and sold, she was actually bought by undercover agents again and once more returned to work as a blockade runner.

The last purchase involving John McLeod

Peter Campbell. This picture of the Rangers and Scotland winger from the 1877 Scottish Cup final team is the only one currently known to be in existence.

Campbell and Alexander Campbell was the Ardencaple in 1869, which ran on the Glasgow to Dumbarton route, with afternoon excursions to Greenock and Garelochhead. However, by the latter half of the 1860s the Campbell brothers had begun to progressively withdraw from the business they had founded, allowing their nephew Robert Campbell, 'Captain Bob' of Kilmun, to take it forward. In the case of John McLeod Campbell, poor health undoubtedly contributed to his decision to step back and allow Captain Bob to assume fuller control.

Peter's father died on 13 May 1871 in Glasgow after a brief illness, aged only 56. His obituary in the Dumbarton Herald the week after his death described him as "one of the best known and most popular steamboat captains." It went on: "Few of any of the Firth stations were better liked by passengers and brother professionals than John Campbell. Shrewd, well-informed, careful, courteous and honourable, he merited the estimation in which he was held."[3] John left almost £1,300 in his will and the family continued to live at Craigellan for many decades, including his wife Mary, who died there on 12 May 1912, aged 89.

Even after the death of his father, Peter Campbell was clearly close to his cousin Captain Bob and his application for his certificate of marine competence in 1882 listed his address as No. 2 Parkgrove Terrace in Glasgow, the city residence of the steamship entrepreneur, who died in 1888. A year earlier, Captain Bob's sons Peter and Alec had relocated the company to the Bristol Channel, their eyes having been opened by the financial possibilities of a business in a corner of England that had a sizeable population, but few passenger services of note. The company P. and A. Campbell dominated for decades, seeing off all competitors and in some cases buying out their fleets. It survived until the early 1980s when increased fuel and maintenance costs and an inevitable drop off in demand as the vogue for foreign holidays put paid to its existence.

The success and longevity of P and A Campbell, borne from the entrepreneurial zeal of John McLeod Campbell and his brother Alexander, made the death of Peter at the age of 25 all the more tragic, as fate denied him the opportunities afforded his relatives. The history of the Campbells of Kilmun makes no reference to Peter of Rangers fame – naturally, perhaps, as he played no role in their Clyde operations. However, the impact he had on Scottish sporting culture has lasted longer than the considerable maritime achievements of his other family members. Peter was present at the birth of Rangers, but brothers John and James also gave the club sterling service in its early years and the family links with the McNeils remained strong in the second half of the 19th century. The 1881 census, for example, listed James as living with Moses, Peter and William McNeil and their sister Elizabeth at No. 169 Berkeley Street in Charing Cross, Glasgow.

Peter had arrived in Glasgow a decade earlier and was the youngest founder of Rangers, having just turned 15 when he embraced the idea of organising a team with his three friends, not least as a release from the toils of the work on the Glasgow shipyards where he was employed. His employment records, accessed from the historical vaults at Greenwich, show he spent five years as an apprentice with the oldest shipbuilding company on the Clyde in Glasgow, Barclay Curle, at Stobcross Engine Works between 1872 and 1877.

John Barclay had started shipbuilding on the Clyde in 1818 and his yard lay half a mile outside the city boundary, on a patch of land near to the present-day Finnieston Crane, surrounded on three sides by open countryside. Facing the Stobcross Shipyard, on the south bank of the river, was the estate of Plantation, with the huts of the river's salmon fishermen standing back from the river bank. It is almost impossible to imagine the site in the present day, where the Squinty Bridge now connects north and south of the river, alongside the Mecca bingo hall and Odeon cinema that make up one of the city's best-known leisure parks.

In today's post-industrial era the shipyards of the Clyde often struggle to compete, financially at least, with other areas of the world but in the 1860s, shortly before Peter began his apprenticeship with Barclay Curle, 80 per cent of British shipping tonnage was constructed on the Clyde. He would have worked in an industry at its peak in the 1870s as bigger and faster ships were built up and down the river. They included the exotic, such as the Livadia, built in 1880 at Fairfield for the Czar of Russia, and government contracts, not only in Britain, but estimated at half the maritime nations of the world – including Japan, who took control of the Asahi from the Clyde in 1899.

Throughout most of the 19th century the shipyards of Glasgow proudly held the record for the speediest transatlantic crossings, with the firm grip of a rivet in an iron hull as Clyde-built ships were successful from 1840 to 1851, 1863 to 1872, 1880 to 1891 and 1892 to 1899. By the end of the century, Fairfield-built vessels Campania and Lucania could make the journey in five days and eight hours. In the 20th century great liners would maintain the reputation of Clyde shipbuilding, including the Lusitania, Queen Mary and Queen Elizabeth.

Peter stayed an additional two years with Barclay Curle as a journeyman from 1877–79 before leaving for at least seven spells at sea on board the London-registered merchant ship Margaret Banks, ranging in time from a fortnight to over six months. His apprenticeship served on the Clyde in Glasgow, he was clearly keen to extend his education to the waters of the wider world. As part of the process he sat engineering exams in March 1882, at Greenock and Glasgow, but failed each time on a poor grasp of arithmetic before passing at the third attempt the following month, on 12 April. Even the most mathematically gifted would surely have offered long odds on his death within 12 months, but betting on an extended life at sea has always been a dangerous gamble.

Peter's passion for the water was matched by his enthusiasm for football and he was an inspired supporter of Rangers, not to mention one of its most outstanding players throughout the 1870s, playing for the team in its very first match against Callander in May 1872 until he bowed out in a 5–1 Scottish Cup defeat to Queen's Park in September 1879. He also spent part of a season at Blackburn Rovers from 1879 and was one of the first Rangers players to cross the border, at a time when the English game was being criticised for its 'shameful' move towards professionalism.

Peter was also a keen shinty player and was recorded by the Southland Times newspaper on May 15 1876 representing the Vale of Leven club in a game against the Glasgow Camanachd, who featured Harry McNeil in their ranks. The Vale of Leven Shinty club were the forerunners to the football club - Queen's Park taught them the game in 1872 - and within a few short years the sticks had been retired for good as the leather ball was grasped with glee. The game, a 3-0 defeat for Glasgow, was played at Burnbank and many of those who featured for Vale of Leven would go on to represent the club in the Scottish Cup final the following year against Rangers.

However, football was his true sporting passion and Peter and Moses McNeil had become the first Rangers players to win representative honours when they turned out for a Glasgow select against Sheffield at Bramall Lane in February 1876, helping their adopted city to a 2–0 victory. Campbell was twice chosen to represent Scotland, scoring a double in a 9–0 demolition of the Welsh at the first Hampden Park in March 1878 and following it up in April the following year with a single strike in a 3–0 victory against the same opposition at the Racecourse in Wrexham. He was also named vice-captain of the club in its earliest years and was renowned as a forward player of some repute, earning praise from Victorian sports historian D.D. Bone as "the life and soul of the forward division."[+]

In the Scottish Football Annual of 1876–77 Campbell was described as a "very fast forward on the left, plays judiciously to his centre-forwards and is very dangerous among loose backs." Three years later, the same review book gushed: "Peter Campbell: one of Scotland's choice forwards; has good speed, splendid dribbler and dodger and is most unselfish in his passing." Sadly, the last mention of Campbell in the Scottish Football Annual of 1881–82 featured him in a list of 'Old Association Players Now Retired'. It read simply: "Peter Campbell: one of Scotland's choice forwards; has good speed, splendid dribbler and dodger and is most unselfish in passing; gone to sea."

Peter's love for football and Rangers was passed to siblings John and James, who played for the club in its earliest years before they sought a new life in other parts of the world. In February 1884, James left Glasgow for Australia to take up a post with the Union Bank of Melbourne. He lived to a ripe old age, dying in Brisbane in 1950. His unmarked grave in the city has recently been discovered by delighted Brisbane bluenoses and plans are already underway to commemorate his final resting place. His younger brother Allan had also joined him in Australia and died in the same city in 1932, aged 72.

John Campbell also emigrated, this time to the United States, and died in Middletown, New York, in 1902, aged approximately 46. Jessie Campbell lived until her late 70s before her death in 1931. The Campbell connection with Craigellan remained strong until 1939 when youngest daughter Mary, then aged 78, passed away at the family home.

Peter set off on Sunday 28 January 1883 from Penarth in South Wales on his second voyage with the St Columba, a 321-foot-long steamer of over 2,200 tons, which had been built on Merseyside in November 1880 for Liverpool company Rankin, Gilmour and Co., although the roots of the firm were Glaswegian. The St Columba was bound for Bombay with a cargo of coal, but it never got beyond the dangerous waters off the west coast of France and, with hindsight, it should never have left its berth near Cardiff Bay in the first place.

The weather that weekend was dreadful and merited mention in the press at the time, as several disabled vessels ran into Plymouth harbour for shelter. The St Columba clearly entered a maelstrom and God only knows the horrors suffered by the crew in those final moments as the waves lashed the vessel, cruelly whipping them into the sea and certain death. The report sent from Cardiff five weeks later confirmed the terrifying circumstances and stated: "The missing steamer…was under the control of Captain Dumaresq and there is no doubt she was overpowered by the terrible weather which prevailed in the Bay of Biscay at the commencement of February."₅

The passing of Peter did not go unnoticed in the Scottish game and 'Scotsman', writing in national publication 'Football: A Weekly Record of the Game', paid a particularly warm tribute. He wrote: "To most of us it is allotted that our virtues are not discovered till we cross the narrow isthmus that separates us from the great majority, but in the case of Mr Campbell, although our appreciation of his never failing amiability, his unchanging kindness, his tact as a club official and his brilliant play on the field may be intensified owing to the dire calamity, still, when in our midst he was so universally beloved that even his opponents on the field could not for a moment harbour any angry thought about him. It was he who, along with Thomas Vallance and Moses McNeil, nursed the Rangers in its days of infancy and brought it to the position which it held so honourably, and since business engagements forced these players to retire, the once famous and popular "Light Blues" have had rather an uneven career. Mr Campbell played for Scotland against Wales and for Glasgow against Sheffield, but he retired before representing his country against England. Memory is said to be short but it will be long – aye, very long, ere one of the truest and best of fellows shall be forgotten by his many friends."[6]

The warm tribute of 'Scotsman' contrasted sharply with company owner Rankin's words in a vanity publishing tome from the turn of the 20th century, A History of Our Firm, which, no doubt unwittingly, managed to read as disregarding and uncaring. His somewhat indifferent tone shone through as he discussed the company's penchants for naming its vessels after saints in the 1880s. He rattled through the alphabet, from St Alban to St Winifred, before adding: "On our adverse experience of the letter "C" we have not repeated St Columba and St Cuthbert, whose losses were both accompanied by some loss of life. My brother always favoured Saints' names taken from his favourite Sir Walter Scott."[7]

In a later chapter, however, he reflects on the company's low points. He wrote: "I draw a veil over the ghastly period wherein the ships St Mirren, St Maur and St Malcolm disappeared with all on board. It was a terrible time. At a later date the St Columba under Captain Dumaresq was never heard of. I may have been overwrought, but a vivid dream wherein I saw her sinking is often times with me still. I pray that we may never have again to pass through such a time. Captain Davey, who has revised these notes, told me Mrs Dumaresq had a similar dream, of which she informed Mrs Davey at the time. If I have written mostly of disasters it is to be said they have been relatively few. Successful voyages have largely predominated, but these are usually uneventful."

Back in East Kilbride in 2013, Stephen McCafferty nods in agreement with Rankin's words.

He said: "Like Peter, I was in the merchant navy as a young man. I spent six years at sea and quit at the age of 25, the same age as Peter when he died on the St Columba. You know, I've sailed the Bay of Biscay many, many times and must have passed over the spot where his ship went down on several occasions.

"Maybe fate determined I would find that medal as a boy and return it to Ibrox. It seems too strange a coincidence, doesn't it?"

Chapter 8
The End of the Innocence

The Glasgow Charity Cup success of 1879, on the back of a controversial loss in the Scottish Cup Final, should have ushered in a new era of success for Rangers. At the annual members' meeting in June that year, held at the Dewar's Hotel in Bridge Street, it was reckoned "the club has never been in such a flourishing condition since its formation in 1872, also now possessing the title of being the premier club in Scotland."[1] There was a comforting stability around Kinning Park as the Light Blues approached their first decade of existence. William McBeath had since left, but at the annual meeting Tom Vallance had been returned as first-team captain and Peter McNeil as honorary secretary, while fellow founders Peter Campbell and Moses McNeil sat on the committee.

There was order and consistency but, if there was a criticism to be made, little new blood to sustain the momentum built throughout the 1870s. In time, the subsequent five years would be recognised less as the start of the big push and more as the end of the innocence and a worrying decline towards financial crisis and an unpopularity that could never have been predicted in 1877 when so many thousands of Glasgow's citizens first thronged to Hamilton Crescent and Hampden to embrace their new association football favourites.

Success on the field, then as now, brought with it problems associated with their new-found popularity. Rapacious English football agents plundered the Light Blues in the aftermath of their two Scottish Cup Final appearances, not least because the game was growing at an increasing pace south of the border. Peter Campbell ultimately left for Blackburn Rovers, who had been formed in 1875, as did Hugh McIntyre, who became landlord at the Castle Inn in the town. McIntyre was an upholsterer by trade, but it was the Lancashire club who were undoubtedly feathering the nest of his future financial prosperity with the offer of a profitable pub. McIntyre, who also went on to gain notoriety as one of the earliest Mr Fixits, was widely criticised for accepting the move to the English club. Bolton added to

Kinning Park woes in 1881 when they persuaded Archie Steel, William Struthers and John Christie to join. Not surprisingly, the following season, for the first time in their short history, a Rangers side shorn of its most talented stars lost more matches than they won.

The departure of Campbell and McBeath left only the McNeil brothers and Tom Vallance as the original pioneers, but changes were afoot that, in the short term at least, would loosen the bonds between the club and the band of teenagers who had brought it into existence. Firstly, Tom Vallance accepted a position on the tea plantations at Assam and left Glasgow in February 1882. Such was the affection in which he was held that he was presented with 50 sovereigns by the club at his farewell reception at the Bridge Street Hotel and as he boarded the train for London the platform was thronged with well-wishers.

Moses McNeil had been a committee member from the beginning of the club's existence until as late as 1879, but the nature of his relationship with the team he helped to form had begun to change as Rangers entered the 1880s. He remained a regular in the side until February 1881, when he played his last game of the season in an 8–2 defeat of Partick Thistle. It would be over 13 months before he would pull on the Rangers shirt again, for a 3–2 defeat at Aston Villa on 25 March 1882. Moses played his last first-team game for Rangers a fortnight later, on 5 April, in a goalless draw with South Western. In subsequent years he would feature for the 'ancients', an old boys' XI who frequently played charity and exhibition matches around the country, but his days at the sharp end were over. It is entirely likely that Moses was sidelined or usurped by others keener to grab the club's key executive positions. Apart from a 12-month stint as honorary treasurer in 1876, he became a bit-part player in the running of the club. Few would argue against the fact that in helping to create Rangers in the first place he had made more than a sizeable contribution.

The club was also thrown into a state of flux in the early 1880s by events outwith its making. Firstly, in November 1882 club president Archie Harkness tragically died from typhoid fever at the age of just 26, leaving a widow whom he had wed less than five months previously. He had been suffering ill health for several months, but still insisted on taking training at Kinning Park on summer evenings and was acknowledged as an influential member of the club he had first joined in 1874 as a friend of the McNeils.

Secondly, the club lost one of its longest serving officials when Peter McNeil was forced to step down from the post of honorary match secretary as a

The stricken Daphne, which went down following its launch at Alexander Stephen's Linthouse shipyard on the Clyde. In total, 124 lives were lost in the tragedy, in July 1883. Picture courtesy of Mitchell Library.

result of business pressures at the end of the 1882–83 season. The sports outfitting store owned by Peter and his brother Harry had moved from its original premises to a new building at No. 91 Union Street and the switch necessitated a focus on their business enterprise at the expense of the club the McNeils had helped to form. Peter also stood down from his post as treasurer of the SFA at the same time.

At this stage Rangers were rudderless and this was reflected in the end of season stats, which showed only eight matches won and 16 lost from 29 games played. The club played the season in white and blue hoops. Their faces were almost permanently red. It came as no great surprise when they ditched the shirts at the end of that solitary campaign. In its end-of-season review the Scottish Athletic Journal was moved to warn: "One has always to be particularly cautious in forecasting the form of such a shifty, uncertain set of players as the Rangers. Today they do something extraordinary and tomorrow they exhibit such a falling off that one is perforce compelled to write them down a very ordinary lot indeed."[2]

Sarcasm dripped from the pages of the Journal like the self-confidence from the very soul of the club. A few weeks earlier, a reader had written to the newspaper asking for details of the club's defeats over the previous months. They replied mischievously: "It is impossible to give the exact number of defeats as these have been so numerous. In fact, it is only an average of once a month they get what is popularly called 'a look in' and when that happens it is generally against second rate clubs."[3]

Financially, the club was in a precarious position. By the summer of 1883 the praise of four years earlier, when the club was described as "flourishing" and lauded as the biggest and strongest in the country, rang hollow. The club were £100 in debt, despite a £30 bail out from new president George Goudie, who had replaced Harkness. Membership numbers had stalled as little attention was paid to the recruitment of those who could have brought fresh ideas and impetus to the Kinning Park set-up. Throughout the second half of the 1870s membership numbers had remained stable at between 70 and 80 per season, but there was a fine line between close knit and clique.

Admittedly, it would have troubled few on the back of two appearances in the Scottish Cup Final in the space of three years and a Charity Cup success, but it would prove problematic to those who wisely took a more long-sighted view of the club's sustainability. In 1880, for example, Queen's Park attracted 97 new members and their numbers exceeded 300. Indeed, the Hampden club were so popular that they were forced to restrict membership numbers to 350, while season-ticket holders were limited to 600. The financial crisis of 1883 brought to a head the need to widen the sphere of influence around Kinning Park and a recruitment drive proved so successful that by the start of the 1884–85 season Rangers boasted 180 members, a record number.

It had become clear that there was a void at the heart of Rangers and that the club needed a radical restructure, which duly took place at the annual general meeting in May 1883 at the Athole Arms. Tom Vallance was back from India and, although he had suffered poor health which had forced his return so quickly and his playing career had been compromised as a result, he was too valuable an ally not to be welcomed again to Kinning Park with open arms. He was quickly named president, with the club's delicate finances placed in the hands of treasurer Robert White. The post of captain was deleted from the list of office bearers and instead a 10-man committee was appointed to oversee team selection. It was a break with tradition for the Light Blues, but acknowledged at the time as a wise move and one that had proved successful for other clubs in Scotland and England.

The situation had improved markedly by the time of the six-monthly meeting in November 1883. The new treasurer had stemmed the losses and his report to members was greeted with enthusiastic applause. All debt had been paid off bar some "trifling sums"+ and it was promised that the club would soon be in credit after forthcoming matches against Queen's Park and Dumbarton at Kinning Park. Nevertheless, this period of transition had also left the club open to opportunists keen to use the good name Rangers had built over the previous decade to their own advantage. John Wallace Mackay shares his first two names with one of Rangers' best known bosses, but jungle fighter Jock would surely have given short shrift to the match secretary from the 19th century, who manoeuvred himself into such a position of dominance that it quickly threatened to destroy the very reputation the club had worked so hard to forge among its contemporaries. Single-handedly, he almost emptied the reservoir of goodwill and respect Rangers had built in their first years of existence.

Mackay first came to prominence at the club in 1882 when he was named honorary secretary and by the following summer he had stepped up to fill the role of honorary match secretary, replacing Peter McNeil. The Scottish Athletic Journal welcomed his appointment at the time, claiming him to be an amenable figurehead with whom other clubs could do business, but within two years they had performed a complete volte-face.

Not even three months had passed since his appointment as match secretary in May 1883 before Mackay was attracting scorn for his handling of the aftermath of the charity game played between Rangers and Dumbarton for the families of the victims of the Daphne Disaster, which still stands today as the greatest tragedy in Clyde shipyard history (memorials to the victims were erected in Elder and Victoria Parks in Glasgow as recently as 1996). There had seemed little amiss when a bottle was broken across the hull of the 449-ton Irish Sea ferry on the morning of 3 July 1883 and it slipped gently into the Clyde from its mooring at the Linthouse shipyard of Alexander Stephen and Co.

However, within five minutes the Daphne capsized to port and 124 men and boys, who had been working inside its hull, died in the murky waters of the river, dragged to their deaths by the weight of the equipment they were wearing and by blind panic as they gasped for breath in the pitch darkness. One woman, a Jane Drysdale from Tranent, lost her husband and son and for almost a fortnight afterwards turned up at the shipyard gate in the vain hope that they had survived. One victim left a wife with eight children, including a mentally disabled son and a daughter paralysed from the waist down. His wife was forced to sell her own clothes to survive and the children were given two bowls of porridge a day to eat. The mother rushed home after hearing the news of the ship's capsize to find her children screaming and the clock on the mantelpiece, which had been in perfect order until that point, stopped forever at the time of her husband's death. [5]

A Disaster Relief Fund was established, which provided regular but modest payments to those who needed it most. It should have been bolstered by a sum of £73 11 shillings and ninepence from the football game, played in front of a crowd of 2,500 at Kinning Park and which Rangers won 4–2. However, to the astonishment of almost everyone involved, most especially those Dumbarton officials who provided their time and team for free, Mackay took game-day expenses for Rangers. The sorry state of affairs first came to light when a letter was sent to the Lennox Herald in Dumbarton, which was re-published in the Scottish Athletic Journal. Dumbarton officials denied sending the information to the press, although they confirmed the facts were substantially correct.

The letter started: "A case of smartness combined with shabbiness on the part of a football club has just come to light which deserves publication." [6] The letter went on to explain the belief and expectation that both clubs would take care of their own expenses, as Dumbarton had demanded and which was an example, as intimated in the Glasgow press, Rangers were expected to follow. However, the Kinning Park committee deducted £10 three shillings and threepence for costs. Appalled, club officials at Dumbarton immediately forwarded half the sum, £5 one shilling and eightpence, to the Daphne Fund from its own coffers to add to the £68 eight shillings and sixpence sent by Rangers.

Angered by the bad press, Rangers immediately withdrew its advertising account from the Scottish Athletic Journal, which hit back by thundering: "The Rangers are wrong if they think our opinions are to be purchased in this way. All along we have been independent, which is the secret of our success. Perhaps there is no club that has benefited so much by our free criticism as the Rangers." [7] For his part Mackay wrote an irate letter to the Journal and – changed days indeed – effectively complained that it was all right for big clubs such as Dumbarton to show such largesse, which was beyond the means of the cash-strapped Light Blues, still mindful of their delicate financial position.

Mackay said: "From the very first I made it clear to Dumbarton that…we could not, as a matter of prudence, undertake to bear a part of the expenses involved in the arrangements for the match…While pleased to know that the Dumbarton intend sending in their share of the expense of the match I have, at the same time, to regret that they should insist by such action, generous though it be, in placing the Rangers in unfavourable contrast to them in this respect, but I am sure were the Rangers in the same enviable financial position as the Dumbarton are at present in, they would not soon be outstripped in generosity."[8]

In addition to the Daphne fund debacle, Mackay also attracted fierce criticism for the 'Cooking the Books' scandal that beset their Scottish Cup ties with Third Lanark throughout October 1884. The second-round tie finished at 2–2 but Thirds lodged a complaint over the involvement in the Rangers team of their former player Sam Thomson, who had been playing as a professional with Preston. Professionals were banned from playing for Scottish clubs and, furthermore, only registered players who had their names lodged with the SFA before the tie could play for their clubs.

Mackay rode roughshod over the rules on both accounts and was fortunate the SFA demanded only a replay of the game. The second match, played a week later in front of 5,000 at Kinning Park, finished goalless and bad feeling was such that it ended in a brawl. To compound matters still further, Rangers fielded another professional, Bolton star Archie Steel, but Thirds threw in the towel on the idea of protesting again and under the rules of the time both sides progressed into the third round.

As fate would have it, the same sides were drawn from the hat to play again in the next round and this time Rangers won comfortably 3–0 at Cathkin, with goals from Lawrie, Morton and new signing Tommy Cook. However, the latter's involvement aroused suspicion in the Thirds ranks, who suspected he belonged to another club. Closer examination of the books indicated, indeed, that a T. Cook had been registered with Rangers, but not in time to turn out in the game. Another player with the surname Cook, first initial J., was also associated with Rangers at the time and would have been eligible. A clumsy attempt had been made to cover the club's path as the 'J' was doctored to make it look like the letter 'T'. The Scottish Athletic Journal accused Mackay in all but name of sneaking into the office of SFA secretary John McDowall and making the change. As an SFA committee member, he would certainly have had access, literally, to the corridors of power.[9]

Astonishingly, Rangers dodged the bullet of cup expulsion or, worse still, expulsion from the association, but their actions were succeeding only in making the club look increasingly tawdry. In the next round of the cup they lost 4–3 at Arbroath, but they dared not lose with dignity and as soon as the game had finished Kinning Park officials appeared with a tape measure and, after running it across the pitch, declared the playing surface a yard short of regulation width. The protest went in. After a discussion, the SFA agreed to a replay and Rangers won 8–1. They eventually tumbled out of the competition at the quarter-final stage following a 5–3 defeat at Renton. The Scottish Athletic Journal jibed four days after the defeat: "So far there has been no protest from Rangers."[10]

Mackay clearly felt himself to be untouchable, but he was occasionally called to task by club members, not least when he berated Third Lanark for their role in the Cook scandal and suggested Rangers never play them again for their insolence in protesting. His call, at the half-yearly meeting of the club in November 1884, was dismissed, as most members claimed Rangers would have done exactly the same. At the same meeting he was also pulled up for claiming Queen's Park were in the financial grubber as a result of costs associated with the construction of the new Hampden Park (the second Hampden. The current national stadium, the third, was opened in 1903). The mighty amateurs had refused Rangers a game at Kinning Park the previous season, unless they were presented with half the gate and stand money. Generously, Rangers gave them the money from the terraces, which amounted to £60, while they banked the takings from the pavilion, a more modest £10. The prudent financial management of Queen's Park meant they were on course to pay off the cost of construction of their new ground within 12 months of it opening. The Scottish Athletic Journal, ever alert, admonished Mackay: "Those who live in glass houses shouldn't throw stones…Mr Mackay is not the Rangers club, nor the Rangers team."[11]

Mackay also had a nefarious influence over the players, which saw a revolt against Tom Vallance on the way to play a game at Dumbarton in October 1883. The players refused to sanction the popular president as their umpire (one in each half in those days, each chosen from the ranks of the competing teams to assist the referee) because he was too honest. Vallance resigned in disgust, only to be talked back the following week following a grovelling apology from his squad.

However, Mackay continued to referee and his lack of balance and judgement soon forced other clubs into appointing their own partisan officials, with the result that games became increasingly bad-tempered. Rangers reached their nadir, according to the Scottish Athletic Journal at least, in September 1885 following a 3–2 defeat at Queen's Park. Indiscipline on the field led to rowdy scenes off it and at one point it was feared the pitch itself would be invaded. There was more than a hint of sarcasm in the Journal's coverage as it revealed: "The rowdy element from Kinning Park hooted and yelled in the style most approved in that aristocratic suburb and the usually serene air of Hampden Park was a perfect pandemonium."[12] The scenes so sickened the editor of the Scottish Athletic Journal that he condemned the Light Blues in print and, the following week, issued a public challenge to Rangers in general, and Mackay in particular, to clean up their act.

He hit out: "My remarks last week on the match between the Rangers and Queen's Park have created no little sensation and the 'light blues' are smarting very sorely under the lash. I do not trim my remarks to suit any club or any individual and I am as indifferent to threats as I am to cajolery. I stated the Queen's Park as a club are composed of gentlemen and the Rangers as a club are not. I stated the Rangers are not now socially the same set of fellows they were when Tom Vallance and Alick Vallance commanded them, and I stated they are no longer a first class club. I stated the game was the most unpleasant ever played between two clubs of standing. All this I repeat with emphasis. I take this opportunity of laying before the public the reason why I give the Rangers on every occasion their exact desserts. The social decadence of the Rangers may be dated from the day Mr Peter McNeil resigned the match secretaryship and J.W. Mackay took it up. Then began that system of trickery which has brought the club to its present low level."[13]

Players and officials were also criticised for their boorish behaviour at club smokers, where alcohol was more than prominent. Rangers were even chided by the Journal for their lack of concern for good causes following a Charity Cup tie against Queen's Park. The Hampden club refused to turn up at a social in the Athole Arms afterwards, where food and drink had been arranged, because they felt it was an unnecessary expense and against the spirit of the tournament's fundraising ethos. Rangers agreed to differ and "turned up to a man and, aided by some friends, disposed of the viands."[14]

The war of words between Mackay and the Scottish Athletic Journal had long since grown personal and severe criticisms became a feature of the newspaper's coverage as it delved into the Rangers official's background, including his church membership. It revealed Mackay had once been a part of the Christian Institute, but resigned after being caught using "unchristian language". It added: "Coward-like, rather than face the indignant and grave seigniors, he sent in his resignation and beat an undignified retreat, thus saving himself from expulsion." Then came the twist of the mighty pen: "This, together with the fact Mackay failed to pass an examination which any fifth standard schoolboy could manage, has left him what he is – a working compositor – and ruined his aspirations forever. His conduct over the Daphne match proves charity is not in his composition." The article was delivered on the pages of the Journal on 5 January 1886. A Happy New Year indeed.

Criticism of Mackay in the pages of the Scottish Athletic Journal must be seen in the context of the loss of advertising revenue from the Kinning Park club in the aftermath of the Daphne fiasco and also the involvement of the Rangers official with a rival publication, the Scottish Umpire, which was published for the first time in August 1884. It had been set up by those, including Mackay, who were disgruntled at the occasionally scurrilous tone of the Journal, which had been on the go since September 1882. Ultimately, by 1888 the two papers had merged to form the twice weekly Scottish Sport. However, the personal nature of the criticism aside (the Journal, in reference to its new rival on the news-stands, frequently referred to Mackay and his publication as the 'Vampire'), many of Mackay's actions were still worthy of being called to account.

Mackay's hypocrisy extended to the thorny issue of professionalism. He was moved to bring up the issue surrounding the plundering of Scottish teams by English outfits at an SFA meeting in April 1884. The report read: "Mr Mackay said…when in England the other day his team was besieged by professionals and every effort was made to induce them to join English clubs – not only that, but they were followed home to Scotland by certain players who had left Glasgow some time before and who made every effort to find out the address of some of the Rangers team. These fellows went about in Lancashire with their hands in their pockets, apparently doing nothing but living on the money they received from football. Mr Mackay spoke very warmly and the committee were entirely in sympathy with him."[15]

However, little more than a week after his report on the evils of professionalism which had elicited nods of support and understanding, Rangers were welcoming an ex-pro, John Inglis, back into the fold. The move was, at the very least, against the spirit of the times in which Scottish clubs – outwardly anyway – railed fiercely against the payment of players. As the Scottish Athletic Journal wryly commented: "The Rangers are a strange lot. In a fit of virtue the other day they ejected Inglis from their club because he chose to assist the Blackburn Rovers in their Cup ties rather than play for his own club. Mr Mackay, too, delivered a virtuous speech on professionalism at the last meeting of the SFA committee. The virtuous fit did not last long and Inglis has been taken back into the fold again and played against Thistle for his old club last Saturday."[16]

Clearly, Rangers were no innocents on the issue of professionalism and, as early as October 1885, they were lobbying other Scottish clubs to follow the route of the English towards the paid ranks. With the aid of hindsight, the opposition to their plans to have professionalism even discussed appears quaintly romantic, but it was a burning issue of the football age and, typically, the Scottish Athletic Journal took no prisoners as it thundered against the Light Blues for earlier breaches of rules and etiquette. Its 'Echoes' columnist rapped: "The pseudo-opposition to the recent edict of the SFA which is being organised by the Rangers is sufficient to damn it in the eyes of the public. A member of the Rangers' committee has sent out circulars to the clubs asking them to attend an anti-amateur meeting tonight. The Queen's Park and other leading clubs will not be represented. No wonder the Rangers desire professionalism. The club has before now paid its players and one of its present office bearers has been dependent on the bounty of the club [no doubt they meant Mackay]; while Hugh McIntyre does not deny he and other members of the team received 10 shillings a week as training expenses. (Sam) Thomson of Lugar Boswell got 15 shillings a week for expenses from Lugar to Glasgow. He is now a Lancashire professional and so is McIntyre. The recent action of the Rangers in trying to induce players to join them has caused no little scandal. Tonight's meeting will fall through, like its predecessors."[17]

In fairness to Rangers and Mackay, under-the-table payments were rife in Scottish football at the time, with Hearts the first club to feel the ire of the SFA following an 11–1 victory over Dunfermline in the Scottish Cup in October 1884. The Pars protested the result, claiming the Jambos had two paid professionals in their line up, Maxwell and McNee. Maxwell was employed at the Fountainbridge Rubber Works on a salary supplemented by the club's fans, while McNee was paid 25 shillings a week from the man with whom he lodged, George Barbour, who received the cash in the first instance to pass on from a grocer friend of the club.

It was difficult not to feel a pang of sympathy for Hearts, who had lost arguably their greatest-ever player, Nick Ross, to Preston North End at the age of just 20 only 12 months earlier. Ross was already skipper of the club – a role he went on to perform with the Invincibles – and had recently married an Edinburgh girl when the English outfit came calling. It was claimed he would have stayed at Hearts for 10 shillings a week and the estimation in which he was held at Tynecastle was symbolised by the expensive clock he was gifted by the club when he married. He vowed never to leave the Edinburgh side, but when he was offered 30 shillings a week under the guise of work as a slater in Preston, he moved south, much to the chagrin of the fans.

Dunfermline's original Scottish Cup protest was upheld and they were awarded the tie. Maxwell and McNee were banned for two years and Hearts were suspended from the SFA. Nevertheless, they continued to play while under suspension and when the erring committee was disbanded and other club members took their place they were quietly welcomed back into the fold.

The formation of Celtic in November 1887 also hastened the advent of professionalism in the Scottish game as they quickly became one of the powerhouses of the sport. There was nothing serendipitous about it – Celtic raided Hibs for players with the promise of greater riches and left the Easter Road club, champions of the world only three months earlier following their 2–1 defeat of Preston at Leith, in a depressed state as the mantle of foremost Catholic club in the country was seized by the canny businessmen in control of the east end of Glasgow.

To highlight the farce of the situation, Celtic players even threatened to go on strike in 1891, two years before professionalism was introduced in Scotland, if their wages were not raised to the levels of new signings recently secured from the English League. The Parkhead players were paid a bonus of £3 and presented with a new suit for winning the Scottish Cup in 1892 and three years earlier it had been noted that Celtic donated £432 to charity at the same time as captain James Kelly, a young joiner from Renton, had bought a pub for £650. The Athletic News posed the relevant question: "Where did he get the money?"[18]

Hibs had also been under investigation for payment to their star player Willie Groves after Vale of Leven hired a private detective following a Scottish Cup tie to investigate his dubious amateur status amid allegations he was being paid up to four times his salary as a stonemason in 'broken time'. Clubs were permitted to make these 'broken time' payments to players who missed work shifts to prepare for or play in important matches, but Queen of the South Wanderers took it a stage too far when they were caught making payments to two of their players – both of whom were unemployed. In addition, clubs frequently kept two sets of books, only one of which was displayed with a flourish whenever SFA auditors came knocking and whose fictional figures had been created with all the craft of a Hans Christian Andersen fairytale. Cowlairs and St Bernard's were caught out and suspended. The Scottish Sport newspaper estimated in 1892 that one unnamed club had paid out £1,150 in salaries the previous year.

However, the commercialism of the sport was becoming less of a trickle and more of a torrent. Celtic secretary John McLaughlin, who, coincidentally, acted as pianist and accompanist at the Rangers Glee Clubs for many years in those more innocent times, famously declared: "You might as well attempt to stem the flow of Niagara with a kitchen chair as to endeavour to stem the tide of professionalism."[19]

His observation could not be disputed – Rangers announced a profit of £500 when they won the first Scottish League championship in 1890–91 and the Light Blues and Celtic were regularly turning over £5,000 a year by that time. The Glasgow Charities Cup alone helped raise £10,000 for the needy of the city from 1877–1890.

The popular newspapers of the time disliked the idea of clubs paying their players and Scottish Sport summed up press feelings best when it carried an editorial on rules for professionalism which had recently been introduced by the Scottish Football League. The Sport loftily declared: "Our first and last objection to them is that they exist. The entire rules stink of finance – money making and money grabbing."[20] Rangers were included in this mix, of course, but there was more than the financial expansion of the game causing unrest about the way the Kinning Park club was running its business. Mackay in his position as honorary match secretary had become exceedingly unpopular. His politicking had made him a major player at the club but not without winning enemies elsewhere, particularly within the pages of the Journal.

The farce of the situation, not to say the depth of control he held over others at the club, was highlighted at the annual meeting in May 1885, held at Ancell's Restaurant on Glassford Street. The income of the year was listed at £804, with an expenditure of £604. Astonishingly, approximately one sixth of the expenditure was paid to Mackay for printing costs associated with the club – bills, members' tickets and advertising. In comparison, the printing and stationery bill at Queen's Park that year was only £29. His 'Vampire' nickname was never more appropriate, as the Journal said: "Mackay proves his capacity for blood sucking by bleeding the Rangers to the extent of about £100…honestly, of course – all in the way of trade! It is a very profitable thing to be match secretary of the Rangers when it brings grist to your own mill." [21]

And Rangers fans thought their club had never seen the likes of Charles Green, Brian Stockbridge and their snought-in-the-trough cronies before.

The excesses of Mackay may have been less of a talking point had Rangers continued their success of the late 1870s into the new decade, but further trophy success proved elusive. Admittedly, the low of only eight victories in 1882–83 was not repeated, but the campaigns that followed were far from vintage. In 1883–84, for example, Rangers won 22 of 36 games played and in 1884–85 there were 24 wins from 40 matches, most of which took place at Kinning Park. Crowds of only 500 were not uncommon at home matches the following year, with modest opposition like Battlefield and Fifth Kirkudbrightshire Volunteer Rifles. As president, Tom Vallance had promised at the start of the season that the Scottish Cup and Charity Cup would be on the table by the end of the campaign. For once, he proved not to be a man of his word.

Eventually, the pressure told and by the summer of 1886 Mackay had resigned, 12 months after he had been knocked off the executive committee and on to the general committee of the club. Rangers turned to a familiar face to steady the ship as Peter McNeil returned and assumed the role of vice-president, his first period of office at the club since business pressures had forced his resignation three years earlier. The Journal noted the return of McNeil on 8 June with great warmth and claimed it was "delighted...this denotes a change. I hope the new committee will inaugurate a new policy now that they have got rid of J.W. Mackay...if the old policy is carried about, bankruptcy awaits them."[22]

However, the Journal could not resist one final dig. "By the way," it added "who is to represent the club on the Glasgow Association Committee? J.W. Mackay has been appointed treasurer without a club and, of course, the printing bill is a substantial sum as he can fix his own prices. Should the Rangers or any other club father him, they know the consequences. If he cannot get a club, he must give place to a less notorious man."

Chapter 9

William McBeath

It takes a lot to reduce grown men to tears, but as Frankie Shanks picked out the notes to Follow Follow on his penny whistle at the graveside of William McBeath, the emotional iron curtain of the Rangers fans gathered in the Lincoln cemetery was finally breached. Around 30 supporters had gathered at Canwick Road to honour the final resting place of William, the founding father whose life was touch by terrible tragedy. Now, finally and thankfully, he has a fitting resting place that acknowledges his role and contribution of the formation of Rangers.

The original Gallant Pioneers was written to inform Rangers fans of the humble beginnings of the men who formed the club and hopefully, in turn, provoke discussion and debate. Fans from the Vanguard Bears supporters group took it a step further when they read of William's burial in a pauper's grave on the fringes of Canwick Road. In October 2009 they launched a public subscription appeal to purchase a 50-year lease from Lincoln Council on his final resting place and within days fans had rallied and sufficient funds had been pledged for the burial plot and a handsome stone.

Over the last weekend of July 2010 fans made the pilgrimage south for three days of remembrance, reported in the local media, that no-one present would forget. The Lincoln Echo reported: "Haunting music and more than a few tears accompanied a ceremony dedicating a gravestone to a footballing legend. Devoted Rangers fans travelled 300 miles to a Lincoln cemetery to see the culmination of months of work to get the grave of one of the club's founding fathers properly marked."

Fan John McCrae said: "Only some of the group had met before, not everyone knew each other. We ranged in age from our twenties to our sixties. We varied in background, in hobbies, in upbringing. But from the first minute, there was a bonding, a kinship, a oneness. We all shared the same glowing pride at being there. The Friday was spent socialising, getting to know each other, and when we met up again at lunchtime the following day, we were in good spirits. Not even the threatening rain – a sharp contrast to the previous day's brilliant sunshine – bothered us. Some of the party had taken the trouble to dress for the occasion, white shirts, dark ties, suits. One of the group was posted missing, but a phone call revealed he had gone to the graveside to clean and polish the stone so that it would be in pristine condition for what was to come. The rain arrived, as it had promised. We made our way to the available cars and convoyed to the cemetery. As we neared the place where William lay - and only one or two of us knew exactly where it was - the group fell silent.

"As though the good Lord was directing the occasion, and nothing should spoil it, the rain stopped and the sun broke through. I was asked to speak and reminded all present we were standing on a site that only ten months previously had been nothing more than an overgrown, unkempt piece of land, overridden by bushes. The ground contained the remains of two souls, I added, buried together in a common grave, both of them dying penniless - William McBeath and Catherine Brumby.

"I struggled once or twice, I admit. Strangely, it was when I mentioned Catherine, of whom I knew nothing, that I lost my composure. A tear formed in my eye and my voice went. When I finished, we bowed our heads. We stood in silence, each thinking his or her own thoughts. Unscripted, Frankie took out his penny whistle and played Follow Follow slowly, as a lament. When he was done, many more than me were crying with the sheer enormity of the emotion. Flowers were laid, we chatted. I stood around, trying not to feel like some sort of idiot, having cried. Men don't cry, do they? Well, almost every one of the bears there did."

The tears were justified. William Shakespeare may have written in Hamlet that sorrow comes not as single spies, but always in battalions. However, it could equally have been written about MacBeth. Or McBeth. Or McBeath. Or McBeith, or any one of the many derivatives of the surname used throughout the life of the founding father about whom least has, until now, been chronicled. If William McBeath had proved as adept at evading tackles on the field of play as his historical footprints have been at slipping the best efforts of researchers off it he would surely have followed in the path of fellow pioneers Moses McNeil and Peter Campbell and won representative honours for Scotland.

Unfortunately, the faint tracks he did leave, which have required expert genealogical assistance to help trace back in time, lead along a sad path of poverty and the poorhouse, mental decline and the tag of 'certified imbecile', two marriages (the latter of which appears to have been bigamous) and even a criminal charge for attempted fraud. His final resting place in that pauper's grave, in a lair shared with a total stranger, lay unmarked, literally under a holly bush in scrubland at the forgotten fringes of a Lincoln cemetery for almost a century.

Until now the life of William McBeath, beyond his contribution to the formation of the football club, has remained a mystery. He is first mentioned in reference to Rangers in 1872 as a family friend of the McNeils and one of the four founding fathers of the club. However, he played his last game for Rangers in November 1875 and disappeared from club records soon after. Not even a photograph of him has ever been uncovered.

In truth, the game of football did not appear to be his forte, despite his best efforts – he was forced to take to his bed for a week after the club's first game against Callander, so exhausted was he by the effort required to participate in the developing sport. However, like Peter McNeil, he clearly enjoyed the respect of his peers for his organisational skills and W.D. McBeath was the first president of the club, listed in the roll of office bearers for the 1874–75 season.

The last recorded mention of William in connection with Rangers came in the pages of the Scottish Athletic Journal in April 1884 when he was honoured by the club at its half-yearly meeting for the role he played in its conception and subsequent birth. The paper reported: "Mr William McBeath, one of the founders of Rangers FC, was presented with a beautiful gold badge by a few of those who were intimately associated with

Members of the Vanguard Bears raised funds to place a commemorative headstone to honour William at his final resting place in Canwick Road Cemetery, Lincoln.

Main Street, Callander circa 1890. The Annetta Building on the left, now the Waverley Hotel, is the site of Peter McBeath's grocery store. The family lived above the shop.

him in the management of the club when he was one of its active members. The presentation was made by Tom Vallance, who is a sort of connecting link between the ancient and modern members, and the grateful manner in which he did so was worthy of the occasion. Mr McBeath replied briefly and after thanking those who had been good enough to honour him, said that he looked upon the days when he played for the Rangers as the brightest and jolliest of his life. Mr McBeath, I may mention, was one of the four who were at that birth of Rangers. One of the number, Peter Campbell, was drowned some time ago, the other two, Messrs Moses and Peter McNeil, live to tell that the management of the Rangers now is very different to what it was then. Mr McBeath, many of his old friends will be happy to learn, is doing well and is still cultivating those tastes for high art which made his company so pleasant to the more scholarly of his companions." ₁

William's love for art, like team-mate Tom Vallance, would see him exhibit his paintings in local shows when he moved to England around 1881. The Cornishman newspaper, in March 1881, mentioned his work at one such event and his Highland roots were recognised in his choice of 'Rob Roy's Cottage' as a subject, along with 'Cattle at Brook'. His love of art clearly continued throughout the 1880s and in December 1886 The Bristol Mercury also noted he was a contributor to a show at the local Fine Arts Academy.

Unfortunately, relating the life story of William is more akin to painting by numbers than flourishing wide brush strokes on a canvas coloured by rich memory, warm anecdote and bountiful documentation because, quite frankly, very little exists. However, a fuller picture has finally emerged from the faint sketches of yesteryear on which research for this chapter has been painstakingly drawn. Confidence about the conclusions here remains absolute, even if there is a wish for a happier tale to tell than the sad story that developed over the 61 years of his life.

William McBeath was born in Callander, Perthshire, on 7 May 1856. He was the son of Peter McBeath, a draper and general merchant born in Callander in 1803, and Jane Duncanson, 16 years his junior (his second wife) and was also born in the village that provided the team for the first Rangers game at Flesher's Haugh in the spring of 1872. Callander FC have long since been confined to the archives of Scottish football history but they were a popular enough club at the time. They grew out of an earlier Glasgow Green team known as The Thistle and were, unsurprisingly, formed by the men who came from the town from which they would take their name.

On the face of it, the McBeath family appeared to lead a comfortable enough existence at their home on Callander's Main Street. The family's general store and their home upstairs is occupied today by the Waverley Hotel. Peter was 52 when William was born, a brother for Jane, aged seven, and Peter, aged nine. Another child, a boy, was born after William, but did not survive beyond infancy. William also had another four half-brothers and sisters from his father's previous

relationships, including two from his first marriage to a Jean McFarlane, who died in 1841 at the age of 39.

Unfortunately, Peter McBeath did not live long enough to profit from the soaring popularity of his birthplace through the Victorian tourist trade as he died of heart disease in November 1864, aged

The Waverley Hotel, Callander, stands today on the site of Peter McBeath's grocery store. Pioneer William was brought up in the house above the shop.

60. His wife and two of the children, William and Jane, moved to Glasgow soon afterwards to start a new life, drawn away from their countryside roots towards the rapidly expanding industrial heartland of Scotland, a million miles away from the picture postcard image Callander was beginning to portray to the wider world.

It was in Glasgow that the teenage William would make the friendships which would earn his name a place in Scottish sporting history. By the time of the census in 1871 William was 14 and working as an assistant salesman. He lived with his sister Jane, a 21-year-old saleswoman, and mother Jane, 50, who was listed as a housekeeper and head of the family home. Their surname, in what would become a consistent scenario of administrative blunders and careless pen strokes, was listed as McBeth. Crucially, they lived at No. 17 Cleveland Street in the Sandyford area of the city – a street that still stands today (although the address no longer exists) running parallel with North Street, a stone's throw from the Mitchell Library. At the same address – that is, living in the same tenement close – were five members of the McNeil family, including eldest daughter Elizabeth, 30, the housekeeper, eldest son James, 27, a commercial traveller, brothers Henry, 21, a commercial clerk, William, 19, a seedsman, and Peter, 16, a clerk. (Moses was at this time still living at home on the Gareloch.)

This is the most compelling evidence that links William McBeath of Callander with the McNeils in the early 1870s and the formation of Rangers, although the birth of the club would have represented a period of mixed emotions for a boy who was still two months short of his 16th birthday. At the same time that he and his friends were planning their new adventure in association football, William's mother died, aged just 53, in March 1872. Her death certificate, signed by her youngest son, again confirmed the family address as No. 17 Cleveland Street and noted her passing was a result of chronic bronchitis, which she had suffered for several months and had, in turn, led to heart disease.

It was undoubtedly a crushing blow to young William to lose his second parent so early in life and, sadly, death was a spectre that was to

Je(a)nnie MacBeth ran the MacBeth Hotel, later known as the Windsor, in Weston Super Mare in the late 1890s.

shadow his existence throughout the second half of the 19th century. The most distressing tale of all the McBeaths, including even William himself, was the terribly tragic short life of sister Jane, who must have felt she was preparing for decades of happiness when she fell in love with and married shipping clerk Daniel Lang in Glasgow in June 1873.

However, by December of that year Daniel, aged just 22, had died from consumption. The effect on his new wife must have been devastating and sadly, in July 1879, when she was only 28 years old, widower Jane also passed away, killed by the scourge of tuberculosis at her home in Kirk Street in the Perthshire cathedral town of Dunblane, a few miles from the original family home in Callander. Once again, it was left to William to sign the death certificate.

In 1878 William moved across the Clyde to Kelburne Terrace in the Crosshill district of Glasgow, following his marriage to Jeannie Yates (or Yeates) Harris, 21, who had been born in the Govanhill area of the city, the daughter of a hosier, David Harris, and his wife Agnes. At the time of their wedding in Glasgow on 28 March 1878, by United Presbyterian minister Alexander Wallace, William was working as a draper's traveller and living at No. 41 Elderslie Street, a short free-kick from Cleveland Street.

The marriage certificate noted the groom's full name as William Duncanson MacBeth, which is significant for two reasons. Firstly, as far as can be established, William's middle name of Duncanson was acknowledged for the first time on official documents and his mother's maiden name was possibly adopted by a loving son following her death six years earlier. Secondly, a slip of a registrar's pen consigned the name of McBeath to the annals of history. William would never again be known, in official documents at least, by the name with which he was born.

Initially, the marriage of William and Jeannie MacBeth seemed to follow a happy and familiar pattern. Two years after their wedding Jeannie gave birth, in April 1880, to a son, also named William Duncanson MacBeth. However, within 12 months the family left Scotland and set up home in Bristol. Almost certainly the demands of William's job as a commercial traveller took the family south, although the nature of his business and the company for whom he worked are, unfortunately, unknown.

At first the family lived in the St Paul district of the city, at No. 16 Albert Park (the street still exists) and they remained there until at least 1886. The family was expanded still further in 1882 with the birth of a daughter named Agnes Isabella and another son, named Norman Douglas, in 1890. Business must have been going well for William because the family had taken an upwardly mobile step by 1889 when they moved to a more upmarket address, No. 2 Chestnut Villas in the Stapleton area of Bristol.

It is impossible not to read the entry for the MacBeths in the census of 1891 and conclude anything other than that the family, like man of the match William against Callander in 1872, were at the top of their game. Their residence at Chestnut Villas was well established and William and Jeannie were affluent enough to employ a domestic servant, 15-year-old Somerset girl Lillie Field.

However, some time after 1893 (the last known date linking them with their home in Stapleton) the family unit collapsed in such a spectacular style that it would never again be reunited. What devastating episode would eventually force them to send young Norman northwards to live with his grandmother in Glasgow? What caused the breakdown of the relationship between William and Jeannie? Agnes would eventually find refuge working as a nursery governess in Torquay, but what became of her after 1901, when she seemed to fall off the face of the earth? What became of William junior, who has also proved impossible to trace beyond his 10th birthday in the 1891 census?

It is tempting, knowing the events that were to follow in the spring of 1897, to conclude that whatever employment William enjoyed throughout the 1880s and into the early half of the 1890s was somehow compromised, perhaps by unemployment or some other economic fate. Perhaps the situation was more prosaic – a lack of health or plain bad fortune, or simply a marriage doomed to failure from the start and which no number of children conceived in hope could ever help to heal. Unfortunately, a lack of evidence leaves them as frustrating and unanswered threads that even Rumpelstiltskin himself would struggle to weave into a definitive narrative pattern.

In the spring of 1897 the headlines in the British press were dominated by world events, including the ongoing funding and engineering crises surrounding the construction of the Panama Canal. German Kaiser Wilhelm II was at loggerheads with his own budget committee in the Reichstag over the country's naval spending, while famine in India and flooding along the Mississippi in the US had left hundreds of thousands homeless and facing illness and starvation. However, it is unlikely that affairs of state or other political intrigues weighed heavily on the mind of William in March and April of that year as he trudged from one boarding house to another around the favoured holiday resorts that fringe the Severn Estuary, including Weston-super-Mare, Clevedon, Clifton and Portishead.

It was not events at the front of newspapers he would have found taxing so much as the pressure of filling the space traditionally given over at the back of the daily publications to classified and display advertisements. As career choices go, it seemed that he had hit rock bottom, accepting in February the kind of employment opportunity that would have made the position of snake oil salesman appear as credible as the post of Prime Minister.

It was not as if he was selling space on behalf of the standard-bearers of the Fourth Estate – Emmott's Seaside Advertiser hardly ranked alongside The London Times as society's great guardian of the truth, as the few copies of the newspaper that did exist were certainly not published by a character with a strong sense of Victorian morality.

On the face of it, the position was hardly the most challenging. For 10 shillings a week and a 25 per cent commission it was the duty of William, most often accompanied by his newspaper's publisher, John Burgoyne Emmott – as it transpired, a conman whose entrepreneurial zeal was clearly in inverse proportion to his sense of ethics – to persuade hoteliers and boarding house owners to advertise in the weekly journal, Emmott's Seaside Advertiser.

The career choice made sense in as much as William knew the market. Recent research has uncovered details of a 'MacBeth Hotel' in Salisbury Terrace in Weston-Super-Mare whose proprietress was Mrs JY MacBeth. The hotel faced the sea, boasted the "lowest commercial tariffs in town" and advertised in the local press between October 1896 and September 1898.

Potential clients of Emmott's Seaside Advertiser were assured the paper was widely distributed each week to 5,000 households throughout the north of England and the Midlands, from where the bulk of their holidaying guests arrived throughout the year. A standard advertisement usually cost at least five shillings for six months, but on immediate payment of cash it could be secured for half the price. On the face of it, a good deal seemed to have been secured, but nagging doubts soon surfaced among those who had paid up front – and they were confirmed when William and Emmott were arrested in Portishead under suspicion of securing money under false pretences.

The full story was recounted in May 1897 in the pages of the Bristol Times and Mirror and the Western Daily Press and exposed William as a weak, naive and impressionable character – sadly pathetic, driven (most probably as a result of recent events in his family life) to accept a job working for a convicted criminal whose ability to sweet-talk over 1,000 gullible souls out of up to £600 in the previous 18 months was as impressive as the depth of his greed and lack of scruples.

On Monday 17 May 1897 the story commanded most of page three of the Western Daily Press under the heading 'Alleged False Pretences in Somerset.' The story read: "A special sitting of the Long Ashton division magistrates was held on Saturday at Flax Bourton for the investigation of charges of obtaining money by false pretences preferred against two respectably dressed men, named John Burgoyne Emmott (45) and William Duncanson MacBeth (40). The proceedings, which were conducted before Sir Edward Fry and Major Thorne, lasted some hours.

"The original charges against the prisoners were obtaining by false pretences 2s 6d from Joseph John Dobbs at Portishead, on 29 April; 3s from Henry

Cranwell Street, Lincoln: One of the last places William McBeath called home.

Charles Barrington, at Portishead, on 30 April; and 2s 6d from Albert Thomas Cross, also of Portishead. Mr Dobbs, corn factor, of Beach Road, Portishead, said at the first hearing that on 29 April Emmott came to his house and, representing himself to be the agent for Emmott's Seaside Advertiser, asked him to advertise his lodgings in that paper. In answer to witness, Emmott said the paper was circulated in the Midlands and had proved such a success in advertising watering places they had decided to take in Portishead and Clevedon. The usual charge, added Emmott, was 5s and upwards per advertisement but as the witness's house was a small one they would advertise it for 2s 6d. Witness agreed to advertise his lodgings for six months for 2s 6d, the defendant promising to send the paper every week while the advertisement was running. Emmott produced a copy of the paper and witness paid him the 2s 6d."

The fraud was repeated with Barrington, who paid three shillings, and also with Mrs Ellen Cross, wife of Albert Thomas, who told how William had first knocked on her door and engaged in conversation on 28 April while Emmott waited at the garden gate. Persistence was clearly a strong characteristic of William's as he returned twice before finally securing 2s 6d from the Cross family on 30 April.

The court then called Arthur Baker, a Birmingham printer, who outlined further details of the fraud. Baker revealed that in 1896 his company printed Emmott's Seaside Advertiser but that he had never met Emmott before. The work was carried out on a written order received from Emmott in Bournemouth and Baker's firm, the Aston Steam Printing Works, agreed to publish the paper monthly for a year. However, Baker's company only printed the paper twice in total and half the initial print run of 1,000 copies was sent to Emmott at a London railway station, with the other 500 retained by the printers awaiting further instructions, which never came.

A lengthy correspondence passed between Emmott and his printer throughout 1896 before he finally wrote from Torquay to complain about business being bad and requesting another batch of 500 papers – his second edition – at a reduced cost of 15 shillings. Surprisingly, the printer agreed and confessed under questioning that, despite extensive experience of publishing in the Midlands, he had never heard of Emmott's Seaside Advertiser being distributed in Birmingham or its surrounding areas.

Emmott and William had clearly aroused suspicion in the local community and it came as no surprise when they were arrested by a PC Sharpe in Portishead on 1 May for alleged offences stretching back two months. Details of their arrests were reported in the 17 May edition of the Bristol Times and Mirror as William pleaded, "I am only an agent for Mr Emmott, receiving so much per week, and he owes me now over £6 in wages. I did not know [anything] but this paper was printed every week in Birmingham and circulated in Birmingham, Manchester, Derby, Liverpool, Nottingham and several other places. I can't see how I can be convicted."

William had been caught with counterfoil receipts in his pockets relating to money received from witnesses in the case. Charitably, Emmott damned William with faint praise, telling police, "I wish to say that he is innocent of the charge. He has worked for me faithfully for the last three months, though not successfully. He has handed over all monies, or accounted for them, which he has received." Emmott added: "I never intended from the first to obtain any money by false pretences."

William's desperation to avoid a longer spell in prison was clear to every reader of the Bristol Times and Mirror as they read over details of his defence. The paper reported he "read a long statement, in which he stated that he was engaged in February last at Weston-Super-Mare by Emmott…His salary was 10s a week, all railway expenses paid, and 25 per cent commission on the amount of advertisements, paid weekly. All monies he collected were handed over at the time of receiving them or the same evening. All the working of districts was directed by Emmott and he had no permission to alter the ground without his authority.

"In canvassing for advertisements he was to make it clear that Emmott's Seaside Advertiser had a wide circulation in the Midlands as a paper devoted to the advertising of boarding houses, hotels, restaurants etc and that 5,000 copies were distributed weekly in Leeds, Manchester, Derby, Liverpool, Leicester, Northampton, London and several other places and that the advertisements would appear every week for 52 weeks unless ordered for six months only.

"These things he represented to all he called on and 60 advertisements were taken in Weston-super-Mare alone, some from personal friends, including others for Clevedon, Burnham, Clifton and Portishead…He had been working for Emmott for 10 weeks only and it was utterly impossible for him to know of anything between Emmott and his printer beyond that they were on good terms. The real facts only came to light with the examination of Emmott at the Portishead police station. He declared that he had nothing to do with the paper called Emmott's Seaside Advertiser further than a paid servant to Emmott as advertising agent. His engagement was to have continued until he had worked Blackpool and district and the Isle of Man."

William's pleas of innocence fell on deaf ears and he was committed for trial with Emmott the following month. Bail was set at £50 for William and £100 for Emmott. Surely, justice was done on Friday 11 June when William was acquitted, but Emmott found guilty of dishonesty. The Western Daily Press noted in its edition of 12 June that the prosecution appeared willing to give Emmott the benefit of the doubt in his dubious publishing venture. It said: "A thousand copies

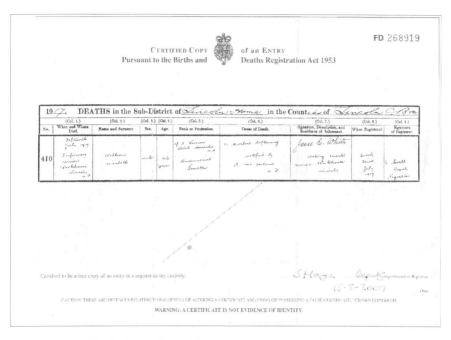

William McBeath's death certificate: There are discrepancies in his age and address, not unfamiliar at the time. Not surprisingly, his passing in 1917 went entirely unreported in the Scottish press.

[of Emmott's Seaside Advertiser] were printed and the prosecution admitted that at the time Emmott may have been acting perfectly honestly. The paper, however, started under unfavourable auspices, only 500 copies being taken by Emmott. Last October he was supplied with another 100 copies and no further trace of the publication could be found. In the following March, however, advertisements were solicited and it was upon this the prosecution relied for a conviction...Mr Garland [William's lawyer] urged that MacBeth acted bona fide and himself thoroughly believed in Emmott's representations."

The jury found Emmott guilty, and acquitted MacBeth. Emmott admitted a previous conviction at Liverpool (for felony, in October 1889). Sergeant Sharpe informed the learned judge that he had received a large number of complaints of this kind of conduct on Emmott's part. Since 1896 the prisoner had collected money from over 1,000 people, receiving between £500 and £600. His Lordship said he was glad the police had taken pains to acquire information about Emmott and he passed sentence of 21 months' imprisonment with hard labour.

Following his escape from the clutches of the courts, William clearly felt he had little alternative but to seek a new start elsewhere in England, leaving behind whatever family he still had left in Bristol. By the end of 1898 and around the time adverts for the MacBeth Hotel stopped appearing in print, he was in Bradford.

However, he clearly ran the risk of falling foul of the law once again when he married for the second time, to a Sarah Ann Lambert, with whom he was sharing an address at 28 Marshall Street in the Horton district of the Yorkshire town.

There is no doubt that the marriage solemnised at the Register Office in Bradford

Canwick Road cemetery in Lincoln: The last resting place of William McBeath.

on Boxing Day of 1898 involved William of Rangers fame – the wedding certificate noted his age as 40, his profession was given as commission agent and his father's name was listed as Peter MacBeth (deceased), whose occupation had been a 'stuff merchant'. Intriguingly, however, William listed himself as a widower when there is no documented evidence to suggest that his first wife Jeannie had even died. In fact, it seems she continued to live until 1915, at which point she passed away in Bristol from ovarian cancer.

The evidence to suggest William's second marriage was bigamous is persuasive, not least for the lack of any official confirmation of Jeannie's passing in the first place. Indeed, in the 1901 census she appeared to have adopted the more anglicised Christian name of Jennie and was living in a boarding house in the town of Rochford in Essex. This Jennie MacBeth also listed a middle initial of 'Y' (as in Yeates or Yates, Jeannie's unusual middle name). To add to the weight of evidence, her birthplace was confirmed as Glasgow, just like William's first bride. She listed herself as a widow who was 'living on her own means' and this marital status is likely to have been a front to maintain respectability.

It is no surprise she was not listed as living with any of her three children – William disappears completely from the records after 1890, while, in 1901, Agnes would have been 19 and was working as a nursery governess in Torquay. Norman, then aged 11, had been sent north to live with his grandmother, also Agnes, and

A Sorry End: William McBeath lies under this holly bush, sharing a lair with a total stranger, in a pauper's plot that was, unsurprisingly, never marked.

aunts Jessie and Mary in their home at No. 26 Stanmore Road, Cathcart, further underlining the strife the marriage break up had caused to the family unit. (As an aside, it appears that Norman lived the majority of his life in Scotland until his death in 1973, aged 83. A customs official, he never married and died of prostate cancer at his home in the west end of Glasgow, a stone's throw from the former Rangers ground at Burnbank).

Following the trail of Jennie to her sad death in 1915 also adds strongly to the belief she was William's estranged wife. Significantly, Jennie had returned to Bristol from Essex in the early years of the 20th century and died on 23 January 1915 at No. 18 Canton Street in the St Paul district of the city, only a few streets from the home at Albert Park where William and Jeannie had first moved in around 1880. The death certificate for Jennie MacBeth lists her age as 51 (again, like the 1901 census, seven years out) and her husband's occupation was listed as commercial traveller, although his name was given as James, not William. The records for Scotland, England and Wales show that no such marriage between a James MacBeth and anyone named Jeannie or Jennie took place in the 40 years before 1915. On the basis of extensive research efforts, it is highly unlikely to have been anyone other than William's first wife from their marriage in Glasgow in 1878.

If William was hoping for greater happiness from his second marriage, however questionable its legitimacy, he would not find it, as his life deteriorated towards a sad conclusion in 1917 when he died in the workhouse at Lincoln; penniless, forgotten and most likely the victim of dementia that led him to be officially cast as a 'certified imbecile'. Soon after his second marriage to Sarah Ann in Bradford they moved to Lincoln, nearer his new wife's birthplace of Welton-Le-Marsh, a few miles from Skegness. Born in 1859, she grew up in the Lincolnshire village with her five siblings and half siblings. Sarah Ann's life, like her husband's, was also fated to be spent in poverty, with several spells in and out of the workhouse at Bradford and Lincoln.

On the surface, all appeared well in their lives and by the time of the 1901 census they appeared to be happily settled at No. 34 Vernon Street in Lincoln, a row of modest terraced houses which had been built in the late 19th century and that could nowadays double as the set for Coronation Street, even down to the pub on the corner. Incidentally, there is no disputing the identities of the couple at No. 34 Vernon Street. Sarah Ann's birthplace is listed as Welton-Le-Marsh in the 1901 census, while her husband's is given as Callander, Perthshire.

The Lincoln Post Office Directory of the time, published every second year, listed William's occupation as insurance agent and by 1903 the couple had moved along Vernon Street to No. 5, where they lived until at least 1907. By 1909 their address was published as No. 57 Cranwell Street, four streets parallel to Vernon Street and only a mile from Lincoln town centre. From 1907 William's occupation was listed simply as 'agent', but after 1910 the name of MacBeth disappeared from the index of addresses for good.

Unfortunately, as he approached his 55th birthday, William was heading down to the lowest rung of society, where the only succour for the needy and infirm was provided by the workhouse. Lincoln had had a workhouse, also often referred to as a poorhouse, since around 1740, with accommodation for up to 350 people in an 'H' shaped building, made up of two dormitory wings and a central dining area in between. A resident could give three hours notice and leave at any time, but it was not a realistic option for all. A parliamentary report of 1861 found one in five residents had been in the workhouse for five years or more, mostly the elderly, chronically sick and mentally ill.

Undoubtedly, William (and also Sarah Ann) fell into this category, because as economic conditions improved in the latter part of the 19th century fewer and fewer able-bodied people were entering workhouses. Indeed, by 1900 many were voluntarily entering the workhouse, particularly the elderly and physically and mentally infirm, because the standards of care and living were better than those on offer outside. Life in the workhouse may have been repetitive, but at least it was healthier than the poorest living quarters outside its walls and from 1870 onwards there was a relaxation of the rules that allowed books, newspapers and snuff for the elderly.

It was against this backdrop that William was admitted in January 1910 and it is not only his age, listed as approximately 15 years out at 39, that raises an eyebrow. The Creed Register for Lincoln Workhouse, held at the Lincoln Archives, notes the 'name of informant' on William's entry records as simply 'prison warder'. Unfortunately, very few records for Lincoln Prison, first opened in 1872, survive from the turn of the 20th century and those that do are still closed under the 100-year rule. Workhouse historian Peter Higginbotham[2] called on his experience to back the suspicion that William may have spent a short spell in gaol at around this time, most probably for a petty offence. He was quite possibly referred on his release to the workhouse, which was situated only a couple of hundred yards from the Lincoln Assize Court.

The Creed Register discloses that William was discharged from Lincoln Workhouse on 3 June 1911, 18 months after he first entered, but he was back behind its gates within seven days. This time, on 10 June 1911, the records reveal he was "brought in by police". It is difficult to escape the conclusion, particularly on the back of evidence from later workhouse records, that law officers were fulfilling a social work function by directing William to a more suitable environment. Frustratingly, although the Creed Register and board minutes of the Lincoln

Workhouse are available, many of the more in-depth records, including medical reports, remain secured under the 100-year rule, so a clearer picture may not emerge for some years to come.

William's personal decline appears marked and it is clear he could not look to his equally troubled second wife for support. She had admitted herself into Lincoln Workhouse on 6 December 1910 and was discharged six months later on 12 May 1911 (a month before William, which may have prompted her husband to return to the outside world). The relationship was clearly not loveless and at least once in August 1912 Sarah Ann made an attempt to secure her husband's release.

The Lincoln Workhouse minutes from 6 August noted: "Mrs MacBeth appeared before the board and asked for her husband, who is a certified imbecile, to be discharged from the workhouse into her care and the question was deferred for a report by Dr McFarland upon MacBeth's state of mind." A fortnight later, on 20 August, the minutes noted a second request, adding: "Mrs MacBeth...asked for her husband to be discharged from the Imbecile Ward into her care and it was agreed to allow Mrs MacBeth to take her husband if the Medical Officer would certify him as fit to be discharged from the Imbecile Ward."

The Mental Deficiency Act of 1913 officially defined four grades of mental defect, listing an imbecile as someone "incapable of managing themselves or their affairs." The 1913 Act specifically stated the condition had to exist "from birth or from an early age." Clearly, that did not apply to William, but there was no one in his life when he was first admitted to Lincoln Workhouse in 1910 to clarify a medical history from childhood that would enable doctors to make a rigorous medical assessment in terms that would dovetail with the official criteria three years later.

In fact, the term 'imbecile' originally came from French via Latin, where it was defined similarly to the condition we now recognise as Alzheimer's, a dementia in which sufferers mentally regress towards childhood. Certainly, the minutes of the Lincoln Workhouse indicate the inhabitants of the imbecile ward could not have been treated less like Oliver Twist. The notes of 15 May 1915 sympathetically recorded: "The clerk was directed to invite tenders for taking the imbeciles for drives during the summer months, as in previous years." Residents were occasionally taken on trips to Cleethorpes and there were also concerts held in the dining hall.

There is no doubt that the William in the Lincoln poorhouse was the same boy from Callander, despite the 15-year difference in the age recorded by the official workhouse documents. As we know, Sarah Ann MacBeth also spent six months in the same establishment in the first half of 1911, before pleading for his release the following year. Her appeals to have William given over to her care fell on deaf ears and it was clearly not just a result of authority's concerns about his declining mental health.

By 1911, the MacBeths had given up their home at No. 57 Cranwell Street and Sarah Ann gravitated back to Bradford soon after, confirmed by the Lincoln Workhouse minutes from 30 March 1915. They revealed: "A letter was read from the Bradford Union (workhouse) alleging the settlement of Sarah Ann MacBeth, aged 56, to be in this union. The clerk reported that her husband had been an inmate of this workhouse for several years and the settlement was accepted."

In effect, Bradford turned Sarah Ann over to the workhouse where she had previously spent some time, claiming Lincoln was responsible for her care because her husband was a long-term resident there, which was acknowledged. Bradford Archives have confirmed the workhouse records of the town from the first decades of the 20th century. Sarah Ann admitted herself to Bradford Workhouse on 3 March 1915. Her address, before admission, was given as No. 149 Manningham Lane, Bradford. Her nearest relative lived at the same address and was named Adelaide Townsend – Sarah Ann's half sister, four years her senior, confirmed by census records dating back to 1861 from their birthplace in Welton-Le-Marsh. Adelaide's husband, Adolphe Townsend, also acted as a witness for the wedding of William and Sarah Ann in 1898.

Unfortunately, the creed register does not recall how long Sarah Ann spent under the same roof as her husband, but it would not have been much beyond two years, as William died in the infirmary at the Lincoln Workhouse on Sunday 15 July 1917. The official cause of death was "cerebral softening", which indicates a stroke or brain haemorrhage, probably relating to his mental state. His death certificate recorded his age at 46 (it should have been 61), his previous address as No. 2 Vernon Street (he lived at Nos 5 and 34) and his occupation as commercial traveller. The informant of his death on the certificate was Jesse E. White, the acting master of the Union Workhouse, Lincoln. The fate of Sarah Ann is unknown.

The Lincoln Workhouse has long gone. The workhouse system was abolished in 1930 and although the Burton Road site was used as an old folks' home for over three decades it was demolished in 1965. However, little has changed in the physical appearance of Vernon Street and Cranwell Street beyond the ubiquitous modern-day sight of cars parked bumper to bumper down the length of each road.

Vernon Street sits around the corner from Frank's Italian barber shop and across the road from Cartridge World and Blockbuster, with the Miller's Arms, not the Rovers Return, sitting on the corner. Further down the street a converted mill development and gaily painted soffits and window frames suggest the street is winning its battle for 21st-century gentrification. However, further along, overgrown gardens and an exterior festive decoration of Santa Claus clambering for the chimney, even though it is the middle of May, suggest it might still have some way to go.

Unfortunately, the net curtains drawn tightly across the bay windows at Nos 5 and 34 do not twitch with the ghosts of Christmas past. A two-minute walk allows the footsteps of William over a century earlier to be followed, although it is doubtful he made his way past three Indian restaurants, a Brazilian foodstore and the Mamma Mia pizzeria on his way to Cranwell Street in 1909. It is slightly more residential than Vernon Street and the red brick of its terraced homes would not look out of place in G51 itself.

Unsurprisingly, William was buried without ceremony on 19 July 1917, four days after his death. The rights to plot A2582 where he lies were never privately purchased, which means they were owned by the council and he was given a pauper's burial. He rests on top of a total stranger, a Catherine Brumby, buried two decades before his death.

The man who helped give birth to a club that spawned Meiklejohn, Morton and McPhail, Woodburn, Waddell and Young, Baxter, Greig and McCoist, lay until recently in that pitiful, indistinct plot, under a holly bush in the forgotten fringes of the burial ground, unmarked and unrecognised behind a neatly tended resting place to a William Edward Kirkby, who died in September 1694, aged 26.

The skilled assistance of cemetery staff and their dog-eared burial chart over a century old are required to even find the site where William is buried – and it is no treasure hunt.

Picking the way back on the path, fine views are afforded up to Lincoln Cathedral, which dominates the horizon for miles around in this flat corner of England. Here is hoping God is looking over William better in death than he ever did in life. Rangers fans will continue to play their part in ensuring he is never again forgotten.

Chapter 10

The FA Cup – From First to Last

The FA Cup has attracted many sponsors in recent years, but the commercial worth of the tournament remained unexploited throughout the latter half of the 19th century. If English football bosses sought financial inspiration from the raucous exploits of the Rangers squad in the only season in which they participated, back in 1886–87, they could surely have attracted a bidding war for competition rights between Alka Seltzer and Andrew's Liver Salts. These were more innocent times (thankfully for Rangers, that also included the media) as they kicked off their campaign at Everton amid accusations of over-drinking and ended it at the semi-final stages against Aston Villa at Crewe surrounded by allegations of over-eating.

The Football Association Challenge Cup has enjoyed a long and distinguished history from its first season in 1871–72, when 15 clubs set out to win a competition that quickly developed into the most democratic in world football, where village green teams can still kick-start a campaign in August and dream of playing at Wembley against Manchester United the following May. Queen's Park were among the first competitors, alongside others whose names reflected the public school roots of the tournament, not to mention its southern bias – the Spiders and Donington Grammar School were the only sides who came from north of Hertfordshire that first season. The first FA Cup trophy cost £20 and Queen's Park contributed a guinea to its purchase, a staggering sum for a club whose annual turnover at the time was no more than £6.

Wanderers Football Club, based near Epping Forest, won the first tournament against the Royal Engineers 1–0 at The Oval, but only after Queen's Park scratched their semi-final replay. In a portent for the zeal with which football would soon be greeted in Glasgow, the inhabitants of the city raised a public subscription to cover the cost of sending the Spiders to London to face the Wanderers, but they could not afford to stay in the capital for a second match and returned home unbowed and unbeaten. In addition to their failure to see through to the end their first FA Cup campaign, there would be other losers as a result of their participation in the competition – keen students of association football in the Borders. Queen's Park were forced to abandon a week-long tour of the Tweed, where they had promised to undertake their fine missionary work in the towns and villages, in order to play in the Cup competition. They never did make their visit and association football lost out to the oval ball game in the affections of a public in an area where the culture of rugby remains strongest to this day.

In the beginning of the game, all British clubs were eligible for membership of the Football Association, their calling card for the FA Cup, so it was no surprise to see sides such as Queen's Park from Scotland and the Druids and Chirk from Wales lining up against sides from the counties and shires of England. However, for the most part Scottish club sides resisted the temptation to turn out in the first decade or so of the competition, particularly as cost was such a significant factor. Indeed, throughout the 1870s Queen's Park regularly received byes to the latter stages of the competition in a bid to keep their expenses low, but either scratched or withdrew as the financial realities restricted their ability to travel.

The FA, responding to the increased popularity of the tournament, particularly in the north of England, began to organise ties on a geographical basis as the 1870s gave way to the 1880s and suddenly Queen's Park returned to the fore to an English audience. In 1884 and 1885 they reached the Final, only to lose narrowly on each occasion to Blackburn Rovers. Until that point, Queen's Park were the only Scottish team to have made significant strides in the FA Cup but, perhaps buoyed by the success of the Spiders, by the third round of the 1886–87 competition there were four Scottish teams who had won through from an original entry of 126 clubs – Partick Thistle, Renton, Cowlairs and Rangers.

In actual fact, the Rangers name had been represented in the FA Cup as early as 1880, when they advanced to the third round before being humbled 6–0 at The Oval by the 1875 tournament winners, the Royal Engineers, but the information is misleading. The Rangers team who competed in 1880 and 1881 were an English outfit who included in their ranks an F.J. Wall, who would later become secretary of the Football Association. He seemed none too disheartened to be on the end of such a heavy defeat, particularly against such illustrious opponents as the Royal Engineers, and later admitted fortifying himself for the game "with a splendid rump steak for lunch."[1]

It was not – at that stage anyway – the state of the pre-match meal that concerned the Rangers as they prepared for their first game in the competition against Everton on Saturday 30 October 1886, but the demon drink. Excitement must have been high among Rangers' players during the 1886–87 season at the prospect of playing in the FA Cup as they boarded the train at Glasgow, bound for a game in a competition in which they had only once before come close to competing.

Rangers had decided to take up membership of the Football Association at a committee meeting in June 1885 and Walter Crichton, who would soon be named honorary secretary of the club, was listed as its delegate to the FA. Subsequently, Rangers were drawn to face Rawtenstall in the first round of the Cup, but Rangers refused the match on the basis that the Lancashire club had paid professionals among their ranks of registered players.

Professionalism had finally been legalised within the English game at a meeting of clubs in July 1885, but with strict conditions for participation in the FA Cup, including birth and residence criteria, with all players also subject to annual registration demands. Of course, at this stage the payment of players was still a strict taboo – publicly at least – in Scotland and the SFA frowned upon games played against English teams who knowingly employed professionals. The FA fined Rangers 10 shillings 'for infringement of rules', although stopped short of telling the Kinning Park committee which rule had been broken. Rawtenstall were subsequently banned from the competition after playing out a 3–3 draw against near neighbours Bolton in the next round, apparently for breaches of the strict FA conditions in their Cup competition relating to the employment of professionals.

Tensions had eased slightly 12 months later as Rangers arrived in Liverpool in high spirits for a game against the underdogs of Everton. The previous campaign had been a miserable one for the Kinning Park regulars, with an early exit from the Scottish Cup at the hands of Clyde following a 1–0 defeat

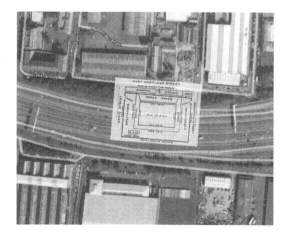

The Rangers Way . . . Kinning Park stood on the site of today's M8 motorway, a historical reference to raise a smile on the slow traffic snarl to the city centre after games at Ibrox.

and an indifferent series of results against often mediocre opposition. Tom Vallance, who had just been returned for his third year as president, had promised three trophies at the start of the season – the Scottish Cup, the FA Cup and the Charity Cup.

However, the club's hopes of winning silverware proved as elusive as their bid to turn a profit – Rangers lost £90 that season, mostly as a result of their early Scottish Cup exit, although the Kinning Park bank book still held funds of almost £130. Still, the Scottish Athletic Journal could not contain its glee as it threatened to present Vallance with three teacups to parade to members at the club's next annual general meeting.

The start of season 1886–87 promised better to come, despite the spectre of relocation from Kinning Park hanging over the club as its lease on its third ground neared its end, but the squad would not be fortified with the Assam blends so familiar to Vallance following his time in India. There was certainly mischief in mind when Rangers travelled to Liverpool the evening before the game against Everton, who had been knocked out of the FA Cup the previous season 3–0 by Partick Thistle.

The Kinning Park squad arrived in Liverpool the worse for wear for a game in which they were overwhelming favourites. These days, the former Compton Hotel in the city's Church Street houses a branch of Marks and Spencer, but it was bed and not bargains on the mind of the bedraggled Rangers squad as they trooped in there on the morning of the game after being thrown out of their original digs. The columnist 'Lancashire Chat' noted matter-of-factly in the Scottish Umpire of 2 November 1886: "The Rangers arrived (in Liverpool) soon after midnight and roused the ire of the hotel proprietor in their night revels. In fact, the Rangers squad were bundled out bag and baggage without breakfast and took up their quarters at the Compton Hotel…They dressed at the hotel and the game was started pretty punctually."[2]

In the 21st century the media would enjoy a field day with the story, but in those more innocent times observers of the fledgling football scene were less inclined to saddle up on moral high horses at a lack of professionalism among players who were entirely amateur, or purported to be so.

Historically, the Victorian era has been regarded as one of austerity and respect for place and position, but in truth, anti-social behaviour was never far from the fore in the Scottish game, which is hardly surprising when by 1890 it was estimated that one third of the total national revenue in Britain came from alcohol.[3]

In 1872, the year of Rangers' formation, 54,446 people in Glasgow were apprehended by police for being drunk, incapable and disorderly.[4] Social commentator Sir John Hammerton painted a vivid and horrifying picture of a drink-soaked society which, sadly, does not appear to have improved much in the century since his publication of Books and Myself. He wrote: "In 1889 Glasgow was probably the most drink-sodden city in Great Britain. The Trongate and Argyle Street, and worst of all the High Street, were scenes of disgusting debauchery, almost incredible today. Many of the younger generation thought it manly to get 'paralytic' and 'dead to the world'; at least on Saturday there was lots of tipsy rowdyism in the genteel promenade in Sauchiehall Street, but nothing to compare to the degrading spectacle of the other thoroughfares, where there were drunken brawls at every corner and a high proportion of the passers-by were reeling drunk; at the corners of the darker side streets the reek of vomit befouled the evening air, never very salubrious. Jollity was everywhere absent: sheer loathsome, swinish inebriation prevailed."[5]

Football then, as now, mirrored society and Rangers players occasionally let themselves down. In March 1883, a columnist in the Scottish Athletic Journal commented: "High jinks in hotels by football teams are becoming such a nuisance that something must be done to put an end to the gross misconduct which goes on. I was witness to a ruffianly trick in the Athole Arms on Saturday night. A fellow – I will call him nothing less – as a waiter passed with a tray full of valuable crystal deliberately kicked the bottom of the tray and broke a dozen of the wine glasses to atoms. In the crowd he escaped notice, but the Rangers will, of course, have to pay for the damage. I cannot see any fun in a low act of this kind."[6]

Of course, Rangers were not alone in drawing criticism for their alcohol-related antics on and off the field. Dumbarton won the Scottish Cup after a replay in 1883, for instance, but only after it had been hinted by football columnist 'Rover' in the Lennox Herald that one or two of their players had partaken of whisky before the first match, which finished 2–2. After the second game, a 2–1 win over arch rivals Vale of Leven, a group of Dumbarton players headed for a few days' celebration at Loch Lomond with assorted wives, partners and pals. Returning home on two wagonettes on the Monday and "boldened by excessive refreshments" they took no time to remind locals of the weekend scoreline as they lurched through Vale of Leven. Predictably, a rammy ensued, during which two buckets of slaughterhouse blood were thrown over the Dumbarton group.

Public houses were regularly used as changing rooms for teams,

West Scotland Street, Kinning Park, circa 1905. The Kinning Park ground was at the very bottom of the street, behind the tenement to the left of the lamp post. Residents feared the site was haunted in the lead-up to the 1877 Scottish Cup final. In fact, the howls and yells came from the Rangers 'moonlighters', practising all hours in preparation for the challenge of Vale of Leven. The baths were pulled down in the 1970s to make way for the M8 motorway.

particularly in Ayrshire, and while the Highlands are synonymous with hospitality, it was another matter in Angus as Forfar treated their players to a half bottle of whisky and a bottle of port after every game, while visitors were restricted to a pie and a pint in 1890. One club, the Pilgrims, vowed never to visit Dundee again after the Strathmore club tried to entertain them after a game on the derisory sum of only five shillings and sixpence. Reporting on the Pilgrims' point of view, the Scottish Athletic Journal lamented: "Can one blame them?"[7] Not even Queen's Park, the grand standard-bearers of the time, could escape the negative influence of alcohol when two players were fined 20 shillings each by Nottingham magistrates for being drunk and disorderly after a match in the town in January 1878.

For the non-professional Scots, trips to England generally took place at holiday times, with New Year and Easter particular favourites. Football often came a poor second to the festivities and the attitude of the press was as schizophrenic as the nation's relationship with alcohol itself. Therefore, the Scottish Athletic Journal reasoned early in 1885 that "a New Year holiday trip does not come every day and youthful blood must have its fling…the honour and glory of Scottish football is cast to the winds and the present is only remembered."[8]

This was a complete reversal from its stern editorial two years previously when it noted: "Generally, when any of our association teams go to England they run riot with everything and everybody they come across. They stick at nothing, not even dressing themselves in policeman's clothes and running pantomime-like through the streets with roasts of beef not of their own. This was what the frolics of one of our leading teams consisted of when in Manchester last Christmas."[9] By sheer coincidence, Rangers were in Lancashire at that time for a game against local club Darwen.

In these days of Premiership millions it is perhaps surprising to learn that Rangers were strong favourites in the first round against Everton, even though the home side had recently won the Liverpool Cup and had been undefeated all season. In a burst of patriotism, the Scottish Umpire declared in its preview to the game: "Dobson, Farmer and Gibson are not eligible [for Everton]. And without them they have not much chance of winning…without the three named, Everton cannot possibly defeat a decent team of the Rangers."[10] The match was played at Anfield and the Scottish Umpire remarked that the ground was not a very good one, particularly as it was situated a couple of miles from the nearest railway station. However, football in Liverpool at that stage was, according to the newspaper, "leaping and bounding".

Rangers were handed the tie before kick-off – unsurprisingly, delayed 15 minutes to give the players time to arrive at the ground after shaking off their excesses – when Everton 'scratched' the tie to give their three ineligible players the chance to play and make the encounter more competitive. The game almost did not start as a result of a morning deluge that had turned the playing surface into a mudbath, but the skies cleared to blue by lunchtime and soon the crowds were rolling up in their thousands. The match report from the Liverpool Courier gives an idea of how established Rangers had become in the 14 years since the club's pioneers had first taken to the game at Flesher's Haugh.

The Courier reported: "The visit of the Glasgow team to the popular Anfield enclosure on Saturday excited such a large amount of interest that there could not have been less than 6,000 persons present to witness the play. Not only were the capacious stands well filled but every available point of vantage was early taken possession of, so long before the game commenced the enclosure presented an animated scene. The game was undoubtedly one of the best that has been witnessed on the Anfield ground during the present season. It was fully a quarter of an hour after the advertised time before the teams put in an appearance. When they did so the Rangers, by their fine physique, gained many friends, but this could not diminish confidence in the ability of the Evertonians to uphold the credit of the district."[11]

Rangers won the game courtesy of a one-yard tap-in from striker Charlie Heggie after 20 minutes. Everton fought valiantly to get back into the game, but Rangers held out and even had a second goal disallowed late on. 'Lancashire Chat' later recalled in the Scottish Umpire: "Tuck McIntyre was in a happy mood and seemed to enjoy himself, whether knocking an opponent over or kicking the ball. [Afterwards] the Rangers drove off to the Compton and [then] returned to the Everton headquarters, where a pleasant evening was spent. The Glasgow men were accompanied by about half a dozen of their supporters and Hugh McIntyre came down to see his old comrades perform. Tom Vallance made a pretty speech, the remarks of the handsome international being received with great cheering. The smoking concerts have evidently improved the vocal attainments of the team and [John] Muir made a very successful debut at Everton. The Liverpool club's vice-president turned out in full force to welcome the Rangers, who left well pleased with their outing."[12]

The club's subsequent early round cup ties, all played at Kinning Park, were to prove less eventful than the trip to Liverpool. Three weeks after the defeat of Everton another English outfit, Church, were put to the sword in a 2–1 victory, with two goals from Matt Lawrie, a dribbling winger who had been signed from Cessnockbank in the summer of 1884. Lawrie found the net again on 4 December when Springburn side Cowlairs were knocked out 3–2 at Kinning Park, with Bob Fraser and Matt Peacock also scoring for the Light Blues. Rangers were guaranteed to be playing FA Cup football into 1887 when they received a bye in the fourth round and were drawn, again at home, to Lincoln on 29 January.

On the face of it, the 3–0 victory over the English side that set the Light Blues up for a quarter-final crack at Old Westminsters seemed academic. A swirling wind made playing conditions difficult at Kinning Park, but Rangers scored twice in the first half courtesy of strikes from Fraser and new boy Joe Lindsay, a Scotland forward who had previously played at Dumbarton but who had been tempted to Kinning Park during the festive period of 1886 as it was closer to his workplace in Govan. The third goal from Peacock sealed a comfortable win and Donald Gow so impressed Lincoln with his performance in defence that he was immediately offered a weekly wage of £2 10 shillings, a king's ransom at the time, to move south.

Gow refused the offer, but the English press were far from happy at the presence of Lindsay in the side and chided the amateur Rangers for alleged professionalism, which was still a strict no-no in the Scottish game under the terms of the SFA, even in the FA Cup. The Midland Athlete newspaper bemoaned the fact that Lincoln City had to meet "a team called Glasgow Rangers, but an eleven that would never be allowed to compete for the Scottish Cup under that name…the Rangers have called in extraneous aid for their national Cup ties."[13]

An editorial in the Scottish Umpire hit back in a fit of nationalist pique: "The Light Blues played on the occasion referred to a team that could, if strong enough, have done duty in the Scottish ties without let or hindrance. Be sure of your fact, friend Athlete, before you launch out. It is awkward to be caught on the hop."[14]

Nevertheless, the Midland Athlete had shone the spotlight on an issue that was becoming an increasing concern in the Scottish game, which would not embrace professionalism until the AGM of the SFA in 1893, eight years after England. Of course, payment of players had been around even before then, with Glasgow shipyard worker James Lang acknowledged as the first professional player in the history of the game when he left Clydesdale and accepted a financial offer to turn out for Sheffield Wednesday in 1876. Lang literally had one eye on a money-making opportunity – he lost the other in a shipyard accident but somehow managed to keep his handicap hidden from his new employers.

In his latter years, Lang was a regular in the main stand at Ibrox and delighted matchday regulars with details of his ground-breaking claim to fame. The bountiful orchards of Scotland yielded a harvest of impressive players ripe for export over the border and, although many were from the industrial heartlands of the central belt and hungry to advance up the economic ladder, there were still those who were attracted to the game as a leisure pursuit and could afford to adopt a more laid-back attitude to otherwise tempting inducements. Pollokshields Athletic forward Frank Shaw, for example, delayed replying to an offer in 1884 of a handsome salary of £120 a year from English club Accrington after he had come to their attention at an earlier game. He wrote in reply that he could not give the matter his full attention until "my return from a fortnight's cruise among the Western Isles, on my yacht."[15]

English clubs quickly began to burst at the seams with the 'Scots professors', skilled players from north of the border who played and educated their new paymasters with all the zeal of tartan missionaries. The last time England had seen such an invasion of Scots was in the previous century when the Jacobite forces of Charles Edward Stuart marched as far south as Derby. This time, however, the Scots did not turn back, but stayed on and conquered, spreading their influence further across the country.

The Liverpool team established by former Everton landlord Houlding, for example, kicked-off its first League campaign in 1893 with 10 Scots in its line up. The first goal scored in English League football was by a Scot, Jack Gordon, who would never have felt homesick at Preston North End. The greatest-ever Preston team, known as the Invincibles, won the first English League title (the brainchild of Perthshire draper William McGregor, the grand patriarch of Aston Villa) in 1888–89 without losing a match, retained the Championship the following season and also won the FA Cup in 1889 without conceding a goal. The spine of their great team was Scottish, including brothers Nick and Jimmy Ross and internationals David Russell, John Gordon and George Drummond, while former Ranger Sam Thomson also played for the club. Scots also dominated in Sunderland's 'Team of all Talents', who won the English title in 1892, 1893 and 1895 and were even founded by a Scot, teacher James Allan, in 1880.

Undoubtedly, Rangers suffered at the hands – and wallets – of the English clubs, who set up raiding parties that would have been the envy of any 16th-century border reiver. First to go in 1880 was Scottish international Hugh McIntyre, older brother of Tuck and a member of the Cup Final team of 1879, who quit for Blackburn Rovers after they bought him a pub in the town. He went on to win three FA Cup-winners' medals in successive seasons with his new side in 1884, 1885 and 1886. He was followed to the Lancashire club by founding father Peter Campbell and, although he played several times for Blackburn, he never moved to the area. Rangers lost another stalwart of the 1879 team, William Struthers, who signed for Bolton Wanderers in 1881, quickly followed to the same club by half-back John Christie, no doubt lured by the promise of riches extolled by his former team-mate.

The finger lingered around the influence of Hugh McIntyre, in particular, in convincing young Scots to ply their trade in the south because then, as now, there were lucrative finders' fees up for grabs. Agents were despised and routinely beaten up and one G.L. Harrison from Nottingham had cause to wish he had never wandered down the Copland Road on 1 August 1889, when he arrived in Glasgow in a bid to lure defender John Hendry, an early darling of the Light Blues legions, south of the border.

Harrison's plan was cunning, as he roped in then Scotland striker Jimmy Oswald (who later went on to play for Rangers) to accompany him to Ibrox on the promise of a £5 commission if they persuaded Hendry south. They had already trawled the player's home town of Uddingston in a vain bid to track him down, but the fear of losing their top talents was so strong among many of the leading Scots clubs, including Rangers, that they regularly formed vigilance committees to keep their non-professionals (in theory at least) away from the paid ranks of the English game.

Word quickly spread around Ibrox, which was hosting an amateur sports that Thursday evening, of the danger in their midst. Panic ensued and Hendry was quickly shepherded away from the dangerous suitors while Oswald, who played for Notts County, was led to safety, surviving the baying mob only because of his standing in the game and the presence of a team from the Rangers committee around him. Harrison was not so lucky as he attempted to sneak from the ground and down Copland Road, only to be accosted by two irate Bears. The full story then unfolded in the Scottish Sport, filed by 'an eye witness' with more than a hint of eager pleasure[16]:

> '"You are looking for someone?" politely enquired the smallest of the two, as they came up with their prey.
>
> "No-no," replied the tall, handsome swell – for with all his audacity he looked a swell – but he did so with a look and hesitancy which identified him at once.
>
> "We were told you were looking for someone," insisted the sly, self-possessed questioner.
>
> "Oh, no. There...there must be some mistake."
>
> "Were you not wishing to see John Hendry of the Rangers?"
>
> An enquiring glance at his tormentors and a faltering "no" was the reply.
>
> Then the second party spoke, but it was aside, and as if to his companion. "What's the use o' makin' a clown o' me. I thocht it was a good thing. I'll awa' back to Oswald," and he cast a withering look at his apparently perplexed companion.
>
> The trick had fairly trapped the agent however, for in answer

to a last attempt to draw him, his wily inquisitor was at length assured, in a half apologetic tone, that he did want to see Hendry and that he had at first denied his real mission because of the fear he had of the club's supporters, whose attentions were evidently not of the most reassuring.

"Well, this is Hendry," said the sly one, after a little more cross questioning, and pointing to his companion who, I need hardly say, was only a cruel impersonator playing a part in the interests of his club.

The "swell" became reassured, looked more like his audacious self, and prepared to do business.

"Do you want me to go to England?" inquired the bogus Hendry after being duly introduced and informed of the terms.

"Yes, I want you to go to England."

"Are you perfectly sure you want me to go to England?"

"Yes."

"Well, take that!" and before anyone could say Jack Robinson the seducer was sent sprawling on the ground with a lick which could scarcely be described as a baby-duster.

"The elongated representative of the ascendant element in English football was not long in getting to his feet, but there was no fight in him. He took to his heels and, as if pursued by an evil spirit, careered down the road at the most undignified speed imaginable. Unfortunately for him, a crowd of unsympathetic Rangers were coming up the road as he was frantically tearing down and they, taking the situation at a glance, cruelly intercepted him and he was once more in the remorseless hands of the Philistines.

"There is no use in prolonging the sequel; sufficient to say that, after a good bit of running in as earnest an obstacle race as was ever ran, he reached Princes Street, about half a mile away, where he was mercifully taken in by a young Samaritan married couple, and allowed to sufficiently recover from his baptism of fright and fists to be able to be sent to his hotel [St Enoch's] in a cab. When I saw the bold adventurer lying low upon a couch, blanched, speechless, and sick unto death, with several well known members of the Rangers holding his low lying head, and timing his quick beating pulse, I did think that the way of transgressors is hard. Probably G.L. Harrison will not again put his prominent features within a mile of Ibrox Park on a similar errand."

The Scottish Referee was more sympathetic to Harrison's plight, if not his career choice: "We have only one opinion of the treatment which was extended to a professional agent at Ibrox on Thursday night," it thundered. "Namely, that it was a dastardly and brutal assault. If a man has legitimate business and indulges in that business legitimately it is monstrous that he should not only be interfered with, but maltreated in such a way that serious results to his physical welfare are likely to accrue. The business of a professional football agent is a perfectly legitimate one and though we have not the slightest admiration either for the vocation or those who follow it, the law is with it and the law must be respected. The reflection cast on the Rangers Football Club by the assault is a most serious and damaging one." [17]

Meanwhile, back in the FA Cup John Wallace Mackay's influence may have been diluted as Rangers approached the latter stages of the competition almost a year after his departure from the club, but they were still far from a team of choirboys – and certainly not, like the players from Old Westminsters, former public schoolboys. The Londoners pitched up at Kinning Park for the quarter-final tie in February 1887 in an attempt to emulate at least their success of the previous year, when they had reached the semi-final of the FA Cup before being humbled 6–0 by West Bromwich Albion.

Rangers were the sole Scottish representatives left standing in the last eight, as favourites Preston North End were also joined by West Brom, Darwen, Notts County, Aston Villa and Old Caruthians. Old Westminsters may have been former pupils of Westminster College in the capital, but they were no slouches at football and went into the game against the Light Blues on the back of decent form, which had seen them lose only two of their 19 games played that season. However, Rangers put in one of their best performances of the season and ran out 5–1 winners. The crowd was an impressive 6,000 ("the largest seen inside the ground for some considerable time" according to the Scottish Umpire), although only four goalscorers were recorded – Pat Lafferty, Matt Lawrie, Bob Fraser and Joe Lindsay.

As winter prepared to give way to spring, the progress of Rangers into the last four of the FA Cup was being recognised by observers beyond the potential for a Scottish side to lift the greatest prize in the British game for the first time. A move from Kinning Park to their new ground at Ibrox in the coming August was agreed by Rangers at a special meeting of members on 16 February. A seven-year lease, with a break available after three years, was signed for a site of "five or six acres" at the Copeland (sic) Road end of Paisley Road, with £750 being committed to building a pavilion, stand and enclosure, with further terracing taking the capacity of the new ground to around 15,000.

The respect Rangers were winning as they progressed to the latter stages of the FA Cup was also being viewed as a vital marketing aid to enhance the club's finances, as well as its reputation. Not only were they looking to attract glamour sides north for showpiece friendlies to boost gate receipts at their new home, but such matches would also attract a new generation of fans to support the now-established Light Blues at their state-of-the-art ground.

As it reflected on Rangers' march to the semi-final, the Scottish Athletic Journal noted: "They will require several big attractions for the first two or three weeks of their tenancy of the new ground to allow the people to become acquainted with the new order of things. If they make a good appearance now, such English matches as they may desire will be all the more easily arranged. It will thus be seen that the club is looking to its financial standing as well as its reputation. It will be a proud moment for the Rangers if they succeed in getting so far as the Final for the English Cup. Stranger things have happened."[18]

Aston Villa, like Rangers, had reached the semi-final of the competition for the first time that season and were under the management of a Scot, Glaswegian George Ramsay (he is credited with helping establish the lion rampant on the Villa badge, where it still roars to this day, and he also dedicated a staggering 59 years of his life to the club, leading them to six championships and six FA Cup Final successes). Villa were given an immediate advantage by the FA's decision to play the game at Nantwich Road in Crewe, meaning Rangers had to travel 200 miles – four times the distance of their rivals – to fulfil the fixture. For their part, the FA believed playing the game at a ground no more than a stone's throw from a railway station that served Scotland and the Midlands was an appropriate compromise.

Ramsay took his players to Droitwich to prepare for the game, a ploy which was virtually unheard of in those days, and they went through a vigorous regime of training and salt baths to ensure they were in the pink for the biggest game in their history. Their star man was skipper and forward Archie Hunter, another Scot who started his career with Third Lanark and Ayr Thistle before moving south. Tragically, he suffered a heart attack in a League game against

Everton only three years later and died in 1894, aged just 35. Rangers arrived in Crewe at 9.30pm the night before the game in the company of former player Hugh McIntyre, who had met them earlier at Preston. Rangers had previously doled out Villa's record defeat, 7–1 back in April 1882, but history was not to favour a repeat.

The clubs shared the same hotel across the street from the ground, the Royal, and a crowd of 10,000 turned out to watch the tie, the majority of them from the Midlands and bearing cards in the Birmingham club's colours of chocolate and light blue, reading 'Play up Villa!' The sides, who changed at the hotel, took to the field and Hunter opened the scoring after only 13 minutes, maintaining a record he would continue throughout the competition of scoring in every round.

However, Lafferty equalised on 34 minutes and Rangers twice went close to adding to their tally, although Villa were always dangerous on the break against a Rangers defence that was, according to the Scottish Umpire, "not being of the best."[19] The Umpire's reporter, writing under the name 'Forward', had previously tipped Rangers to win through to the Final, but his faith proved unfounded and his fearless punditry was reduced in the second half to barely concealed disgust over the performance of 'keeper Willie Chalmers, who had lunched heartily with McIntyre before the match and was beginning to feel the effects.

'Forward' wrote: "The Rangers defence was much better than it had been in the first half, so far as the backs were concerned, but Chalmers was in very poor trim. A shot was sent across by Hodgetts and though Chalmers had plenty of time to get it away he just touched it along the ground, and Albert Brown dashed it through." Hunter added his second near the end to secure his side's 3–1 victory and 'Forward' concluded: "They [Villa] played a much better game than the Rangers, who were not so good as I expected. Chalmers was the worst of the lot and seemed very nervous on the three occasions, besides the one that ended so fatally…The weak points of the Rangers were in deficient combination and dash of the forwards, rather weak defence and downright poor goalkeeping."[20] It was scant consolation that Rangers, on paper at least, were the only amateur representatives in the last four.

Villa's victory, added to a shock 3–1 semi-final win for their near-neighbours West Brom over the mighty Preston North End, sent the Midlands into meltdown. The Scottish Umpire revealed that: "when the results were made known, the Midlands went about delirious, and many got fou. Poetry cobblers were commissioned to write peans in praise of the respective champions. The Villa almost went off their heads on Saturday night, especially when they heard of the Albion victory. They think they can now win, but did not favour their chances against North End."[21] Villa's confidence was not misplaced, as they defeated West Brom 2–0 in the Final at the Kennington Oval on 2 April in front of more than 15,000 fans.

For Rangers, the recriminations continued for several weeks after the semi-final defeat and the Scottish Umpire noted: "From all accounts, Chalmers cracked his reputation by his Crewe performance. Was it that lunch that did it?" It added: "The Rangers…can't get over their dismissal and the number of 'ifs' they have uttered would fill our columns from end to end. Let them forget the past and prepare for the future."[22]

It was easier said than done for Chalmers, who was ditched by the club before March even came to an end, much to the disgust of the Scottish Athletic Journal, who finger-wagged: "The Rangers have lost the services of Chalmers, who has certainly not been very well treated by the club. It is most unfair to blame him for the loss of the Aston Villa tie…Chalmers has done good service during three years."[23]

A fortnight earlier the Journal's English football writer, who penned his articles under the byline 'Rab', was less forgiving as he mischievously suggested a more sinister motive behind Chalmers' poor form. He wrote: "I have it on the authority of a brother scribe, who was at Crewe seeing the semi-final, that the Rangers would have drawn with the Aston Villa but for the wretched goalkeeping of Chalmers. He says it was vicious such, in fact, as might have been expected from a novice. Chalmers got badly chaffed by the spectators, some even hinting that he had sold the match. Altogether his lot was not a happy one. The Villa were exceedingly lucky in their scores and, but for Chalmers, there was not much difference between them and the Rangers."[24]

John Allan, in his jubilee history of the club, cut straight to it: "William was an excellent trencherman and Hugh McIntyre confessed, with some self-reproach, that it was he who, in a playful spirit, acted as agent to the goalkeeper's little debauch."[25]

Rangers and Chalmers did kiss and make up – he had returned to the club by the start of the following season, though could have been forgiven for wishing he had stayed away as Preston North End rattled eight goals past him to mark the opening of the new Ibrox Park. However, even that was not as bad as the 10–2 defeat Rangers suffered at snow-covered Kinning Park in February 1886 against Airdrie. That scoreline still stands as the Light Blues' heaviest defeat and Chalmers was also slated after that one for refusing to dive around his icy goalmouth.

Rangers' relationship with the FA Cup ended for good at the end of the 1886–87 season as the SFA finally forbade its clubs from competing in the Cup south of the border. Their reasons were straightforward and justified: not only did their members' appearances in the FA Cup undermine their own Scottish Cup competition, they also ran the risk of losing control of football in their own backyard. It was inconceivable to the SFA that if two Scottish clubs met in the FA Cup and came to loggerheads, the association in London could argue for the right to resolve the dispute.

The Scottish Athletic Journal had argued as much in a stern editorial when it said: "It does rile us to see England thus claiming a jurisdiction over Scotland... How can the SFA prevent this assumption of a British jurisdiction by the English association? Easily enough. It only has to pass a rule at the coming annual meeting that no club under its control can take part in any Cup competition, save that of the Scottish Association or one of its affiliated associations. At the same time, the Scottish clubs are to blame. What has the Queen's Park gained by competing for three consecutive seasons for the English Cup? Nothing, save disappointment and humiliation...The Rangers, with more than ordinary luck in the ballot, are now in the semi-final and were they even twice as good as they are they could not win the Cup. If they do, they deserve a public banquet."[26]

They never were so feted. However, Chalmers appears to have eaten on behalf of the whole team anyway.

Chapter 11
Tom Vallance

The shabby goings on around Murray Park as winter gave way to spring in 2012 and Rangers toppled into the financial abyss of administration were an affront to the memory of the man looking down on it all. Day after day the media camped outside the club's training ground at Milngavie, waiting from updates from management and officials, little knowing the final resting place of Tom Vallance, at Hillfoot Cemetery, was framing the scene. Vallance was part of the club when the only mention of Zeus was in relation to his own God-like ability to play, organise and inspire his team-mates and fans.

Former Rangers manager Graeme Souness surely never had Vallance in mind when he memorably opined that one of the biggest problems in Scottish football was the presence of too many hammer throwers. Vallance, dubbed 'Honest Tom' throughout his glorious, one-club career with the Light Blues, could lob 16 pounds of solid steel with as much aplomb as he could run, jump, row or play football. Of all the gallant pioneers, he clearly boasted the richest and most varied talents. This lad o' pairts from the Vale of Leven was a champion athlete and skilled oarsman, international footballer, successful entrepreneur and such an adept artist that his work was exhibited in the Royal Glasgow Institute and Scottish Academy. He would have needed a wide canvas indeed to reflect in oils on all he had achieved.

Tom Vallance was not present at the conception of Rangers in West End Park, nor its birth shortly afterwards against Callander, but he quickly developed a bond with the infant club that would remain virtually unbroken until his death from a stroke in February 1935, aged 78. He nurtured its development to such an extent that he was club captain for nine seasons from 1873 and president for six years from 1883. He represented Scotland seven times, with four caps won against England in 1877, 1878, 1879 and 1881. Not once did he finish on the losing side against the 'Auld Enemy'. Four men are correctly identified with the formation of Rangers but a fifth, Vallance, was also a towering influence – and not just because the powerful full-back stood 6ft 2in tall, a veritable giant of the age on and off the park.

Vallance was born at a small farmhouse known as Succoth, near Renton in the parish of Cardross, in 1856. His father, also Thomas, was an agricultural labourer from Lesmahagow and his mother, Janet, came from Loudon in Ayrshire. They were married in Glasgow in December 1842 and by the time Tom was born there was already a large Vallance family, including Ann aged 12, James 9, Robert 8, and Margaret 2. The family unit would increase still further in later years with the birth of another two boys, Alexander (who also gave sterling service to Rangers) and Andrew (who went on to become head gardener in Helensburgh for Neil Munro, the novelist best known for his 'Para Handy' tales).

When Tom was still young the family moved to the Old Toll House at Shandon, north of Rhu on the Gareloch, and in all likelihood crossed paths with the McNeil brothers for the first time. After all, the new Vallance residence was only a short distance south of Belmore House, where John McNeil, the father of Moses and Peter, was employed as head gardener. Tom Vallance senior is listed in the Helensburgh Directory of 1864 as a 'road man' – in effect, a toll collector for a stretch of highway that once hugged the shore of the Gare Loch between Shandon and Garelochhead, but which has long since been swallowed by the naval base at Faslane.

Captain Fantastic: Tom Vallance, the first great Rangers skipper, who set the standards for many more to follow in the subsequent 130 years.

On the athletics field in his youth, Vallance was a regular prizewinner at the annual Garelochhead Sports, while his love of rowing was nurtured and developed initially on the local regatta circuit. Newspaper reports from the 1870s and 1880s confirm his domination of the local sports scene. For example, on Ne'erday 1878 he competed in the annual Garelochhead Amateur Athletics sports meeting and promptly won the champion mile race for the parishes of Rhu and Rosneath, the 150 yards and 200 yards sprints, as well as the hurdle, 'hop step and leap', and the hammer throw. Three years later, at the same Ne'erday meet, he won the 160 yards and 200 yards races, the steeplechase, the triple jump, another hammer event and the long jump. To rub salt into the wounds of the defeated and dispirited, his team even won the tug-o-war.

By that stage in 1881 Vallance, then aged 25, was at his athletic peak, underlined when he jumped an astonishing 21ft 11in (6.68 metres) at the Queen's Park FC sports. The leap pre-dated the formation of the Scottish Amateur Athletic Association (it would not be established for another two years) but was still passed as the initial Scottish record. It was no fluke either, as Vallance also leapt 21ft 6in and 21ft exactly at two other sports meetings that year. Amazingly, Vallance's Scottish record stood until 1896 when Glaswegian Hugh Barr, another athletic all-rounder, beat it by two inches.

Artist Helen Runciman was commissioned to paint a portrait of Tom Vallance, which is now proudly on display at Ibrox.

By 1871 the Vallance family had moved to Hillhouse in Rhu, where 14-year-old Tom was listed in the census as a "civil engineer's apprentice". If the work was not directly with his father at that time, it was almost certainly a position gained through his influence. However, with a restricted economy based on farming, fishing and the infant industry of tourism, the Gareloch proved inadequate to satisfy the career interests of Vallance and, like the McNeil and Campbell boys before him, he headed to Glasgow where he quickly found work as a mechanical engineer in the shipyards with the company P and W McLellan.

Schoolboy friendships formed would be cherished in the new, alien environment, so it was no surprise when Vallance teamed up with his Gareloch chums soon after his arrival in Glasgow to boost their fledgling football enterprise, nor would it have come

THE "CLUB"
RESTAURANT,
22 PAISLEY ROAD WEST.

THE Proprietor would beg to call the attention of Football, Cricket, Volunteer and every other form of Club to the splendid facilities he has at the above address for conducting Social Meetings, Smoking Concerts, Suppers, etc.

In the large Dining Room in connection with the premises, accommodation can be provided for a company of 200 persons.

For Terms, etc., apply to

THOMAS VALLANCE,
Proprietor.

The popularity of Vallance allowed him to call out to personalities from all Scottish sports to visit establishments such as 'The Club' as a shock to see the teenager seek out a rowing club at which to continue the pastime that had so captured his interest. According to the Scottish Athletic Journal[1] he chose Clyde Amateur Rowing Club – and therein lies a story.

For decades the Clydesdale Rowing Club, neighbours and friendly rivals of Clyde, believed Rangers were formed as an offshoot of their club, but there is no evidence to support their claims beyond anecdotes passed on by members through the generations. Clydesdale generously opened up their minutes and membership lists dating from soon after their formation in 1857 for the research purposes of this book. Unfortunately, none of the names on the membership lists (which are extensive) from the period 1865–1900 match the gallant pioneers, other players or committee members from the earliest years of Rangers.

Of course, that is not to say Tom Vallance, the McNeils or the Campbells never splashed a ripple in the colours of Clydesdale but, more likely, it was Clyde,

Scots Wha Hae: The Scotland team that defeated England 6-1 at The Oval, London on March 12, 1881. The side included three Rangers – Tom Vallance, back row, centre. Striker David Hill, middle row left; with George Gillespie (now goalkeeper, no longer a back) second from right in the middle row. Harry McNeill is middle row, far right. The match was especially significant as it marked the first time a black player, Andrew Watson of Queen's Park, played international football.
Picture courtesy of Scottish Football Museum.

The land of the founding fathers . . . the Gareloch, from above the village of Clynder.

who were formed in 1865. The reported evidence of the time in relation to Vallance apart, there is another strong clue – the blue star on the shirt of the 1877 Scottish Cup Final team, the earliest known picture of a Rangers squad. It has baffled the unknowing for years, but the puzzle is surely solved moments after stepping through the front door of the Clyde HQ at the boathouse on Glasgow Green when visitors are confronted by the club's motif on the wall – a light blue, six-pointed star, identical to the one on the shirts worn by the Rangers team over 130 years previously, which suggests a close relationship between the two clubs. (In the 1877 picture, however, Tom Vallance is pictured with a lion rampant on his shirt, symbolising his status as a Scottish international that season.) Unfortunately, absolute verification of the Clyde link is impossible, not least because their earliest records, unlike those of Clydesdale, were lost long ago.

John Allan's first great history of Rangers paints a somewhat romantic picture of "lusty, laughing lads, mere boys some of them, flushed and happy from the exhilaration of a finishing dash with the oars…seen hauling their craft ashore on the upper reaches of the River Clyde at Glasgow Green." The truth of the rowing exploits of Vallance and Co. was likely to have been somewhat more prosaic. Firstly, opportunities to row would not have been so plentiful, not least because boats would have to be hired from specialist agents on the south of the river at Glasgow Green or loaned from the Clyde or Clydesdale clubs themselves. As recently as the 1960s, as many as six crews would share the use of one four-man boat.

Members of each 'four' would be under strict instruction to return to the boathouse within half an hour and only if there were no crews waiting on the bank for their slot could the time on the water be extended. Furthermore, rowing on the Clyde for much of the latter half of the 19th century often involved a lengthy game of patience. Until 1887 there was a weir on the Clyde at Glasgow Green and, while it helped to hold a high tide longer that usual, it was impossible to take to the water at low tide as the river resembled little more than a narrow stream between two substantial mud flats. [2]

For the most part, four-man teams on Glasgow Green raced a 1,000-yard course upstream between the Albert Bridge and St Andrew's Suspension Bridge, while single rowers favoured longer distances of up to four miles. The demographic make-up of the Clyde and Clydesdale clubs at the time was white-collar – doctors and lawyers, but the gallant pioneers were aspiring middle class, serving professional apprenticeships. Peter Campbell may have been a shipyard worker, but he was from entrepreneurial and privileged stock and he and his brothers, as well as the McNeils and Tom Vallance, would have felt at home on Glasgow Green, not least because rowing was such an integral part of their upbringing on the Gareloch. The clubs may have been perceived as elitist, but the sport was not. Employees of each shipyard on the Clyde, for example, designed, built and rowed their own boats under the auspices of the Trades Rowing Association.

In truth, it is more than likely that the founding fathers of Rangers were social rowers in Glasgow rather than competitive, not least because their new football team took up so much of their time and attention. The highlight of the rowing season in the city was

A reproduction of 'The Charge' by Tom Vallance, which appeared in the Daily Record in February 1934. The original oil painting, a six foot tall canvas, was presented to Cadder Golf Club ahead of its opening in 1935.

undoubtedly the Glasgow Regatta, and it is astonishing to think in the 21st century that as many as 30,000 spectators would cram the banks of the Clyde in the 1870s to watch the best rowers in the country. There is no evidence to suggest that any of the club's founding fathers, even including Vallance, took part in the main event on the Clyde, not least because it was generally held on the first or second weekend in September, when the football season had just got up and running.

An examination of newspaper reports of the event throughout the 1870s failed to throw up the names of anyone connected with the Light Blues although, intriguingly, one ace rower was a Gilbert McNeil, while the regatta's energetic secretary was

Senior statesman: Tom Vallance, pictured in the 1920s.

a certain John Banks McNeil. The latter was the owner of the Clutha Boathouse and one of the principal hirers of small craft on the Clyde, not to mention the founder of the Glasgow Regatta itself. However, no connection between John and Gilbert and the McNeils of Rangers fame could be established.

As a footballer, Tom Vallance was without equal in the Scottish and English game in the latter part of the 1870s, with the skipper, like his team-mates, first shooting to prominence in the memorable Scottish Cup Final ties against Vale of Leven in 1877. He played the Final against the same opposition two years later and, although the Cup would leave the city in controversial circumstances on both occasions, the Charity Cup success of 1879 made some amends for the earlier disappointments. Vallance was revered by commentators at the time, with respected football analysts such as D.D. Bone arguing that "for several seasons, but more particularly that of 1879–80, none in Scotland showed better form. His returns near goal were neat and clean, and without being in any way rough with an opponent Vallance's length of limb

Honest Tom . . . a man of fine sporting and business standing

A picture of the Lansdowne Restaurant in Hope Street showed Tom was catering to a high class of diner in Victorian Glasgow.

DINING SALOON, LANSDOWNE RESTAURANT.

and good judgement often saved his club from losing goals."[3] The Scottish Athletic Journal reckoned: "He was worshipped by a very large section of the football community, and that worship at times had in it all the fire and enthusiasm which are commonly bestowed on a hero."[4]

Were he playing today, Vallance would command a substantial seven-figure transfer fee, but in those innocent, amateur days football was only a pastime for most. Looking to the future, Vallance decided to leave his lodgings at No. 167 Govan Road in February 1882 and forge a career on the tea plantations of Assam in India. It was a bold move as it was a fledgling industry that had only become commercially exploited in the previous 50 years. However, conditions in the north east of India were far from idyllic.

Vallance moved to the foothills of the Himalayas to erect and superintend new machinery being introduced at the Corramore Plantation, which had been established in 1858 by Scot Robert Logan and named after the family farm in Lanarkshire. The Corramore Plantation stayed in the Logan family for 120 years before it was absorbed into Williamson Tea Holdings.

Assam historian Derek Perry[5] has painted a picture of a remote, lonely region at the time of the emigration of Vallance. The conditions would have been daunting, even for a man such as Vallance at his physical peak, but he had little chance to settle as he was struck down by illness within a few months of his arrival. On the basis of later accounts, particularly those which reveal that the illness compromised his football career on his return to Scotland, Perry suggests he was likely debilitated by the dreaded Kala-azar, or black water fever, a form of pernicious malaria. Another attack could have been deadly and it was in light of concerns about his health that Vallance returned to Scotland after only a year away.

A profile on Tom, published in the Victualling Trades Review in May 1891, admitted as much. It read: "Unfortunately, even his strong constitution, hardened as it was by his great athletic career, fairly broke down and he was most reluctantly compelled to abandon his bright prospects of success in this sphere and return to Auld Scotia, where his native air, the bagpipes, the parritch and the mountain dew soon re-inspired him with his wonted vigour."

Tom played three times for Rangers in season 1883–84 but was a spent force. He kicked his last ball for the club in a 9–2 win over Abercorn at Kinning Park on 8 March 1884. The Scottish Athletic Journal sadly noted: "He still had a fancy for the game of football and donned the jersey several times but his eye was dimmed and his leg had lost its cunning and he was not even the shadow of his former self."[6]

His illness had clearly forced Vallance into taking stock of his life and soon after his return from India he abandoned his earlier aspirations of pursuing a career as an engineer to become a travelling salesman in the wine and spirits trade, opening the door to a new and lucrative existence in the hospitality industry. He was employed by James Aitken & Co. Ltd, brewers who operated from Linlithgow and Falkirk, brewing their popular 'Aitken's Ale'. His working life quickly back on track, Vallance also set about re-establishing himself at Kinning Park. If he could not do it on the field any longer, he could certainly contribute off it and he was elected club president for the first of six seasons in May 1883.

During his 12-month absence John Wallace Mackay had come to the fore at Kinning Park. Vallance honourably resigned early in his presidency after that player coup moved to remove him as umpire for a match at Dumbarton and replace him with Mackay because he would not favour his own team in his decision making. However, 'keeper George Gillespie issued a grovelling apology on behalf of the team and Vallance returned within a week, his grip on his portfolio tightened still further. As a salesman he was undoubtedly used to flattery and cajolery to get his own way, but there also appeared to be a genuine streak of honesty and integrity running through Vallance to which people warmed. For example, he was an arch critic of Mackay and frequently stood up against the worst excesses of the honorary match secretary in his seemingly never-ending spats with the Scottish Athletic Journal.

On one occasion, following the half-yearly meeting in November 1884, Mackay attempted to coerce Vallance into lying on his behalf by denying claims in the Journal that the match secretary had said Queen's Park were on their financial uppers ahead of their move to the second Hampden Park. In a fit of pique, Mackay

OUR PORTRAIT GALLERY.

MR. THOMAS VALLANCE, The "Club" Restaurant,
Paisley Road Toll.

To a student of human nature it is always a strange and interesting study to observe the ever-fluctuating evolution of circumstances which tend to make or mar one's destiny. Time and chance happeneth unto all men, but unfortunately the capacity for seizing the opportunity at the proper moment is only granted to the minority.

The subject of this sketch, Mr. Thomas Vallance, the stalwart proprietor of the "Club" Restaurant, Paisley Road Toll, affords a very peculiar example of the vicissitudes which a man may undergo before settling down to his life's work.

Mr. Vallance entered this wicked world in the year 1856, his birthplace being the Vale of Leven, that district noted for the famous athletes it has produced, as well as for the wondrous beauty of its surrounding scenery. He early removed to the Gareloch, remaining there till his 14th year. He thus had the inestimable advantage denied to the dwellers in the murky city of inhaling the health-giving breezes which scattered the mist from off the lofty Ben Lomond, and which ruffled the blue waters of the Queen of Scottish Lakes, and so laying up a store of health for future work.

When a raw young lad of fourteen—tall for his years—he migrated to Glasgow (verily a fuliginous purgatory to the rosy-cheeked country boy) and entered the office of a civil engineer, where he remained for three years. Thereafter he served his apprenticeship as a mechanical engineer in the works of P. & W. M'Lellan, and afterwards increased his knowledge of his profession in various other large engineering works on the Clyde. In 1882 he set sail for India's coral strand, having received an important appointment in the Corramore tea estate to erect and superintend new machinery which was being introduced in tea-planting. Unfortunately, even his strong constitution, hardened as it was by his great athletic career, fairly broke down, and he was most reluctantly compelled to abandon his bright prospects of success in this sphere and return to Auld Scotia, where his native air, the bagpipes, the parritch, and the mountain dew soon re-inspired him with his wonted vigour. He thereupon procured a situation with Colonel James Menzies, agent for Messrs. Usher, brewers, Edinburgh, and thereafter represented for six years the well-known firm of James Aitken & Co., Falkirk, but, owing to his present business assuming such

large proportions, he was compelled to cut his connection with the firm, and devote his whole time to his restaurant.

While ever strictly attentive to business, Mr. Vallance found time to cultivate his physical powers, and is a splendid example of a man possessing the *mens sana in corpore sano*. Standing nearly 6 feet 2 inches in his stockings, and straight as a dart, he has been a conspicuous figure amongst the athletes of Scotland. He captained the Rangers (the famous Light Blues) team for seven years, and gained his international cap four times against England. He has, along with his brother Alexander, agent for Jas. Aitken & Co., won over £300 worth of cups and medals, and at present holds the record in Scotland for the long jump—nearly twenty-two feet.

He further possesses considerable artistic taste, evidence of which is to be found on the walls of the "Club" Restaurant, which are adorned with works of art from his own ready brush, and the clever black-and-white sketch of the "Club" dining-room, reproduced below, is an example of his work. He is modest to a fault, and possessed of that rare virtue of sterling honesty—so much so, that he enjoyed amongst his football club mates the soubriquet of "honest" Tom.

In concluding this article we must give a brief sketch of his premises, now becoming so well known in the district as the "Club," but, as we have transgressed already the usual space allotted for this purpose, it must necessarily be short. The dining-room, a sketch of which we give, is certainly the most prominent

feature of this well-equipped establishment, and, large and commodious as it is, Mr. Vallance is already beginning to find that it is none too big for his rapidly-increasing trade, and what we have no doubt is of inestimable advantage in this respect is, that diners can enter the dining-room direct from the street. Adjoining the dining-room, and entering from it by a glass doorway, is the smoking-room, which is a lofty spacious apartment, quite out of the rut of the usual stuffy smoking-rooms attached even to first-class restaurants. That portion of the premises that faces the Paisley Road is fitted up as a horse-shoe bar, artistic glass panelling representing every branch of British sport being the chief mode of decoration. Underneath, the whole area is taken up with cellars, stores, pantry, kitchen, &c. &c. In fact, the whole premises are fitted up in a manner so thoroughly complete, not only for daily dinners, but suppers of almost any number, that we have no doubt whatever Mr. Vallance will be able to cope with the ever-increasing requirements of the district.

A flattering portrait of Tom was painted by the Victualling Trades Review in its edition of 12 May 1891 had also recommended Rangers never play Third Lanark again after their Glasgow rivals reported them to the SFA for the 'Cooking the books' scandal. Vallance refused and, not surprisingly, was showered with praise the following week by the newspaper.

Increasingly, Vallance was dealing from a position of presidential strength as Rangers moved from a period of financial uncertainty to one of stability under his reign. Membership numbers increased and, with a far-sighted and energetic committee at the club, a move to the purpose-built first Ibrox Park was secured. However, Vallance missed the grand opening of the new ground against Preston North End on 18 August 1887 as he married Marion Dunlop, sister of former team-mate, club president and friend William. Marion was from Glasgow and was six years Tom's junior. The wedding ceremony was held in the Dunlop family home, with Tom's younger brother Alick acting as best man.

Within 18 months the couple's first child was born, Harold Leonard Vallance, on 20 January 1889. By this time they lived at No. 89 Maxwell Drive in the south-west of Glasgow, before moving back into the city to No. 48 Sandyford Street a year later. It was at this point that Tom's career was suddenly injected with an extra impetus, as he moved from his position with brewer James Aitken to become a successful restaurateur. In 1890 he took on his first real business venture – a pub/restaurant located at No. 22 Paisley Road West at Paisley Road Toll. He called the restaurant The Club and it quickly became a popular venue for the Rangers' 'smoker evenings'. He would also go on to own and operate at least two other restaurants in the city: The Metropolitan at No. 40 Hutchison Street and The Lansdowne at No. 183 Hope Street. His reputation among his business contemporaries was underlined in 1906 when he became president of the Restaurateurs and Hotelkeepers Association.

The happiness of Tom and Marion was sealed still further in 1891 when another son, James Douglas, was born. The Vallances seemed to lead a somewhat itinerant life at this stage as James was born in the new family home at No. 219 Paisley Road in Glasgow, before they moved to nearby Lendel Terrace then, soon after, Maxwell Drive and back to Kersland Street in the west end. Finally, in 1908 Tom and Marion settled at No. 189 Pitt Street in Glasgow city centre and the place they would call home for the rest of their lives.

In addition to his work with Rangers and his various business concerns, Vallance was also a member of the 'Old Glasgow Club,' a local history society. He also found time for another passion: art. Self taught, he exhibited at the annual exhibition of the Royal Glasgow Institute at least twice, in 1897 and 1929, and his work was also displayed by the Scottish Academy. He never became as celebrated as contemporaries such as Glasgow Boys James Guthrie and James Paterson, or Scottish colourists Samuel Peploe or John Fergusson, but his work was popular and still occasionally appears at auction.

One of his final commissions was an impressive and dramatic canvas almost six feet in height entitled The Charge, which was presented to Cadder Golf Club in Bishopbriggs on its opening in May 1935. The painting, which featured an army battalion on horseback, was so impressive it was even reproduced in the Daily Record in February 1934. Unfortunately, despite its size, the golf club lost track of the painting when it was removed during World War Two and its current whereabouts is unknown.

Sadly, the events of World War One were to have a lasting impression on

MOTOR CAR RUNS AMOK IN GLASGOW STREET.

Scene of the tragedy at Hillhead, Glasgow, where a motor car, after knocking down and fatally injuring a young man, laid low a lamp-post, carried away several feet of iron railing, and collided with a wall. The driver, a well-known Glasgow man, has been arrested.

The Daily Record of October 6 1922 tells of the full, devastating extent of the damage caused by John Vallance in Gibson Street.

the Vallance family. Harold Vallance joined the 7th Battalion (Blythswood) of the great Glasgow regiment, the Highland Light Infantry. Tragically, on 28 September 1918, just six weeks before the end of the war, Second Lieutenant Harold Leonard Vallance, aged 29, was killed in one of the closing conflicts in the assault on the Hindenburg line in France. He was buried with honour at Abbeville Communal Cemetery. He is commemorated on the memorial board at Glasgow's Western Baths, where he was a member, along with Peter McNeil's son, John Fraser.

Tom would know heartache in his life, not least the death of younger brother Alick at the age of only 38 in 1898, soon after the younger brother had taken over as proprietor of the Red Lion Vaults in Glasgow's West Nile Street. The influence of Alick on the early years of Rangers should never be forgotten. Alick joined Rangers in 1873 as a 13-year-old, shortly after his big brother and, like Tom, was employed by the engineering firm P and W McLellan, initially as an office boy. He was credited, with support from Tom, with securing Burnbank for the use of Rangers in 1875 and, the following year, he put forward the suggestion of Kinning Park, thus taking Rangers to the south side of the city for the first time. He would have known the area around Kinning Park intimately as P and W McLellan had opened the Clutha Ironworks in 1873 and it would stand as a neighbour of the Light Blues in the district for several years.

Alick also kept pace with his big brother in sport and it was estimated the Vallance boys won more than £300 worth of cups and medals across several sporting disciplines. Indeed, Alick even put out a 12 sport challenge to any Scottish athlete in 1884 who fancied taking him on, but there was no-one willing and, as a result, he was lauded in the press as the finest all-round athlete in the country. In addition to their membership of Rangers, the siblings were also long-standing members of the Clydesdale Harriers, which Alick helped establish in 1885. Alick also solely organised the first Rangers Sports. Golf was another passion and he was one of the founder members and the first captain of Garelochhead Golf Club in 1895. He was also Scottish 120 yards hurdles champion in 1888 and he played over 100 times for the Light Blues in a career spanning 12 seasons from 1877–88. Like Tom, he was a defender and, although he had a lighter physique than his older brother, he was every bit as gutsy. They played together in the Glasgow Charity Cup Final in 1879 when Rangers beat Vale of Leven 2–1 to win their first piece of silverware as a club.

Alick, who was a Rangers selector before being named captain in 1881, packed achievement after achievement into his life before his death. He was secretary of the Shandon and Gareloch Rowing Club, the Shandon Mutual Improvement Society, a member of the of the Glasgow Wanderers Angling Club and even a member of the Queen's Own Yeomanry Cavalry. He was an award-winning poultry breeder and his love of dogs shone through as secretary of the Glasgow Canine club and membership of the Scottish Collie Club and the Scottish Kennel Club.

Tom's life was also touched with scandal and sorrow of a different sort in January 1923 when his surviving son James was jailed for nine months and fined £250 for culpable homicide following a car accident on Gibson Street in the west end, a stone's throw from the former home of Peter McNeil. On 4 October 192 James had been driving up Gibson Street in a car purchased for him by his dad, by whom he was employed at the Lansdowne Restaurant in Hope Street. Painfully, no doubt, Tom admitted in court the distance between the accelerator and brake pedals in the vehicle was only an inch-and-a-half and the brakes were slack. He added that if the accelerator was touched at the same time as the brake, the car would shoot forward.

James, aged 30, then stepped forward to give evidence and told the court he had been travelling at 20 miles an hour, but had accelerated going up the hill at Gibson Street towards Bank Street. Suddenly, two men stepped out in front of him and he swerved to the left to avoid them but could only conclude that as he tried to apply the brakes he hit the accelerator instead. The car crashed into a lamp post and although Vallance walked away uninjured one of the poor pedestrians, Alexander Doyle, was struck by the vehicle and died.

The jury returned a guilty verdict by a majority and Lord Alness passed sentence. He told Vallance: "I will not add to your distress by reading a homily with regard to the painful position you find yourself in because you have been convicted of a crime involving the loss of life."[7]

The devastation of the Doyle family, in part, would also have been shared by Tom and Marion Vallance. Tom remained an ever present at Rangers throughout his life. He attended the dinner to mark the 50th anniversary of the club at Ferguson and Forrester's Restaurant on Buchanan Street in April 1923 and it must have been an occasion of mixed emotions following the death of Alexander Doyle and the imprisonment of his surviving son. Tom was also present when the magnificent Main Stand was officially opened on January 1 1929. To think the pride he must have felt that day as he reflected on the club's humble origins at Glasgow Green and how far they had grown in little more than a half century.

Tom was given the Ibrox equivalent of a state funeral following his death at home on the evening of Saturday 16 February 1935, with his burial three days later at Hillfoot. Rangers chairman James Bowie took one of the cords as the gallant pioneer was laid to rest, while former teammate James 'Tuck' McIntyre, also in his late seventies and one of the oldest surviving former players at the time, took another. Bill Struth attended, along with other senior club officials, while a host of former opponents from clubs such as Dumbarton, Clyde and Third Lanark also turned out.

Fittingly, Rangers saw him off on the day of his death with a 3-1 win over Airdrie at Ibrox.

Chapter 12

Happily We Walk Along the Copland Road

It was a measure of the new-found confidence of Glasgow that the city hosted its first International Exhibition in 1888 on the stretch of parkland that had earlier provided a place of contemplation for four youngsters who were interested in forming the football club that quickly became known as Rangers. Glaswegians grew giddy at the thought of the cosmopolitan delights of a showcase for their city that would eventually be nicknamed Baghdad on the Kelvin as a result of the eastern influence on the architectural structures that dominated Kelvingrove Park for seven months between May and November. The Glasgow International Exhibition of Science, Art and Industry attracted almost six million visitors in total and was widely recognised as the first truly international exhibition since the great gathering at Crystal Palace in 1851.

In addition to showing off Glasgow's outstanding achievements as an industrial power and second city of the Empire, the exhibition was also aimed at turning a profit to fund a new gallery and museum at Kelvingrove. Glasgow now boasted such a treasure trove of art and other valuable artefacts there was no longer room to display them at the McLellan Galleries, which was until then its main museum. The art gallery and museum at Kelvingrove opened in time for the next major exhibition in 1901 and still stands today as one of the country's top tourist attractions in all its refurbished splendour.

In total, there were 2,700 exhibits at the 1888 event, including an electrically illuminated fairy fountain of different colours and a Doulton Fountain, now restored to all its former glory and housed at Glasgow Green. The River Kelvin was even deepened and cleaned and the flow of sewage into its waters stemmed to such an extent there were regular swimming galas.

A gondola was brought to Glasgow from Venice especially for the exhibition and two gondoliers, nicknamed Signor Hokey and Signor Pokey, treated visitors to trips up and down the Kelvin. H. and P. McNeil also took the chance to exhibit their wares – at court number two, stand 1241, according to their adverts at the time. Glasgow was letting its hair down, more confident of its place in Britain and the world in general. It was a bold self-assuredness that was being matched at the time by the leaders of Rangers.

The constant creep of industrialisation had long put pressure on land at Kinning Park, the ground Rangers had called their home, if not their own, since 1876. At least twice the Light Blues had fought the threat of eviction from their landlord, but the writing was not so much on the wall as the gable ends of the tenements that began to dominate in the district. The factor, land agents Andersons and Pattison, duly arrived early in the New Year in 1887 and gave Rangers notice to quit their home by 1 March.

It was a sad blow, not least because the £60 per annum Rangers paid in rent was considered extremely cheap for the time and the facility. Nevertheless, the move to evict came as no great surprise. In the 1860s Kinning Park was a pretty patch of meadowland and even as late as 1872 the former ground of the Clydesdale Cricket Club sat in rural isolation. However, by 1873 the Clutha Ironworks had been constructed nearby, followed a couple of years later by a depot for the Caledonian Railway Company. By the turn of the 20th century the green grass at Kinning Park would disappear forever and be replaced by a coating of dust from the sawmill of Anderson and Henderson. A move west to the undeveloped lands of Ibrox beckoned.

In the same weekend that Rangers booked their place in the semi-final of the FA Cup against Aston Villa in February 1887, the club's committee came together and settled on a seven-year lease for a parcel of land of up to six acres at the Copeland (sic) Road end of Paisley Road. They struck a deal with Braby and Company, a building firm from Springburn, to construct a new

Rangers took part in one of football's first floodlit games, against Vale of Leven at the Exhibition Showgrounds in Kelvingrove Park in November 1888.

It may not have boasted a line-up to match Sunday Night at the London Paladium, but the fund-raising concert for the first Ibrox Park at the Waterloo Rooms was a roaring success.

stadium at a cost of £750, which included a pavilion, a 1,200 capacity stand, an enclosure and a four-lane running track inside a terracing amphitheatre.

In addition to the ambitious plans, a playing surface would be laid out 115 yards long by 71 wide and space was even left behind each goal for tennis courts to be introduced at a later stage. The ground, it was claimed, would be little inferior to Hampden Park, then recognised as the best sporting arena in the country.

The Scottish Athletic Journal greeted the decision of the Kinning Park committee to forge ahead with plans for a new ground in February 1887 with glee. It reported: "The meeting was most enthusiastic, harmonious in tone and unmistakenly evidenced the deep desire of the Light Blues to take a higher stand in the football arena than they have hitherto done."[1] However, only three years earlier it had foreseen only doom and gloom if Rangers ever moved from Kinning Park. In March 1884 it warned: "The Rangers have received notice to quit Kinning Park as the ground is to be immediately built upon. This is a serious blow to the Rangers – one from which they will scarcely recover. It almost certainly means extinction. Dissociate the Light Blues from Kinning Park and the club will soon collapse. One cannot think of the Rangers associated with any other park and grounds situated so near the city as Kinning Park is are not to be had."[2]

However, a sub-committee under the guidance of convenor Dan Gillies was formed for the purpose of raising the necessary funds in the spring of 1887. The

Kinning Park closed for good on February 26, 1887 with a game between the Ancients and the Moderns. The Ancients included players such as Tom and Alex Vallance, George Gillespie, Sam Ricketts and William 'Daddy' Dunlop. Moses McNeil (seated second row, far left, with cane) attended but did not play. The Moderns won 3-2.

fears of the Journal would soon prove unfounded.

Rangers hoped the bulk of the finance would come from money already at hand and the following season's gate receipts, but fundraising was also crucial. To that end they organised a benefit concert at the Grand Hall of the Waterloo Rooms in Wellington Street in Glasgow city centre, with Tom Vallance acting as compere. The bill promised acts such as Cinderella, from the Gaiety Theatre pantomime, celebrated tenor Peter Kerr, eminent soprano Isa Grant and Irish comedian Dan Rogers. There was something for everyone, including an American music band, The Dobsons, and even a French equilibrist, Monsieur Trewey, whose trick involved walking along tightropes.

Rangers also got the financial balancing act spot on – the night was a complete sell-out, a roaring success. The licence for the Grand Hall was extended to 2am to allow dancing into the night and, with ticket prices of sixpence and a shilling, the club coffers were swollen substantially and concerns eased that the move was a step too far for an organisation that was still just 15 years old.

These days, with its excellent transport links and relative proximity to Glasgow city centre, Ibrox is the perfect home for Rangers geographically, not to mention the strong spiritual links which have been forged with the district for over a century. However, in the 1880s the move to the relative backwater was considered a risk, but it was championed by the club's honorary secretary Walter Crichton, who foresaw the spread of the booming city further westwards. Glasgow had overtaken Edinburgh in terms of the size of its population as early as 1821 and by the time of the formation of Rangers in 1872 it was home to approximately 500,000 people, which had become almost 660,000 by 1891.

For much of the second half of the 19th century Ibrox was still a rural district – in 1876, fields of corn grew to the very fringes of Clifford Street, which runs parallel between Paisley Road West and the M8 over a century later. An outward sign of the growth and prosperity of the district in the 1870s came with the construction of the original Bellahouston Academy, which still stands today on Paisley Road West near its junction with Edmiston Drive.

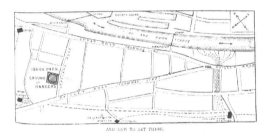

AND HOW TO GET THERE.

The Scottish Umpire.   11

THE RANGERS, NEW GROUND (Looking towards Copeland Road).
Fred Braby & Co., Ltd, Glasgow, Contractors.

Surprisingly, few pictures exist of the first Ibrox Park but the following line drawings, from contractors Fred Braby and Co, appeared in the press ahead of the official opening against Preston North End in August 1887. The gent enjoying a smoke is standing at what today would be the Copland Road stand.

Districts such as Bellahouston, Dumbreck and parts of Ibrox were home to the well-to-do and they shuddered at the prospect of sending their children across the ever sprawling city for a premier education at Glasgow Academy, situated in the west end, and as a result Bellahouston Academy was formed.

Understandably, given its rural status, the history of

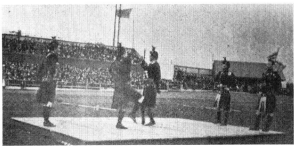

A merry jig. Highland dancers excel at the Govan Police Sports at the first Ibrox Park in May 1897.

Ibrox has tended to be overlooked, certainly in comparison to its near neighbour Govan, once the fifth-largest burgh in Scotland. The oldest recorded mention of the place name now so closely associated with Rangers is Ibrokis, in 1580, and Ybrox in 1590. Indeed, in the 19th century there were still people who lived in and around the district that pronounced it as 'Eebrox'. The name is believed to come from the Gaelic broc, meaning badger, and I or Y, an old Celtic word for island.

According to local lore, a water trough stood just off the head of what is now know as Broomloan Road, with its spring water origins at Bellahouston Hill. The water was so plentiful it occasionally spilled over to join the Powburn, a sluggish stretch of water that meandered through Drumoyne and into the Clyde at Linthouse. A swampy island populated by badgers was formed at the Broomloan Road site where the two stretches of water met, hence Ybrox or Ibrox, the island of the badgers.

In more recent times, the land around Edmiston Drive now associated with the home of Rangers was field and meadowland. There were two large houses on the area now recognised as Bellahouston Park — Bellahouston House, sometimes called Dumbreck House, owned by a famous Govan family, the Rowans. Another estate nearby was known as Ibrox or Ibroxhill and was owned by the Hill family, partners in Hill and Hoggan, the oldest legal firm in the city. Both estates were bought by Glasgow town council in 1895 for £50,000 and within 12 months had been absorbed into the city boundaries, opening their gates as Bellahouston Park.

An historical delve into the origins of the names of Edmiston Drive and Copland Road might also intrigue fans. The former was named after Richard Edmiston, a senior partner in the auctioneer firm J. and R. Edmiston, who operated at West Nile Street for much of the first half of last century. Edmiston's family home, Ibrox House, was in the shadows of the second Ibrox Park and he was

On your marks, get set, go . . . the old ground covers the site of today's Copland Road.

Then and now . . . Ibrox Terrace in the background gives an example of the scale of the first Ibrox Park compared to today.

The pipes of PC . . . the police band marches past the main stand of the first Ibrox Park.

bestowed the honour when the street on which the stadium now stands was first opened. He appeared to have had a philanthropic nature and in 1949 was even named a freeman of Girvan, where he owned a holiday home, after gifting the local museum several paintings by leading artists of the time.

Copland Road was named in the first half of the 19th century after a writer, William Copland, in tribute to the fact that his principal residence was at Dean Park Villa, at the west side of the thoroughfare near its junction with Govan Road. The name of the street was correctly spelled out in maps and journals of the time, but was later changed to Copeland Road after a spelling blunder by builders who were constructing the local Copland Road School. The erroneous letter 'e' was allowed to stand unchallenged for much of the first half of the 20th century, but the street name has long since been restored to the original.

It was long thought the picture above showed Rangers against a touring Canadian select. In fact, research has confirmed it to be the Light Blues lining up against Preston North End before the game to mark the opening of the first Ibrox Park in 1887.

If the few residents who lived in the Ibrox district at the time of the Rangers' arrival had some reservations about their new neighbours, they were probably well founded. A few months before the move, the Scottish Athletic Journal was forced to take Rangers fans to task, not for the first time, for their behaviour at a match, this time against Third Lanark. It reported: "There were several of the Kinning Park rowdies at Cathkin on Saturday. Some of them seemed proud of their swearing abilities as they took advantage of every lull in the play to volley forth a few choice oaths which were heard all over the field. It is a pity an example cannot be made of some of these people."[3]

Rangers toyed with the idea of taking over the lease of a ground in Strathbungo at a rent of £80 a year and the Journal warned that rents in the area would immediately go through the floor. Perhaps Tom Vallance summed it up best of all at the cake and wine banquet for VIP guests the Wednesday before the official opening of the new Ibrox ground. He addressed the throng and admitted that Kinning Park was not always a place for the faint-hearted. He said, "A certain stigma rested on the club owing to their field being in a locality not of the best, while the spectators of the game were not always of the best description, though they were simply such as the locality could afford. I have known very respectable people come to our matches and not renewing their visits but that has all gone and I am sanguine that in our new sphere we will be able to attract to our matches thousands of respectable spectators."[4]

His claims proved prophetic, as almost a year after the opening of the first Ibrox Provost Ferguson of Govan admitted there had been initial private misgivings among the burgh's leading citizens over the arrival of the Light Blues in their district. However, he lavished praise on the Rangers fans, noting there had not been a single arrest in their first season. The Scottish Umpire gushed: "It is satisfactory to have such a testimony from the chief magistrate of such a football constituency as Govan as to the law abiding and peaceful character of the crowds which patronise the pastime."[5]

Bad behaviour was not restricted to Kinning Park. Indeed, one of the most ugly and unsavoury incidents of the period involved Queen's Park, following a 3–0 defeat to Preston in the FA Cup in October 1886 at Hampden. There were 14,000 at the game, including 500 from England, and the crowd invaded the field near the end to attack the visitors following a hefty challenge on star player William Harrower by Preston inside-forward Jimmy Ross, younger brother of former Hearts star Nick. Queen's players were forced to leap to the defence of helpless

Preston players as they were attacked by sticks and umbrellas as they made their way through the throng to the safety of the pavilion. Ross later ordered a cab to take him away from Hampden but "the vehicle was stormed and Ross was severely maltreated."[6]

Nevertheless, despite its occasionally disreputable status, there was still a fondness for the old ground at Kinning Park that was exemplified by the turnout of former players to mark the end of its life as a sporting arena on Saturday 26 February 1887, days before the landlord turned the key on the gates for good. Rangers had tried – and failed – to lure Nottingham Forest and Blackburn Rovers north to play an exhibition match to mark the occasion, but it was perhaps more appropriate to field the moderns against the ancients, although the last-minute nature of the arrangements restricted the number of fans in attendance. Old boys such as Tom and Alick Vallance, George Gillespie, Sam Ricketts and William 'Daddy' Dunlop all turned out and, although Moses McNeil did not feature on the park, the picture taken before the game shows him sitting proudly with his former colleagues, who were unlucky to lose 3–2 to the younger and fitter Light Blues.

Rangers were left to see out the last three months of the 1886–87 season as nomads, with 'home' games played at venues such as Cathkin Park, Hampden and Inchview (Partick Thistle's ground at the time, in the Whiteinch district), while their soon-to-be near neighbours at the other end of Copland Road, Whitefield, offered their own Whitefield Park ground for training purposes, which was gratefully accepted. Throughout the spring and summer work continued unabated on the new ground, while the Rangers committee set about organising a grand opening that would later lead the Scottish News to comment: "The usually quiet district of Ibrox has never before witnessed such an assemblage."[7]

The Rangers committee succeeded in persuading Preston North End to travel north to open their new ground. The visitors demanded a £50 appearance fee, a fair deal for Rangers on the back of eventual gate receipts of £340. The Lancashire side, under manager Major William Sudell, became known as the Invincibles, with a team consisting predominantly of Scots who were among the first professionals in the sport. Players such as Nick and Jimmy Ross, David Russell, John Goodall and Geordie Drummond earned a fortune – comparatively speaking – as Preston won the first English League championship in 1888–89 without losing a game and clinched the double by going all the way in the FA Cup without conceding a goal. They also won the League in 1890, so Rangers fans were watching legends in the making as they turned up at Ibrox that August afternoon.

Rangers were keen to show off their new ground to a select audience ahead of the formal opening and 150 invites were sent out to dignitaries to attend the cake and wine preview the Wednesday before the Preston game (it was also a chance for Vallance to meet the VIPs ahead of his own big match with Marion Dunlop, which forced him to miss the game on the Saturday). On the Tuesday night, a Rangers team playing under the guise of the Ibroxonians fought out a 2–2 draw with Whitefield at Whitefield Park as they prepared for Preston, although the Light Blues could only muster eight men to start the game.

Not surprisingly, the atmosphere at the cake and wine was jovial as the club was complimented for the quality of a facility few in British football could boast. Mr Luther, of builders Braby and Co., even noted that the sharp corrugated fencing around the ground would prevent fans from watching without paying for the privilege, as it made for an uncomfortable seat for supporters keen to snatch an illicit view of their favourites.

Behind the scenes, preparations continued to accommodate fans from all

Footprints of time . . . a line map of the first Ibrox Park, superimposed on an aerial view of the current stadium.

over the city at the new ground. The Rangers committee asked for the 6 o'clock train to Wemyss Bay to make a temporary stop at Ibrox to allow fans easier access to the new site, while the Glasgow Tramway Company agreed to run additional brakes from the city to Paisley Road at only twopence a head. In terms of pre-match entertainment, the Scottish Umpire somewhat snootily noted: "The Fairfield Band offered to assist the Govan Police Band and Pipers at the opening ceremony. Declined regretfully. It is a football match, not a band contest."[8]

The game and the opening of the new ground had clearly captured the public's imagination and, while the event was as popular as all associated with the club could have hoped, the capacity crowd of 20,000 revealed severe organisational problems. Time was called on the action five minutes early amid scenes of chaos, even though many supporters had already given up and headed for home, setting a 19th-century precedent for the 21st century's so-called Subway Loyal, who turn for the exits as soon as the hand of the Ibrox game clock reaches out to touch 80 minutes.

Even the prophecy by Mr Luther of Braby and Co., who cheerfully predicted no climbing on the perimeter fencing, was wide of the mark. The Scottish News lamented that the capacity, by kick-off time of 4pm, was "taxed to its utmost. There was scarcely standing room. Many spectators eager to obtain a good view mounted on the top of the corrugated iron fencing, on the sharp end of which they must have had a most uncomfortable seat. The stand was full to overflowing."[9]

The pain of the posteriors of the Light Blues legions was nothing compared to the assault on their eyes as Preston opened the scoring after only two minutes through Goodall and raced to a 5–0 lead by half-time. Goodall, born in London to Scottish parents and raised in Kilmarnock, notched up at least four goals (even the papers of the time stopped naming the North End scorers after a while). The Lancashire cracks had just scored their eighth goal, right near the end, with only a solitary response from Andy Peacock, when the game was ended prematurely.

Seven minutes from time, as Rangers mounted a rare attack, fans who had been forced by weight of numbers onto the track around the field crowded to the touchlines for a closer look. Inevitably, spectators spilled on to the field itself, crowding the players in the process. The players eventually made their way through the throng to the safety of the dressing rooms. Rangers were victims of their own success, and claims by the builders for a capacity of 20,000 were clearly straining credulity as thin as the patience of the Preston party, who were understandably upset by the conduct of the crowd.

The News explained: "The accommodation outside the railings was found to be too limited and the officials were obliged to allow the spectators to go inside on the track, which made room for thousands demanding admission. The spectators, evidently weary of a very slow game, began to troop out of the game some 15 minutes before the allotted time had run. The policy of allowing the people in on the track proved a fatal one, as the crowd who stood there gradually edged their way in on the field of play and finally all control was lost over them. Before the game was concluded the police tried in vain to clear the spectators off the field. The Rangers coming close on the visitors' goal was the last straw as the people fairly swarmed round the players and the field was a black mass of living beings. It was no use now to attempt further play and the game came to an abrupt close five minutes from time. The players were followed into the pavilion and some were cheered. Others, especially Goodall, being hooted."[10]

Rangers hosted Preston at the official banquet that evening in the favoured restaurant of the Light Blues, Ancell's in Glassford Street. In the absence of Vallance, it was left to vice-president Peter McNeil to address the players and officials and he enthused about the strides the club had made in the previous 15 years and the hopes for a new era symbolised by the new ground. Not surprisingly, the on-field events of a few hours earlier merited only a passing remark.

McNeil said: "I have been a member of the Rangers since it was ushered into the world and I cannot recollect an event which will bear comparison with the event we have been celebrating today and which has ended so gloriously for the club…we, as a club, have reason to congratulate ourselves on the splendid success that has attended the opening ceremony…there was, it is true, a curiosity shared by all to see the new ground but what attracted so large a crowd was the reputation of the North End more than the novelty that surrounded our enterprise.

"I am expressing the sentiments of every member of the committee when I say that we are deeply grateful to the North End for coming at this time and should it ever turn out that building extensions force them from Deepdale to some other ground the Rangers, if they are asked, will willingly go to Preston and perform the part that has been so well performed by the North End today. There is no need to say much about the game. It was played in a spirit of honest rivalry and with a true appreciation of the finer points of the game…I again express the wish that this day, which is undoubtedly the most memorable in the history of the club, will be followed by results, financial and physical, that will place the Rangers in a position that will be the envy of many and the possession of few."[11]

Preston manager Major Sudell replied briefly, complimenting Rangers on the construction of such a spectacular new ground, but calling on the press in

Glasgow to educate local fans in the matter of manners after the events of earlier in the day. The get-together broke up shortly afterwards and Preston players and officials boarded the last train south from Central Station. They did not look back as they headed for the border. Pretty soon, neither did Rangers, and even the brand new home that drew so many admiring glances from rival clubs would soon prove too restrictive for the ambitions of a club that would go on to earn a cherished status as the most successful in Scottish football history.

Chapter 13

A New Era

Alexander Graham Bell had already invented the telephone by the time Rangers and Celtic first crossed swords on 28 May 1888, but thankfully Guglielmo Marconi still had another eight years to go before his work on wireless transmission would reach its defining stages. In truth, even if radio phone-ins had been an integral feature of the media and sporting landscape at the time, it is doubtful whether many among the Light Blues' legions would have rushed to spin the dial and pour out their hearts in dismay at the 5–2 defeat that had just been suffered by their favourites.

Rangers made the short journey to the east end in the spirit of sporting friendship, to help the newly formed Celtic play the opening match at their recently constructed ground at Parkhead, built in their spare time by volunteer supporters of the club. Celtic were following in the footsteps of the country's other great outfits of Irish influence, Hibernian of Edinburgh and Harp of Dundee. The Old Firm has gone on to forge one of the most appealing yet controversial rivalries in world football, but these were more innocent times.

Celtic's 5–2 victory in front of a crowd of 2,000 against opposition featuring more second-string players than usual came courtesy of an opening goal from a former Ranger, Neil McCallum. After the match, played in an atmosphere of genuine bonhomie, both sides retired to the local St Mary's Hall, where a supper was laid on for 70 guests and a concert enjoyed as toasts were raised to the ongoing success of both clubs. The friendship between the teams was strong. The Scottish Sport, reflecting on a forthcoming Scottish Cup tie in 1892, reported: "Financially, Dumbarton or Queen's Park might have pleased treasurer Maley better, but for a genuine good match the Light Blues are favourites with the Parkhead crowd." [1]

Perhaps it was coincidence that brought the two clubs together that early summer evening, a quirk of fate that the two teams who would become so associated with the Scottish game, and indeed each other, would meet at the very first opportunity. It also certainly made sense for Celtic to approach Rangers to play their first match, not least because of the relationship between Celtic secretary John McLaughlin and the Ibrox side, but also because the Light Blues were a draw, a prized first opponent for any club kicking off an infant venture.

However, there is a hitherto unacknowledged relationship between two of the greatest figures in Celtic's history, Tom and Willie Maley, and Rangers players, committee members and other senior club figures, as together they helped establish the first open athletic club in Scotland, the Clydesdale Harriers, bringing the sport to a wider audience than when it had previously belonged to the elite of the university and public school system. This was Glasgow united against the likes of the Fettesian-Lorettonian Club, Edinburgh Collegiate AC and St Andrews University.

In total, 13 clubs joined forces when the Scottish Amateur Athletics Association (SAAA) was formed in February 1883, with a bias towards clubs in the east of Scotland bitterly opposed in the initial months by athletes in the west. However, differences were soon settled and the popularity of the sport boomed, particularly on the back of athletic events sponsored by football clubs such as St Bernard's throughout the 1870s and 1880s, where participants would compete in everything from track and cycling races to five-a-side football challenges. It was against such a backdrop that the Clydesdale Harriers were formed in May 1885 to promote athletics in general and cross-country running in particular.

Immediately, the influence of Rangers on the fledgling venture was there for all to see, not only in the membership list but also on the choice of venue for the club's first event on 3 June 1885. It was a 300-yard handicap which attracted 54 entrants to Kinning Park, with athletes such as a certain William Wilton cheered on by approximately 500 spectators. Wilton failed to emerge from his heat, finishing sixth of seven runners – scant consolation, surely, that he just held off R. Shiels, 'a plucky little youngster of 12 years,' according to the Scottish Umpire.[2] The judges that summer evening included the notorious honorary match secretary J.W. Mackay, the handicapper was committee member W.W. Tait and clerks of the course included former 1877 Scottish Cup Final forward James Watson, who would go on to become vice-president and president of Rangers, further underlining the commitment of the Light Blues to the new cause.

The 300-yard distance was marked around the pitch at Kinning Park and the event was hailed as an enormous success by the Scottish Umpire, which had been in business for less than 10 months under publisher Mackay. It came as no shock that his arch-rivals, the Scottish Athletic Journal, took a more mischievous tone and criticised the fans and the grass track in particular. In another stern editorial it lectured: "I should strongly advise the Clydesdale Harriers to switch their quarters from Kinning Park. Several prominent athletes have told me that so long as these handicaps are run on the Rangers ground they will not compete. I expect several names will be absent from the next handicap on account of the language used by the crowd and also because Kinning Park is not well adapted for running purposes. I know the Clydesdale Harriers are not of the Rangers stamp and hire Kinning Park because none other is available." [3]

The editor of the Athletic Journal needed only to glance at the membership list of the Harriers to recognise the folly of the last part of his statement. Indeed, he recognised it later that year and took a backwards leap on his earlier criticism as he slated Clydesdale for relying too heavily on the Kinning Park influence. "The Clydesdale Harriers are not doing so well as one could wish. I am afraid the members are not pulling very well together," he lamented. "A very attractive programme of club runs was arranged a couple of months ago but only two have come off through the failure of the members to turn up at the rendezvous. A meeting of the club is to take place this week at which some plain speaking will take place. If the truth must be told, the members are finding the Rangers clique in the club more than the other members can bear. I feared this from the very first."[4]

The Journal needed weep no more crocodile tears for the Harriers, as any teething problems it encountered in the early months were soon overcome. By 1887 they boasted 120 members, rising to 650 and then more than 1,000 before World War One. The Rangers influence was striking, from the appearance in the early years as life member of John Stewart of Belmore (one of the brothers credited with gifting Willie McNeil that first ball with which the young Light Blues played on Glasgow Green) to John Mellish, who rose to become vice-president of Clydesdale Harriers and president of the football club.

The membership lists of Clydesdale in its first decade are packed with great names from the history of Rangers. Peter McNeil was a member and H. and P. McNeil were official outfitters to the Harriers. Brother Willie was also a Harrier, although there is no record of Moses, a gifted runner in his youth, ever becoming part of the club. Tom and Alick Vallance were Clydesdale Harriers, as were other players including, but not exclusively, Scottish internationals James 'Tuck' McIntyre, John Cameron, Donald Gow and his brother, John Robertson Gow.

The organisation that had helped bring Rangers to the fore in the decade or so preceding the establishment of the Harriers was also evident in the development of the athletics club. In some cases, future Rangers office holders cut their teeth in the athletics division – for example James Henderson, president of the football club in 1898–99 when they went through the season without dropping a point in the League, was a Clydesdale Harriers committee man in 1887, as was John C. Lawson,

Rangers' honorary secretary between 1891 and 1892. In 1887–88 the Harriers' membership list also included T.C.B. Miller and J.F. Ness, who had each held honorary treasurer positions at Kinning Park.

The Clydesdale Harriers even had a short-lived football division in the late 1880s as Celt Maley joined forces with Rangers men John C. Lawson and A.B. McKenzie (a director at Ibrox between 1899 and 1911) to oversee a new enterprise. The Harriers attracted players from most senior clubs, although Rangers were in the majority. Athletic members also played for clubs including Queen's Park, Third Lanark, Cowlairs, St Mirren, Morton, Hamilton Accies and Celtic. When arranged, football matches were mostly of the challenge variety and clubs such as Third Lanark and even the mighty Preston North End were put to the sword. Clydesdale Harriers also entered a team in the 1889 Scottish Cup and knocked out Celtic from the competition, but football was soon dropped to allow members to focus more fully on the track and countryside run.

Certainly, Tom and Willie Maley were likely to have had more pressing sporting concerns on their minds in 1887, when Celtic were officially formed following a meeting at St Mary's Hall on 6 November. Within a month the founders of the new club, including Brother Walfrid, made the capture of Tom a priority, banking on his sympathies with the charitable Catholic principles of Celtic, initially at least, and relying on his talents as a player with clubs such as Hibs, Partick Thistle and Third Lanark. On a visit to the family home in Cathcart, Brother Walfrid was also impressed by the maturity and physical strength of younger brother Willie, whose stature had grown, in part, as a result of his endeavours on the track as a sprinter with Clydesdale Harriers. A trainee accountant, he also worked at the time for Andrew Dick, then secretary of the Harriers. Willie was thus invited to join his brother at the new club and he accepted the invitation with alacrity. He kept his membership at Clydesdale long after he joined Celtic and also became a promoter of athletics at Parkhead. His career in the sport culminated with him being elected

The Clydesdale Harriers' membership lists 1887-88 highlights the common love of athletics the Maley brothers of Celtic shared with their Rangers rivals – John Mellish, JW Mackay, Peter McNeil and AB McKenzie were all influential members of the football club during its time at Kinning Park and Ibrox.

Maley, W., Argyle Place, New Cathcart -
Maley, T.,   „   „   „   -
Mellish, J., 6 Cleveland St., Glasgow
Mackay, J. W., 18 Westmoreland Street, Glasgow
M'Neil, Peter, Union Street, Glasgow
M'Intyre, J. D , 188 Holm St , Glasgow
M'Kenzie, A. B , 98 Pollok St , Glasgow -

The Rangers team of 1888 were far from the best in even its fledgling history, but it still featured several men of Light Blues renown.

president of the SAAA in 1921.

Rangers had also become members of the SAAA in 1886, in part to facilitate the hosting of their own sports, which remained an integral part of the British athletics calendar until the early 1960s. In the early years at least, the annual athletics meeting was organised with the Harriers. The handbook of the athletics club in 1889 states, for example: "It is hoped that the same arrangements regarding the joint sports with our good friends The Rangers Football Club [will be in place] at which some of the English cracks will be invited to show their paces." The links between Rangers and the Clydesdale Harriers remained strong until the 1920s.

Admittedly, it is still a source of frustration to some club members in the present day as they search for a permanent and suitable home around the Clydebank area that they never took the opportunity to act earlier in their history. For sure, the club handbook in 1889 discussed sourcing their own ground with a cinder track "but so long as the present friendly relations are maintained with the Rangers FC, the committee consider there are no grounds for moving in this matter."

That is only one of many glowing references made to Rangers over the years in the Harriers handbooks, still lovingly treasured by their club historian,

Brian McAusland. For the most part, Clydesdale Harriers trained at the first and second Ibrox Parks and their annual meetings were held on the Rangers' grounds bar a couple of years at the turn of the 20th century when they switched to Parkhead and also Meadowside, then home to Partick Thistle.

The last reference to Rangers hosting the Clydesdale Harriers came in 1921 and the sports day ended on a financial high, but the balance in the bank could not be maintained by the athletics club and they cancelled the meeting the following year as a result of the industrial depression and uncertainty surrounding the response from the paying public. Attempts were made by Clydesdale to resurrect the annual sports in 1923 and 1924, but they were in vain and nothing came of the efforts. Rangers had only recently celebrated its jubilee season, but the Harriers were already on their way to being relegated to a footnote in the history of the football club.

The relationship with Celtic, of course, was to become enduring. The new club had quickly established itself as a major player in the Scottish game and brought new enthusiasm to the scene at an exciting and turbulent time for the development of the sport. Celtic were formed to provide assistance where needed among the Catholic population of the east end of Glasgow, most of whom were first or second generation Irish and many of whom, like local Protestants, suffered appalling living conditions. The main objective of the club was to provide the St Vincent de Paul Society with funds to maintain dinner tables for needy children in the local St Mary's, Sacred Heart and St Michael's diocese, and the Catholic community in the city quickly rallied around their club. Brother Walfrid was also motivated by the fear that his congregation would also be moved to abandon their faith, particularly with a number of Protestant soup kitchens also established in that part of the city.

As latecomers to the scene and with strong political and business acumen to guide them, Celtic decided to go for revolutionary growth rather than organic progress and players were quickly lured from the country's most prominent Catholic club, Hibs. Undoubtedly, financial inducements were offered and the Edinburgh side lost six players to an act of footballing larceny those at Easter Road with long memories and a keen knowledge of their club's history still recall bitterly today. Celtic were admitted to the SFA in August 1888, alongside long-forgotten sides such as Temperance Athletic from Glasgow, Britannia from Auchinleck, Whifflett Shamrock from Lanarkshire and Balaclava Rangers from Oban, and their on-field strength was highlighted in the first season when they reached the Scottish Cup Final, only to lose out to Third Lanark.

Inevitably, perhaps, the cash cow potential of the Parkhead outfit became a source of friction between those labelled by Celtic historians as idealists or opportunists. Celtic had quickly become one of the best-supported clubs in Britain, and in only its second season was attracting attendances of up to 25,000, such as witnessed a Scottish Cup tie against Queen's Park. By December 1897 the club had managed to buy Celtic Park outright from their landlord, even though the lease still had four years to run. Brother Walfrid, the strongest supporter of the club's charitable ethos at its foundation, had been transferred to London by 1892 and the idealists lost their strongest ally. Celtic became a public limited company in March 1897 and within a year they boasted a British record turnover of £16,267 (approximately £3,000 more than Rangers in the same season) and paid a dividend of 20 per cent, but no donations were made to charitable causes.

If Rangers had been blessed with such a privileged existence, their move to the first Ibrox Park in the summer of 1887 would have heralded the beginning of a happy ending to the 19th century for the Light Blues visionaries. However, this was a club to whom nothing had ever come easy. In a short period of time the rise of Celtic undoubtedly focused the minds of the Ibrox hierarchy – between 1889 and 1894 the income of Rangers quadrupled from £1,240 to £5,227, for example. Initially at least, things would have to get worse for the Light Blues before they got better, and their silverware collection would extend to some of the game's other major prizes. As it was, the memory of their sole success in the Charity Cup Final of 1879 was fading fast in the minds of many club members as the 1890s approached.

That 8–1 trouncing against Preston North End in August 1887 apart, the season immediately following the move to Ibrox was not without its merits, financially at least. The club reported an annual income of £2,232 – an impressive sum – almost half of which was allocated to offset the cost of building the new ground. The turnover was boosted by gate receipts of £400 from a demanding five games played at various venues across the city from November 1887 to January 1888 against Springburn side Cowlairs in the inaugural Glasgow Cup. Rangers eventually prevailed, winning the fifth match 3–1, but the tie was not without the element of protest pantomime that was so widespread in the Scottish game in the period.

This time, Rangers were chided by Cowlairs after the fourth game, which they won 2–1, for playing a professional striker, Bob Brand. Cowlairs brought evidence to the SFA claiming Brand had received £1 from his former club Queen of the South Wanderers to buy a suit in 1885. Their allegation was as threadbare as the cloth would have been after almost three years of wear and was dismissed, but Brand was suspended for two months anyway after the officials discovered he had been paid £1 to play for Hearts earlier in the season. Almost inevitably, a replay was ordered. Rangers lost the very first Final played in January 1888 to Cambuslang, going down 3–1. Rangers finally ran out of steam in a season that was also memorable for the first floodlit match staged at Ibrox, with the Scottish Corinthians (in effect, the Scottish national team) turning up for an exhibition under electric light in March. The gate receipts went to Govan charities as the Scots triumphed in the 'sunlight fixture', but the darkest season in the history of the Light Blues lay just around the corner.

The statistics for season 1888–89 were, quite frankly, woeful: 39 games played, 19 lost and seven drawn, with 108 goals conceded as annual turnover dropped by £1,000. Rangers were knocked out of the Scottish Cup in a second-round replay after a 3–0 defeat against Clyde and in the third round of the Glasgow Cup Celtic came to Ibrox and won 6–1. At the start of the season Rangers had taken the innovative step of appointing the club's first trainer, John Taylor, but he was struggling to make an impact.

The club were toiling as much off the field as on it, as the committee structure was in chaos and even the omnipresent Tom Vallance was struggling to make his influence felt as one embarrassment followed another. On New Year's Day 1889 Rangers were losing at Blackburn at the same time as Aston Villa arrived in Glasgow expecting to play their old FA Cup foes in a match they believed had been previously arranged. Nine men turned up for a game against Morton, the team lost 8–0 to Vale of Leven and even the much-heralded Ibrox Park was being criticised for a pitch that resembled a potato patch.

Meanwhile, the concept of a capacity crowd similar to that which witnessed the opening of the ground against Preston was a dim and distant memory – only 500 fans could be bothered turning up for a match against Partick Thistle. One newspaper noted: "Such apathy and the name and fame of grand old Rangers will soon be but a distant memory."

These were desperate times and temperatures were running so high that the club's half-yearly meeting in November 1888 was adjourned for a week. Seven days later resentment was still simmering and after nine hours of debate it was finally agreed to extend the numbers on the committee from five to seven in a bid to widen the circle of experience and expertise. It also marked the end for the direct, decision-making involvement in Rangers of the gallant pioneers, as Vallance stepped down at the end of the season after six years as president to be replaced by John Mellish. Rangers were moving on. Indeed, stagnation was not an option and William Wilton was the man to take them into the 20th century. More than anyone it was his vision, passion and commitment at a crucial watershed in the development of Scottish football that relegated to the annals of history the internecine squabbles that had so characterised much of the 1880s for the Light Blues.

Wilton was born in Largs on 9 June 1865, a son to James and Janet Wilton. William's father, a stonemason, died aged 52 in Millport in March 1873 and soon after the family moved to Govan, where Janet set up home in Crookston Street with William and his brother Daniel, seven years his senior (they had at least one other brother, Charles). By the age of 15, William was working as an office boy at a sugar broker and he would later earn promotion to the position of mercantile clerk, thus setting out on a career path that suggested diligence and discipline, the very traits for which he would soon become so respected and cherished at Rangers.

In his spare time, William was a member of the Glasgow Select Choir, a fine tenor by all accounts, and it is to the eternal benefit of Rangers fans that he could hold a tune better than he could his position on the football field. He became a member of Rangers on 24 September 1883 aged 18, but his skills as a player with the second team 'Swifts' were open to question. What could not be doubted, however, even at such a tender age, were his leadership abilities off the field and he was quickly promoted to match secretary for the second string. His responsibility stopped short of picking the Swifts' team, but he organised fixtures and travel details and soon became an integral and influential figure behind the scenes at Kinning Park and Ibrox.

In 1887 he argued successfully at a members' meeting for an increase in the numbers making up the selection committee after that poor run of results at first-team level. In May 1889, at the age of 23, he was put forward for the key position of match secretary of Rangers and saw off the challenge of James Gossland, an experienced committee man who had been honorary secretary of the club as early as 1883.

The promotion of Wilton was vital for several reasons, not least the drive and energy he brought to the club at a time in which the landscape of Scottish football was changing forever. The Football League had been established in England in the summer of 1888, the brainchild of a Scot, Aston Villa patriarch William McGregor, and a natural consequence of the move to professionalism south of the border in 1885. In total, 12 clubs started the first season in the Football League, all of them from north of Birmingham – Accrington Stanley, Aston Villa, Blackburn Rovers, Bolton Wanderers, Burnley, Derby County, Everton, Notts County, Preston North End, Stoke City, West Bromwich Albion and Wolverhampton Wanderers.

A structured set-up of regular fixtures was crucial, not least for the club moneymen, who were charged with turning over sizeable sums to pay the weekly wage bill. The new division was a roaring success and in its first season the English clubs attracted 602,000 fans to their games, an average of 4,600 per game. By the outbreak of World War One the Football League, by then 20 clubs strong, was attracting almost nine million fans a year, an average of 23,100 at every game.

Inevitably, in 1890, Scotland followed suit, although professionalism would not be officially recognised in the game until 1893, in part to stem the tide of players travelling south to earn their riches legitimately, rather than under the table in their homeland.

Peter Fairly, the secretary of Renton, set the ball rolling on a Scottish League on 13 March 1890 when he sent a letter to 14 clubs across the Clyde–Forth Valley, inviting them to send two representatives to Holton's Commercial Hotel in Glassford Street, Glasgow, on Thursday 20 March to consider the question of organising a league for Scottish clubs (in effect, there was a central belt bias and the Dundee clubs, for example, would soon express fears over their inability to attract clubs to play them on Tayside). Mellish, as president, and Wilton, as match secretary, attended for Rangers.

All but two of the clubs invited sent representatives: Queen's Park and Clyde. Clyde would later be welcomed into the fold, but Queen's Park were opposed to the new set-up as the avowed amateurs correctly foretold the arrival of a professionalism they considered elitist and selfish in what they had always considered a gentleman's game.

In addition to Rangers, the clubs who turned out for the meeting were Abercorn, Cambuslang, Celtic, Cowlairs, Dumbarton, Heart of Midlothian, Renton, St Bernard's, St Mirren, Third Lanark and Vale of Leven. The proposal to form a league was given the backing by the majority of those present, but with conditions. Clubs were still keen to operate under the umbrella of the SFA and there was clearly further discussion to be held on the distribution of gate monies.

The Scottish Sport newspaper admitted it was disappointed with the contribution of Mellish to the debate, chiding him for adding little that had not already been said previously. Journalist Number One went on: "Mr Mellish's words…were few, but were those of a diplomatist. In conjunction with Mr Wilton, he had come there to listen and report. Provided the league was got up in a proper way and for the benefit and furtherance of Scottish football he could see no harm in the departure, but it must be strictly amateur and recognise the SFA as the governing body. He had no instructions to act definitely."[5]

A seven-man sub-committee, including Wilton, was formed to draft rules and a constitution for the fledging Scottish League and it was formally inaugurated on 30 April 1890, with 11 clubs competing (St Bernard's were not elected by their fellow clubs in a dispute over professionalism, in addition to the no-shows from Queen's Park and Clyde). As part of the new set-up it had also been agreed that League games should take precedence over all others, Scottish Cup ties excluded, and teams were forbidden from playing friendlies in a town or city where a Scottish League fixture had been arranged that day.

The boot was now on the other foot and, almost two decades after Queen's Park wrote to Rangers refusing their request for a game because they had no private pitch to call their own, it was now the turn of the Light Blues to send a rejection letter to the amateurs. Along with every other club in the new Scottish League, Rangers politely declined a request from Queen's Park in the summer of 1890 for challenge matches in the forthcoming months as they were already committed to the new structure. Wilton was to remain a key player in the new set-up, firstly as League treasurer and then, in 1895, as secretary.

History records Rangers as the first champions of the Scottish League or, more accurately, co-champions as they shared the trophy with Dumbarton. In truth, the new competition at that stage was still considered a poor relation to the Scottish Cup and Glasgow Charity Cup, although that would soon change. Off the field, Wilton's firm guidance was proving invaluable and on it the leadership of new signing John McPherson was to prove invaluable in the decade that lay ahead as a lynchpin of the first of the Rangers super teams. McPherson, a forward, was signed from Cowlairs in June 1890 and he went on to make a sterling contribution in almost every position for the Light Blues, particularly inside-forward. He scored the first ever hat-trick in the Scottish League, against Cambuslang in the first month of the new competition, and in total he won five championship medals, three Scottish Cup badges and 13 Scotland caps, in addition to seven Glasgow Cups and two Charity Cups. He retired in 1902 and became a director of Rangers in 1907, serving the club diligently until his death in 1926.

Until the closing weeks of that debut League campaign Rangers had lost only once, against Dumbarton, and with three games still to play were just four points behind their rivals. Dumbarton had the chance to clinch the League title when they travelled to Ibrox for their last game of the season, although the Light Blues still had two further games to play. However, Rangers triumphed 4–2 in front of a crowd of 10,000, with such healthy numbers underlining the importance fans had already began to attach to the new competition. McPherson scored once in the hard-fought victory and Rangers knew three points from their last two games would clinch the Championship outright.

They were not secured, thanks to the efforts of Celtic, who won 2–1 at Parkhead on the second last day of the season courtesy of a late winner from Johnnie Madden. Rangers were still two points behind Dumbarton as the final regular game of the League season approached and a 4–1 win over Third Lanark at Ibrox took the title to a play-off at Cathkin Park. Again, a crowd of 10,000 emphasised the importance of the occasion in the eyes of the fans and, although Rangers raced to a two-goal lead at the interval, with strikes from David Hislop and Hugh McCreadie, the Sons hit back in the second half with two goals as the game ended in an admirable draw and a title shared.

Rangers had lost out in the Glasgow Cup that season in the quarter-final stages after three replays against Third Lanark (the free and easy way Third Lanark full-back Smith had used his hands to control the ball during these games was a major factor in the introduction of the penalty kick rule the following season). Rangers did not compete in the Glasgow Charity Cup as a result of pressure of fixtures on the back of the new League season. Their Scottish Cup campaign ended in the first round with a 1–0 defeat at Celtic and, although the season was considered a success, Rangers – and other clubs in the Scottish game – were becoming more and more mindful of the strength of the new team from the east end of Glasgow. The old order of the Scottish game was changing for good as the influence of Queen's Park waned on the back of their stubborn yet noble support for amateurism. Fittingly, perhaps, they won the last of their 10 Scottish Cups in 1893 with a 2–1 win over Celtic, just weeks before professionalism was publicly embraced in the Scottish game.

However, Queen's Park survived into the 20th century and continue to survive to the present day. Within a decade of the establishment of the new Scottish League six standard-bearers had gone to the wall: Abercorn, Cambuslang, Cowlairs, Renton, Vale of Leven and Dumbarton, although the latter would emerge again. To think, as recently as 1888 Renton had been acclaimed champions of the world after the Scottish Cup holders thrashed the FA Cup winners West Brom 4–1 in front of 10,000 fans at Hampden and followed it with another victory against the Invincibles of Preston North End. Financially crippled, they tendered their resignation from the Scottish League five games into the 1897–98 season, with Hamilton Accies stepping in as replacements.

A none-too-subtle shift was taking place as the early clubs from small towns and villages such as Renton and Alexandria gave way to sides from bigger industrial centres.Rangers were at the forefront of the changes, with Wilton the dominant figure as the endeavours of the previous two decades finally helped to deliver a sustained period of success on the field and startling progress off it.

Before the decade was over they had won the Scottish Cup three times, their first success a 3–1 win over Celtic at Hampden in 1894. Old Firm fixtures had quickly vital for bragging rights as the the new rivlary was shaped and formed. Rangers won the Glasgow Cup four times in the 1890s, including a win over Celtic at Cathkin Park in February 1893.

The Scottish Sport of 21 February told the delightful tale of the urchin who ran all the way from the Third Lanark ground to Paisley Road Toll to deliver the score to the customers of Tom Vallance, who were gathered outside 'The Club.' In those innocent times of limited media and no mobile phones or internet access, it reported: "A crowd was patiently waiting the verdict . . .the first news merchant to arrive was an urchin, who had done the distance in record time. He had little more than sufficient wind left to exclaim: 'Rangers 3, Celtic 1.' At first this was considered too good to be true, so the lad was pounced upon, and not until he had solemnly declared: 'Strike me deid if it's no true,' did the crowd break forth into . . . we will leave the rest to the varied imagination of our readers."

Rangers also won the Glasgow Charity Cup twice that decade, to add to their earlier success in 1879. Rangers may have had to wait another eight years for their next championship success after 1891, but it was worth it as they romped through the 18-game card without conceding a single point, a world record that still stands to this day. Business was booming, with the club's annual turnover that year an impressive £15,800.

Wilton, as League secretary, sounded almost abashed as he praised his Rangers for their achievement, "Modesty, born of my close connection with the champions, hampers my eulogising them to the extent their great performance warrants. A world's record, however, especially when it is an unbeatable record, is an achievement that will speak for itself as the years go by."[6] It was a watershed year in more ways than one as Rangers Football Club ceased to exist, replaced on 10 May 1899 by Rangers Football Club Limited. In total, £12,000 of shareholder capital was raised to fund the new Ibrox Park and secure still further the club's long-term future, with Wilton appointed manager and secretary.

The move to a second Ibrox Park had been on the cards for several seasons as the popularity of the team and the booming population of the south side helped push crowds ever upwards. As early as 1892 the club had been forced to extend the first Ibrox Park, including a new grandstand, but even a 36,000 capacity proved inadequate in the end. The arrival of the subway at Copland Road in 1896 added to the already existing railway station that served Ibrox on the Glasgow to Paisley line and made accessing the stadium even easier for fans from other parts of the city. Crowds of upwards of 30,000 for major matches were commonplace and there was another solid economic argument for a new ground as Rangers sought to keep pace with Parkhead and Hampden and attract major Cup Finals and international games to the area.

A new era had been entered in the 1890s and the door to further prosperity had opened by the turn of the 20th century with the move to the new ground. Rangers have known hardships and heartaches since 1872, none more poignant than the memory of almost 100 fans tragically killed in two disasters in 1902 and 1971. All the while the team has carried the hopes and aspiration of millions of supporters at home and abroad onto the field of play wherever and whenever they have performed. There have been rich harvests of success and occasionally the barren crop of failure; however, Rangers have never stood as anything but their club to the proud people who have supported it since those earliest days on Glasgow Green.

The gallant pioneers have long gone, their voluble chatter no longer echoing around West End Park as they discuss the formation of their infant enterprise. However, the passion remains, recorded in every hoarse shout and cry from supporters on a matchday at Ibrox. Moses and Peter McNeil, William McBeath, Peter Campbell and Tom Vallance were the standard-bearers. In their shadows, generation after generation have been happy to follow follow.

Chapter 14

The Founders Trail

Stan Butler and Jack Harper can retire the uniforms because when it comes to On The Buses no-one can hold a candle to Iain McColl and Gordon Bell. As Gordon stamps another ticket for the Founders Trail and Rangers fans pile excitedly onto the open top bus parked outside the club shop at Ibrox, Iain grabs the microphone with all the confidence of a cabaret club veteran and begins to tell a story that will keep his audience spellbound for the next three hours. "To think," he says later, another successful tour negotiated, "there were people, even within Ibrox, who told us Rangers fans wouldn't be interested in the early years' history of the club. Thankfully, we didn't believe it for a second."

At noon on the dot, the bus pulls out onto Edmiston Drive and swings a left towards Paisley Road West with another capacity crowd on board. More than 2,000 fans have follow-followed in the footsteps of the gallant pioneers since the first tour in 2009. We're approaching a half century of them now and tickets are no sooner available than they're snapped up by fans eager to know more about the life of Moses and Peter McNeil, William McBeath, Peter Campbell and Tom Vallance.

Iain adds: "If anything, the history of the club has come to mean more to supporters these last couple of years when, quite frankly, Rangers has been under the control of sharks. You wonder if Craig Whyte or Charles Green would have offered to man the turnstiles, as Tom Vallance did at the first Ibrox Park when he was president of the club. Fans are taking comfort from the past in the hope men of the character and integrity of the Vallances and McNeils will emerge again to lead the club to a brighter future."

Iain and Gordon, who are often joined by fan and fellow historian Neil Stobie, first met via fan website FollowFollow when their shared love of the early years of Rangers collided online. Soon, they were meeting on the south side for a pint and speaking enthusiastically of all they knew and information they had gathered and were keen to share. By coincidence, the research for the original Gallant Pioneers book was already well underway. Serendipity would lead everyone to the point today where generations of Rangers fans have a genuine thirst for knowledge of players and personalities about whom so little had been known only a decade ago.

On we go along Paisley Road West passing, like a million Rangers fans before us, a row of unremarkable tenements on our left. Iain reveals to the supporters on the Trail: "Tom Vallance lived in various locations around Glasgow, one of which was 282 Paisley Road West. This block here was formerly known as Lendl Terrace and Tom lived at number two in 1890." Tom's name features heavily throughout the commentary and, after the tour, Iain isn't afraid to admit to favouritism.

He adds: "Bill Struth is quite rightly acknowledged as the man who established many of the traits we've been proud to see associated with Rangers - honesty, integrity, decency, fair play. But he tipped his hat to the gallant pioneers in that famous speech about the trials to be overcome and I'm sure Tom was at the forefront of his thoughts.

"It was Tom who resigned his position as president in October 1883 before a game against Dumbarton, with whom there had been bad blood. Rangers players refused to sanction his appointment as umpire, fearing he'd be too fair, and Tom was rightly angered. Some of the current board should look to the selflessness of Tom, who organised the fund-raising concerts that raised the money to build the first Ibrox Park. Tom played a crucial, hands-on role in ensuring the club survived and prospered at a difficult time for the amateurs of Scottish football, especially as the English game was packed with professionals and their teams had money to spend.

"It's also amazing to think of the three man strand that links Rangers in 1872 to the club we still love today. Tom was guest of honour at the club for a match against Sporting Club Vienna in 1933 and attended the gala dinner later that evening at the St Enoch's Hotel. One of

C'moan, get aff . . . Ibrox clippies Iain McColl and Gordon Bell prepare for another sell-out Founders Trail tour from the stadium.

our scorers in the 3-3 draw against the Austrians was Bob McPhail. Mr McPhail was also in the stadium in 1997 when Ally McCoist broke his Rangers league scoring record. Tom Vallance would have spoken with Bob McPhail, who chatted to Ally McCoist. Three Rangers greats linked, from Flesher's Haugh right through to the present day. Amazing."

The bus meanders along, past the William Hill's at 219 Paisley Road West, next door to which Tom also lived, and The Viceroy Pub at Paisley Road Toll, which Vallance also owned as bar/restaurant 'The Club' in the 1890s. Astonishingly many of its features, including the dining room, survive to this day. On we go, past another boozer, The Angel, once owned by Sir Alex Ferguson and, decades before him, gallant pioneer James 'Tuck' McIntyre, before the bus swings into Bridge Street.

Dewar's Temperance Hotel once stood at number 11 and hosted the meeting which led to the formation of the SFA in 1873 - Rangers, as mere pups, were not invited to join. Across the road, at number 14, was the entrance to Bridge Street railway station, where hundreds of Rangers fans gathered in 1882 to bid Tom Vallance a fond farewell on his move to Assam to work in the tea plantations.

After 20 minutes the bus makes its first stop at Glasgow Green where, over the years, scrubland and red ash have given may to manicured show pitches and state-of-the-art artificial surfaces. The pitches are also several metres higher than in Victorian times as earth removed during the construction of the Glasgow underground system, which began in 1891, was piled here by contractors. Nevertheless, the geography remains the same and even the clump of trees and bushes, behind which the earliest Rangers players stripped and changed - when they were not turning out in their civvies - can still be picked out from the earliest maps. Supporters gather to hear of the trials and tribulations of the club in its earliest years and then move inside to the modern new sports pavilion Moses and his friends could never have imagined in 1872.

Here, on the wall, is fixed a plaque in honour of the Rangers forefathers, commissioned and funded by fans on the back of Iain's efforts when the Founders' Trail was but a dream. He said: "I approached Glasgow City Council back in 2006 with a proposal to place a plaque within the Football Centre on Flesher's Haugh marking the birthplace of our club and to acknowledge the determination to succeed shown by our four kids back in 1872. After lengthy negotiations, we reached agreement to honour our founders by way of a plaque that was to be placed at the reception area. Artwork and text was chosen and given to our plaque manufacturer. The club these lads formed has given so much to the city of Glasgow that it was time the city gave something back."

The plaque was unveiled Sunday 6th September 2009 when, fittingly, Peter McNeil's grand-daughter Heather Lang drew back the curtain in front of a gathering of fans and Rangers VIPs, including Sandy Jardine and John MacMillan of the Rangers Supporters Association. Local councillor Alison Thewliss also attended, along with George Parsonage, the honorary president of Clyde Amateur Rowing Club. Iain added: "It was a poignant and emotional day. It was wonderful to have Heather unveil the plaque as her grandfather played such a huge role in establishing the club. Interest in the boys and the early years history has just continued to grow and grow."

Back onboard, the bus continues its route from the east end back into the city centre, passing Hutchison Street, where Tom Vallance owned the Metropolitan Restaurant at number 40. He hosted a dinner there in April 1898 to mark the 21st

Anniversary of the Gers' first Scottish Cup final in against Vale of Leven. On we go, past number 28 Glassford St, where Holton's Commercial Hotel once stood. The Scottish Football League was formed there in March 1890, with William Wilton one of its architects and Rangers, of course, shared the first title with Dumbarton.

Further up the

Former team-mates Tom Vallance and Tuck McIntyre owned pubs and restaurants that were just a stone's throw from each other at Paisley Road Toll. The dining room of Tom's Club restaurant still exists today at the Viceroy Bar.

"THE CLUB"

Tom Vallance & James 'Tuck' McIntyre.

Tuck McIntyre's Pub Then & Now.

It no longer stands, but Bridge Street train station, where Rangers fans gathered to see off Tom Vallance on his journey to India, was once a Glasgow landmark.

BRIDGE STREET 1865

BRIDGE STREET TRAIN STATION

street, on the left hand side, is the most important building in Glasgow's business history and yet one about which few Rangers fans in the modern era would ever have given much thought. The Trades House was built in 1605 and, the medieval Glasgow Cathedral apart, is the oldest building in the city still used for its original purpose. Its membership is still active today and is involved with key educational and charitable projects aimed at developing the craft skills of the youth of the city.

However, in the second half of the 19th century is was an important administrative and social hub for Rangers, along with Ancell's restaurant next door. Monthly and annual gatherings were held at the Trades House, including the first ever annual meeting in 1873. Ancell's also hosted the after-match banquet with Preston North End to celebrate the opening of the first Ibrox Park in 1887. Founder Peter McNeil recalled in a rousing speech: "I have been a member of the Rangers since it was first ushered into the world and I cannot recollect an event which will bear comparison with today." Wilton was also appointed the club's first manager there on 1 June 1899 and the club held its first meeting as a limited company there three months later.

The tour bus turns left into Ingram Street and left again into Queen Street as the easy flow of the conversation among fans is matched the Iain's commentary. All the time, eyes flicker among supporters with fresh recognition of a city that is slowly giving up its secret history of Rangers. Iain nods down to the right of the bus

In the spring of 1872 four young boys, Moses McNeil, Peter McNeil, Peter Campbell and William McBeath left their rowing boat on the nearby River Clyde and upon these fields formed a football team.

This team was to be known as The Rangers Football Club.

It was their determination to succeed that led to The Rangers becoming one of the world's most famous clubs.

Perseverance paid off for Iain McColl of the Founders Trail when city fathers agreed to pay tribute to the Gallant Pioneers at Glasgow Green.

as we approach Argyle Street and says: "Rangers set up headquarters in the Steels Hotel in 1888 when they decided all club business would be discussed on a weekly basis. The Hotel stood at the corner of Queen St and Argyle Street and meetings were also held just along the road at the McCulloch Hotel, now part of the St Enoch's Centre."

Passing the side of Queen Street Station, the Buchanan Street underground entrance on Dundas Street swallows up thousands of Rangers fans every other Saturday as they make their way to Ibrox by train and subway. As they head down the moving escalator, few realise on the same spot 140 years ago the boys who formed the club would meet to celebrate their triumphs and shake off defeats with a few drinks.

The Athole Arms Hotel once stood here and it was where Rangers and Vale of Leven players retired after the famous 1877 Scottish Cup final. Tom Vallance was also elected president of the club in the Athole in 1883 on his return from India. Monthly meetings took place in the hostelry and membership requests were processed, including one from a certain Samuel Dow, whose former pub still stands next door proudly bearing his name.

The bus meanders around George Square and along St Vincent Street before turning into Renfield Street and towards Union Street. Suddenly, Iain has to quicken the pace of his commentary to include all this stretch of a few hundred metres has incorporated in the story of Rangers. He says: "Harry and Peter McNeil went into business together as sports goods retailers and were frequent advertisers

TRADES HOUSE, GLASSFORD STREET

The following intimation which appeared in the *Glasgow Herald* of Friday last will interest a large portion of our readers :—

"VALLANCE—DUNLOP.—At 3 Kersland Street, Hillhead, on the 18th inst., by the Rev. J. Fraser Grahame, B.D., of Belmont Church, Hillhead, Thomas Vallance, jun., to Marion, eldest daughter of James Dunlop, Esq."

We extend our hearty congratulations to Tom and his good lady, who, we may mention, is a sister of W. Dunlop, who in the heyday of the Rangers played extreme right with Hill. We are sure that even on such a happy occasion, and with such an excellent excuse, Tom would feel a pang of regret at being absent from Ibrox Park on Saturday. We have no doubt, however, that, although absent in the body, he was present in the spirit. Wonder what he ejaculated when he read the result?

The Trades House is one of the best known buildings in Glasgow city centre, but few Rangers fans are aware of its connection to the earliest days of the club's history.

in the press. They had premises at 21-23 Renfield Street from 1878-1883.

"Originally, they were at 105 Union Street, which is now a Money Shop, but left after a year in 1878 to move up the road. Their brothers John and Willie took over the premises and ran a florists. Harry and Peter moved back down to Union Street in 1883 to number 91, which is now a Chinese restaurant and stayed there until 1896, when the business partnership was dissolved. Bizarrely, for sports shop owners, adverts for the period also reveal the brothers offered a barbershop

The move in 1888 to Steel's Hotel, on the corner of Queen Street and Argyle Street, underlined the growing admin responsibilities as Scottish football moved to become even more structured and organised.

STEEL'S HOTEL, QUEENS STREET.

The Rangers have resolved to have official head-quarters in the centre of the city, where their committee and sub-committee meetings can be held, where the members can make sure of meeting the officials, and where all communications regarding club business can be addressed with the certainty of reaching its proper destination. This is a step in the right direction, and we congratulate the committee upon the indication which it affords of a definite desire on their part to raise the status of the club. The rendezvous has not yet been definitely fixed, but we understand that negotiations are pending with Steel's Hotel in Queen St.

THE SCOTTISH UMPIRE, 12TH MAY 1888

The Rangers official head-quarters is now Steel's Hotel, Queen Street. Business communications for any of the officials of the club left there will be forwarded to their proper destination. The match committee meets there every Monday.

THE SCOTTISH UMPIRE, 19TH MAY 1888

and shampoo service for a spell. Moses was also employed as a salesman for almost 20 years at 70 Union Street by draper Hugh Lang."

The passion of Iain and Gordon for the club's story is reflected at every turn of phrase, every turn of the guide book lovingly designed and distributed to supporters on the tour and in every turn of the road in Glasgow city centre. The tone doesn't drop as we pass Wellington Street, where the club held those fund-raising concerts at the Waterloo Rooms in March and December 1887. Under the guidance of Vallance, enough money was quickly raised to build a new ground on the meadowlands of Ibrox.

We continue up Hope Street, Iain excitedly pointing number 183, where Tom owned the Monico Restaurant, which later became the Landsdowne. The Monico's walls were adorned with paintings by local artists, including some of Tom's own work. He was president of the Restaurant and Hotel-Keepers Association of Glasgow for several years and Iain also nods in the direction of number 211, the former offices of Aitken's Brewers, where Tom and his brother Alick were both employed.

Later, Ian adds: "The overwhelming response of fans who have taken the tour these last four years is to say they feel closer to the club. You think of the Victorian era and you imagine sober old men in dark suits and a gulf between boardroom and support. Nothing could have been further from the truth. Rangers were a club of the people from the very start and I never tire of reading that quote about the working class of Glasgow rushing straight from the factories to watch the team play the 1877 Scottish Cup final. It's not always about share issues and administration. Like many Rangers fans I've worked in the city centre and passed places such as Trades House a thousands times without ever realising its significance in the history of our club. The tour helps visualise all that and takes you back to a time of innocence in our history. If only those who have been running our club the last few years could invoke the spirit of the past."

Slowly, the city centre is left behind although not without a nod to number 148 Bath Street, the site of the former Alexandra Hotel, where Rangers were presented with the Scottish Cup for the first time in history following their 3-1 defeat of Celtic at Hampden on 17 February 1894. It's a pub question that stands the test of time today: "How many times does the name of Rangers appear on the Scottish Cup?" The answer is none at all - the cup quickly filled with the engraved names of its earliest winners, mostly Queen's Park, and Rangers were relegated to its supporting plinth.

Suddenly, we're over the M8 and into the heartlands of the founding fathers, the Sandyford area, where they lived on moving to the city in the 1870s. There are nods of acknowledgment to various home addresses around Berkeley Street and Cleveland Street, as well as the entry gates of Kelvingrove Park, through which the boys strolled that spring day in 1872 to discuss and ferment the idea for their new club. Across the road sits the Queens Rooms in Clifton Street, where the club held their annual meetings in 1875 and 1877 and also hosted a ball in 1884.

Further west we travel along Dumbarton Road before pulling in at Partick Bus Station for the short stroll to Hamilton Crescent, which hosted two of the three cup final matches against Vale of Leven in 1877 in which the young Rangers sealed their reputation. The West of Scotland Cricket Ground was also the venue for the first ever international football match, a goalless draw between Scotland and England in 1872. Little has changed at the club in the intervening 150 years, with only a small plaque mounted almost out of sight on a side wall paying tribute to its place in world football history.

The hungry bears are offered the chance of a sandwich and a pint and the fans,

THE RED LION 1888

In the 1890s the licence for the Red Lion was transferred to former captain of the Rangers Football Club Alexander Vallance paying an annual rent of £175. There was only one brand of ale stocked in the Red Lion, Aitken's Pale ale, however the pub was very busy and one could always get their rarebits at any time of the day.

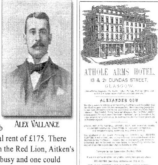

ALEX VALLANCE

Alick Vallance, like his brother Tom, was a successful Glasgow publican and a towering influence on Rangers in the early years.

GEORGE SQUARE 1870

most of whom were unknown to each other just a couple of hours ago, chat easily in the comfort of their shared heritage of support for Rangers. In between the raffle and herding everyone back on the bus Iain and Gordon reflect on the pride they feel at connecting fans with the club via its historical links. Iain says: "It's heartwarming and encouraging to see the way the fans have rallied behind the Founders Trail, especially the younger generation, who can take the story forward for us all.

"We've welcomed groups from supporters clubs including Port Glasgow and Greenock, Cumbernauld, Kirkintilloch, Tannochside, Carronshore, the Arthur Numan loyal, the Baku Bears, District Bar, Hong Kong Bears, Isle of Harris Rangers and the Coulport Naval Base Bears. Supporters come from all walks of life and from all over the country. The club have embraced it. We've had Rangers TV on the tour and we work closely with the Ibrox marketing department to ensure we have a presence in the club shop on tour days and everyone is given a merchandise voucher.

"We did our first couple of tours on foot, but there was just too much distance to cover and they were almost sending out the search parties for us at the end of the day. We've also run a couple of tours out to Rosneath and Garelochhead to see the birthplaces of the founding fathers and they have proved overwhelmingly popular and we'd like to do even more. We're recognised by Visitscotland and have an excellent relationship with Glasgow City Marketing. Still, we're always keen to expand and maybe team up with local hotels and other organisations, such as schools and colleges and introduce an education programme.

"We're also working on creating the Founders Trail road show which we hope, with the backing of the club, will see us host presentation evenings at supporters clubs where distance from Glasgow is an issue. We also had a stall at the West End Festival on Byres Road in 2013. It was a huge success and raised fantastic sums of money for Erskine and Yorkhill Hospitals. We're proud of the money we have raised along the way for good causes, which also includes the Rangers Youth Development Fund."

Fed and watered, the fans return to the bus for another mini-tour

The Monico Restaurant in Hope Street, also known as The Lansdowne, became recognised by other names when it was under the control of Tom Vallance - including The Strand. Tom was a regular advertiser in the city's newspapers.

Tom Vallance's restaurants in Glasgow appealed to a broad mix of the Victorian citizens in the second city of the Empire.

A smart thing in Post Cards.

around the west end, with a thumbs up at the Kelvingrove Museum and Art Gallery, built in 1901 on the back of funds raised by the Great Glasgow Exhibition of 1888. One of the main events was a game between the Rangers Ancients and Queens Park played on a makeshift pitch on what is now part of the Western Infirmary. The bus turns along the Kelvin Walkway and into Gibson Street, past the tenement flat where Peter McNeil lived with his young family before he was sadly declared insane and sent to Hawkhead Asylum.

The roads are getting narrower now, especially when the bus turns off Woodlands road and into the streets where Burnbank, the second home of Rangers, once stood. Rangers opened their 12 month tenure at the ground in 1875 with a game against Vale of Leven and ended it with a match against Clydesdale. However, it has long since been covered by tenement flats and other developments. Moses also lived nearby in 29 Baliol Street, then known as Stanley Street, at the turn of the 20th century.

The tour also passes the site of Grant Street, where former Rangers president George Goudie lived at number 89. His name was referenced during the club's recent financial crisis for his selfless dedication in loaning the club £30 to pay off mounting debts in 1883 to prevent it from going under. He is buried in Lambhill cemetery, but when Iain, Gordon and Neil Stobie found his final resting place the stone was lying face down. A discreet word with council staff who know all about the founding fathers and the stone was lifted and put back in place.

THE QUEENS ROOMS

KELVINGROVE PARK

The Queen's Rooms in the Sandyford district, a venue for agms and even a club ball in the late 1870s and early 1880s.

The tour is drawing to a close, but not before crossing the river again for a visit to Kinning Park, where the club played its home games for 11 years from September 1876 until the creep of industrialisation forced Rangers further west to Ibrox. Those who question the suggestion of the remote positioning of the district that has long since become the club's spiritual home are left in no doubt when Iain refers them to one of the pictures on the handout as the bus passes Ibrox Parish Church. These days, it is a popular climbing centre and it has featured heavily in the history of Rangers, not least as the church which opened its doors for Bill Struth's funeral in 1956. it is remarkable to think that, in 1875, it stood in almost splendid isolation, surrounded by fields and meadows.

There is one last stop to be made before the bus pulls up outside the front entrance at Edmiston Drive and that's Craigton Cemetery to pay tribute at the gravesides of both the McNeils and, further up the hill, Mr Struth himself. The fans stand in quiet remembrance, their link and support of their club reinforced by all they have seen and learned in the previous few hours. Iain adds: "It wasn't enough for the founding fathers to establish a boys club, it had to be the best football club it could possibly be. No-one who takes the tour thinks anything other than they succeeded in their goal."

Appendix

References

Foreword

1.   - STV website, www.sport.stv.tv 14 December 2012: 'European clubs' body downgrades Rangers' status but recognises history.'

2.   - Sunday Mail, 23 September 2012.

Chapter 1 – The Gallant Pioneers

1.   -The Times, 9 October 2004.

2.   -Bill Leckie, The Sun, 19 March 2007.

3.   -The Only Game, Roddy Forsyth, page 19.

Chapter 2 – The Birth of the Blues

1.   -Daily Record, 10 April 1953, page 7.

2.   -100 Years of Scottish Sport by Rodger Baillie, page 20.

3.   -Among Friends by Alastair Dunnett, page 27.

4.   -Rangers Supporters' Association Annual 1954, page 47.

5.   -Daily Record and Mail, 22 April 1935.

6.   -Helensburgh and Garelochhead Times, 4 January 1882.

7.   -Evening Times, 10 April 1923.

8.   -Scottish Football Annual 1878–79.

9.   -'Association Football and the Men Who Made It', by Alfred Gibson and William Pickford, volume four The Game in Scotland, by Robert Livingstone.

10.   -Scottish Athletic Journal, 23 August 1887.

11.   -25 Years Football by Old International.

12.   -The Story of the Rangers by John Allan (Desert Island Books edition), page 11.

13.   -Sport and Patronage: Evidence from 19th Century Argyllshire by Lorna Jackson, Edinburgh University.

14.   -The Story of the Rangers by John Allan, page 10.

15.   -ibid, page 10.

16.   -Daily Record and Mail, 22 April 1935, page 20.

Chapter 3 – Moses McNeil

1.   -The Queen's Park Football Club by Richard Robinson, 1920, page 258.
2.   -North British Daily Mail, 7 February 1876.
3.   -Evening Times, 10 April 1923.
4.   -Daily Record, 18 April 1938.

Chapter 4 – Valiant, Virtuous – and Vale of Leven

1.   -The Old Vale and its Memories by James Ferguson and James Graham Temple, page 175.
2.   -ibid, pages 180–81.
3.   -Scottish Football Annual 1877–78 edition, page 76.
4.   -The Queen's Park Football Club by Richard Robinson, 1924, page 423.
5.   -Scottish Athletic Journal, 27 September 1887.
6.   -50 Years of Reminiscences of Scottish Cricket by D.D. Bone.
7.   -The Story of the Rangers by John Allan, pages 20–21.
8.   -25 Years Football by Old International, pages 28–33.
9.   -North British Daily Mail, 19 March 1877.
10.   -Glasgow News, 9 April 1877.
11.   -Scottish Football Annual 1877–78, page 76.
12.   -Glasgow News, 13 April 1877.

Chapter 5 – Peter McNeil

1.   -The Rangers FC by True Blue, Scottish Football Annual 1881–82.
2.   -Scottish Athletic Journal, 27 April 1883.
3.   -Minutes from SFA AGM on 25 April 1883.
4.   -Scottish Athletic Journal, 23 February 1883.
5.   -ibid, 16 March 1883.
6.   -ibid, 18 February 1885.
7.   -ibid, 25 May 1883.
8.   -Evening Times/Glasgow Herald, 1 April 1901.
9.   -Information from Parish of Govan Combination, Application for Relief (Assistant Inspector's Report), Mitchell Library.
10.   -Hawkhead Health Records for Peter McNeil, from NHS Archives.
11.   -Scottish Referee, 5 April 1901.

Chapter 6 – Sweet Charity

1.   -Glasgow News, 21 April 1879.
2.   -North British Daily Mail, 22 April 1879.
3.   -Glasgow News, 21 April 1879.
4.   -ibid, 30 April 1879.
5.   -ibid, 1 May 1879.
6.   -ibid, 2 May 1879.
7.   -ibid, 2 May 1879.
8.   -ibid, 3 May 1879.
9.   -Glasgow Evening Citizen, 21 May 1879.

Chapter 7 – Peter Campbell

1.   -Accessed at Caird Library, National Maritime Museum, Greenwich.
2.   -'The Folklores and Genealogies of Uppermost Nithsdale', courtesy of Dumfries Library.
3.   -Dumbarton Herald, 18 May 1871.
4.   -Scottish Football Reminiscences and Sketches by D.D. Bone, page 39.
5.   -Accessed at Caird Library, National Maritime Museum, Greenwich.
6.   -Football: A Weekly Record of the Game, 7 March 1883.
7.   -A History of our Firm. Published privately by Rankin, Gilmour and Co., from a collection at Caird Library, National Maritime Museum, Greenwich.

Chapter 8 – The End of the Innocence

1.   -Glasgow News, 9 June 1879.
2.   -Scottish Athletic Journal, 11 May 1883.
3.   -ibid, 27 April 1883.
4.   -ibid, 16 November 1883.
5.   -'Glasgow and West of Scotland Family Historical Society' newsletter, October 2004, pages 19–24.
6.   -Scottish Athletic Journal, 24 August 1883.
7.   -ibid, 14 September 1883.
8.   -ibid, 31 August 1883.
9.   -ibid, 6 October 1885.
10.   -ibid, 31 December 1884.
11.   -ibid, 24 November 1884.
12.   -ibid, 29 September 1885.

13.   -ibid, 6 October 1885.

14.   -ibid, 9 November 1883.

15.   -SFA committee minutes, April 1884.

16.   -Scottish Athletic Journal, 11 April 1884.

17.   -ibid, 6 October 1885.

18.   -The Glory and the Dream – the History of Celtic 1887–1987 by Tom Campbell and Pat Woods, page 29.

19.   -ibid, page 32.

20.   -Quote taken from Scottish Football League – The First 100 Years by Bob Crampsey, page 15.

21.   -Scottish Athletic Journal, 27 May 1885.

22.   -ibid, 8 June 1886.

Chapter 9 – William McBeath

1.   -Scottish Athletic Journal, 25 April 1884.

2.   -Administrator of www.workhouses.org.uk

Chapter 10 – The FA Cup – From First to Last

1.   -The Official History of the FA Cup, Geoffrey Green, page 27.

2.   -Scottish Umpire, 2 November 1886.

3.   -Drink, Religion and Scottish Football 1873–1890 by John Weir.

4.   -One Hundred Years of Scottish Football by John Rafferty, page one.

5.   -Quote taken from The Second City by C.A. Oakley, page 233.

6.   -Scottish Athletic Journal, 30 March 1883.

7.   ibid, 1-2 October 1883.

8.   -ibid, 7 January 1885.

9.   -ibid, 13 April 1883.

10.   -Scottish Umpire, 26 October 1886.

11.   -Liverpool Courier, 1 November 1886.

12.   -Scottish Umpire, 2 November 1886.

13.   -ibid, 8 February 1886.

14.   -ibid, 8 February 1886.

15.   -The Only Game by Roddy Forsyth, page 22.

16.   -Scottish Sport, 6 August 1889.

17.   -Scottish Referee, Monday 5 August 1889.

18.   -Scottish Umpire, 22 February 1887.

19.   -Scottish Athletic Journal, 22 February 1887.

20.   ibid.

21.   -Scottish Umpire, 8 March 1887.

22.   -Scottish Athletic Journal, 15 March 1887.

23.   -ibid, 29 March 1887.

24.   -ibid, 15 March 1887.

25.   -The Story of the Rangers by John Allan, pages 44–45.

26.   -Scottish Athletic Journal, 1 March 1887.

Chapter 11 – Tom Vallance

1.   -A profile of Vallance appeared in the Scottish Athletic Journal of 25 March 1885.

2.   -I am indebted to George Parsonage of the Glasgow Humane Society for his good humoured and patient assistance, expertise and historical knowledge of the period in question, not to mention his knowledge of rowing from then until now.

3.   -Scottish Football Reminiscences and Sketches by D.D. Bone (1890).

4.   -Scottish Athletic Journal 25 March 1885–86.

5.   -Many thanks to Paul Rowland, editor of the Indiaman Magazine, the only genealogical and history magazine dedicated to the lives of the British in India between the 16th–20th centuries. He kindly put me in touch with Derek Perry in Australia, a former tea planter and Assam historian who agreed with marvellous alacrity to write a sketch based on his research of the conditions Tom Vallance would have faced in the region in the 1880s.

6.   -Scottish Football Journal, 25 March 1885.

Chapter 12 – Happily We Walk Along the Copland Road

1.   -Scottish Athletic Journal, 22 February 1887.

2.   -ibid, 21 March 1884.

3.   -ibid, 12 October 1886.

4.   -ibid, 23 August 1887.

5.   -Scottish Umpire, 10 July 1888.

6.   -Liverpool Echo, 1 November 1886.

7.   -Scottish News, 22 August 1887.

8.   -Scottish Umpire, 9 August 1887.

9.   -Scottish News, 22 August 1887.

10.   -ibid.

11.   -Scottish Athletic Journal, 23 August 1887.

Chapter 13 – A New Era

1.   -Scottish Sport, 29 January 1892.
2.   -Scottish Umpire, 10 June 1885.
3.   -Scottish Athletic Journal, 19 June 1885.
4.   -ibid, 8 December 1885.
5.   -Scottish Sport, 22 March 1890.
6.   -Scottish Football League – The First 100 Years by Bob Crampsey, p 40.

Bibliography

The Story of the Rangers, 50 Years Football 1873–1923 by John Allan (Desert Island Books)

Rangers: The Complete Record by Bob Ferrier and Robert McElroy (Breedon Books)

Rangers: The Managers by David Mason (Mainstream Publishing)

Neil Munro: The Biography by Lesley Lendrum (House of Lochar)

Celtic: A Century With Honour by Brian Wilson (Collins Willow)

The Glory and the Dream: The History of Celtic FC 1887–1987 by Tom Campbell and Pat Woods (Grafton Publishing)

The Scottish Footballer by Bob Crampsey (William Blackwood)

As Centuries Blend: 106 Years of Clydesdale Cricket Club by S. Courtney (John Miller Ltd)

One Hundred Years of Scottish Football by John Rafferty (Pan Books)

The Only Game: Scots and World Football by Roddy Forsyth (Mainstream)

Scottish Football: A Pictoral History by Kevin McCarra (Third Eye Centre/Polygon)

Pay Up and Play The Game by Wray Vamplew (Cambridge)

Victoria's Daughters by Jerrold M. Packard (St Martin's Griffin)

Rosneath and the Gareloch by Keith Hall (Tempus Publishing)

Around Gareloch and Rosneath Peninsula by Keith Hall (Tempus Publishing)

Among Friends: an Autobiography by Alastair Dunnett (Century Publishing)

The Official History of the FA Cup by Geoffrey Green (Sportsman's Book Club)

Scotland: The Team by Andrew Ward (Breedon Books)

The Second City by C.A. Oakley (Blackie)

Scottish Football: A Sourcebook by John Weir (Stewart Davidson Publishing)

25 Years of Football by Old International

The Campbells of Kilmun by Iain Hope (Aggregate Publications)

Clyde Passenger Steamers from 1812–1901 by Captain James Williamson (James MacLehose and Sons)

Made in the USA
Charleston, SC
10 November 2013